EDUCATION, POLITICS, AND PUBLIC LIFE

Series Editors:

Henry A. Giroux, McMaster University

Susan Searls Giroux, McMaster University

Within the last three decades, education as a political, moral, and ideological practice has become central to rethinking not only the role of public and higher education, but also the emergence of pedagogical sites outside of the schools—which include but are not limited to the Internet, television, film, magazines, and the media of print culture. Education as both a form of schooling and public pedagogy reaches into every aspect of political, economic, and social life. What is particularly important in this highly interdisciplinary and politically nuanced view of education are a number of issues that now connect learning to social change, the operations of democratic public life, and the formation of critically engaged individual and social agents. At the center of this series will be questions regarding what young people, adults, academics, artists, and cultural workers need to know to be able to live in an inclusive and just democracy and what it would mean to develop institutional capacities to reintroduce politics and public commitment into everyday life. Books in this series aim to play a vital role in rethinking the entire project of the related themes of politics, democratic struggles, and critical education within the global public sphere.

SERIES EDITORS:

HENRY A. GIROUX holds the Global TV Network Chair in English and Cultural Studies at McMaster University in Canada. He is on the editorial and advisory boards of numerous national and international scholarly journals.Professor Giroux was selected as a Kappa Delta Pi Laureate in 1998 and was the recipient of a Getty Research Institute Visiting Scholar Award in 1999. He was the recipient of the Hooker Distinguished Professor Award for 2001. He received an Honorary Doctorate of Letters from Memorial University of Newfoundland in 2005. His most recent books include *Take Back Higher Education* (co-authored with Susan Searls Giroux, 2006); *America on the Edge* (2006); *Beyond the Spectacle of Terrorism* (2006), *Stormy Weather: Katrina and the Politics of Disposability* (2006), *The University in Chains: Confronting the Military-Industrial-Academic Complex* (2007), and *Against the Terror of Neoliberalism: Politics Beyond the Age of Greed* (2008).

SUSAN SEARLS GIROUX is Asso
Cultural Studies at McMaster University.
The Theory Toolbox (co-authored with Jef
Higher Education (co-authored with Henr

D1592775

Race and Reason: Violence, Intellectual Responsibility, and the University to Come (2010). Professor Giroux is also the Managing Editor of *The Review of Education, Pedagogy, and Cultural Studies*.

Critical Pedagogy in Uncertain Times: Hope and Possibilities
Edited by Sheila L. Macrine

The Gift of Education: Public Education and Venture Philanthropy
Kenneth J. Saltman

Feminist Theory in Pursuit of the Public: Women and the "Re-Privatization" of Labor
Robin Truth Goodman

Hollywood's Exploited: Public Pedagogy, Corporate Movies, and Cultural Crisis
Edited by Benjamin Frymer, Tony Kashani, Anthony J. Nocella, II, and Richard Van Heertum; with a Foreword by Lawrence Grossberg

Education out of Bounds: Reimagining Cultural Studies for a Posthuman Age
Tyson E. Lewis and Richard Kahn

Academic Freedom in the Post-9/11 Era
Edited by Edward J. Carvalho and David B. Downing

Educating Youth for a World beyond Violence: A Pedagogy for Peace
H. Svi Shapiro

Rituals and Student Identity in Education: Ritual Critique for a New Pedagogy
Richard A. Quantz with Terry O'Connor and Peter Magolda

Citizen Youth: Culture, Activism, and Agency in a Neoliberal Era
Jacqueline Kennelly

Conflicts in Curriculum Theory: Challenging Hegemonic Epistemologies
João M. Paraskeva; Foreword by Donaldo Macedo

Sport, Spectacle, and NASCAR Nation: Consumption and the Cultural Politics of Neoliberalism
Joshua I. Newman and Michael D. Giardina

Immigration and the Challenge of Education: A Social Drama Analysis in South Central Los Angeles
Nathalia E. Jaramillo

Colbert's America: Satire and Democracy
Sophia A. McClennen

COLBERT'S AMERICA

SATIRE AND DEMOCRACY

Sophia A. McClennen

COLBERT'S AMERICA
Copyright © Sophia A. McClennen, 2011.

All rights reserved.

First published in hardcover in 2011 by PALGRAVE MACMILLAN® in the United States—a division of St. Martin's Press LLC, 175 Fifth Avenue, New York, NY 10010.

Where this book is distributed in the UK, Europe and the rest of the world, this is by Palgrave Macmillan, a division of Macmillan Publishers Limited, registered in England, company number 785998, of Houndmills, Basingstoke, Hampshire RG21 6XS.

Palgrave Macmillan is the global academic imprint of the above companies and has companies and representatives throughout the world.

Palgrave® and Macmillan® are registered trademarks in the United States, the United Kingdom, Europe and other countries.

ISBN: 978–1–137–01472–6

The Library of Congress has cataloged the hardcover edition as follows:

McClennen, Sophia A.
    America according to Colbert : satire as public pedagogy /
Sophia A. McClennen.
        p. cm.—(Education, politics and public life)
      ISBN 978–0–230–10466–2 (hardback)
        1. Colbert, Stephen, 1964—Criticism and interpretation. 2. Political satire, American. 3. United States—Politics and government—1989–1993—Humor. I. Title.

PN2287.C5695M44 2011
973.92902'07—dc23   2011017102

A catalogue record of the book is available from the British Library.

Design by Newgen Imaging Systems (P) Ltd., Chennai, India.

First PALGRAVE MACMILLAN paperback edition: July 2012

10 9 8 7 6 5 4 3 2 1

Transferred to Digital Printing in 2012

For Isabel and Sebastian
Future Members of the Colbert Nation

CONTENTS

PREFACE

"Hey, you've got to see this!" These are the words that first introduced me to the art of Stephen Colbert's satire as I sat down to watch a streaming video of a comedian roasting the President on a site called ThankYouStephenColbert.org in the spring of 2006. Watching that video goes on record for me (and for many others) as a turning point during those years. It would be fair to say that many of us marked the Bush years according to the temporal shift from BC (Before Colbert) to AD (After Dinner). There was something thoroughly extraordinary about his performance that night. This was a form of satire that was totally outrageous—outrageous for its humor, for its boldness, and for its creative way of speaking truth to power. It wasn't long after seeing his performance that I began thinking about writing this book.

Colbert is always on the move. His persona and his show are ever evolving and the reference points he makes to current events are inexhaustible. This broad range of material meant that it would not be possible to cover every part of his work that I thought would be of interest to readers. I opted instead to focus on ongoing themes and to analyze major moments in his satire within that context. It was hard not to be infected by Colbert's charisma, and I found myself laughing out loud constantly as I rescreened pieces from *The Colbert Report* and read over transcripts of his work. All writing should be this fun.

Thanks not only to Colbert but also to all of his staff and writers who work together on his material. While I write about the Colbert persona as the product of Stephen Colbert, it is important to remember that the creation of the Colbert persona has been a collective effort.

We always want to thank those that helped us during the process of writing, but it remains clear that it is never possible to fully acknowledge all of those who helped, encouraged, and lent a hand. Possibly because of the nature of the book topic, this was the least solitary writing experience I've had and I was very fortunate to have a large group of colleagues and friends accompany me through this process. Among these, a few deserve special mention.

This book would not have been possible without the friendship and the critical work of Henry Giroux. He remains one of my most valued friends and one of my greatest sources of scholarly insight. I was also privileged to have the ongoing support of Ariel Dorfman, who continues to be a valued mentor and collaborator. John "Rio" Riofrio was an enormous source of support as well, reading chapters on the fly, offering encouragement, and acting as a sounding board throughout this process. Special thanks to all three of them.

As anyone who has written on Colbert well knows, the Colbert Nation is the premier source of information and insight into his work. Without their blogs, websites, tweets, Wikipedia entries, and other sources about Colbert, this book would simply not have been possible.

Thanks are also due to Henry Morello, who first introduced me to the video of Colbert at the White House Correspondents' Association Dinner.

During my college years, I had the extraordinary good fortune to be a part of the *Harvard Lampoon* staff. I am absolutely certain I would not have written this book had I not had that experience. From brief moments spent partying with Conan O'Brian when he returned to hang out with his fellow lampooners to years working with staff members Bill Oakley, Bob Neer, Dan Greaney, Steve Young, Steve Tompkins, and too many others to mention, I learned about humor—especially satirical humor. The memories I have of my time at the *Lampoon* remain some of my best moments from college, and I want to thank both fellow staff members as well as the institution of the *Lampoon* itself.

At The Pennsylvania State University, I have been grateful for the extraordinary support of all of my colleagues and especially for the encouragement of Carey Eckhardt. Jon Abel, Tom Beebee, Jeremy Engels, Chip Gerfen, Eric Hayot, Jonathan Marks, and Dan Purdy, each deserve thanks for their collegiality, critical feedback, and support.

Special thanks to Joaquín Dorfman, who gave me helpful pointers and passed on useful comments during the writing process.

A number of colleagues and good friends lent an ear, provided important dialogue, and offered insights to me while I was writing this book. Gene Bell-Villada, Debra Castillo, Deb Cohn, Angela Dadak, Greg Dawes, James Dawes, Rodrigo Dorfman, Jeffrey Di Leo, David Downing, Claire Fox, Susan Searls Giroux, Jeffrey Middents, Robin Goodman, Ricardo Gutiérrez-Mouat, Jennifer Harford Vargas, Peter Hitchcock, Leerom Medovoi, Uppinder Mehan, Julie Minich, Bill

Mullen, Silvia Nagy-Zekmi, Donald Pease, Claudia Sadowski-Smith, Rob Schwaller, Joseph Slaughter, Paul Smith, Jeffrey Williams, Zahi Zalloua and many others have been valued sources of engaged critique and friendship.

This book would not be what it is without the tremendous efforts of a number of research assistants who tracked down research materials, did literature surveys, found websites and other Colbert resources, and helped with the citations and editing of the manuscript. Special thanks to Michelle Decker, Caroline Egan, Cory Hahn, Sara Marzioli, and Leisa Rothlisberger. Thanks also to my students who offered me opportunities to share my work and get their feedback, especially José Alvarez, Germán Campos-Muñoz, Spencer Delbridge, Lorena Cuya Gavilano, and Nicole Sparling.

I have also had the good friendship of a series of colleagues in Germany who have become important interlocutors for my work. Thanks especially to Luz Kirschner, and to Alexander Greiffenstern, Markus Heide, Willy Raussert, Josef Raab, and Stefan Rinke.

Special mention must go to the staff with which I have had the good fortune to work this past year. Their hard work and eye for detail freed up needed space and time for me to write. Thanks to Jamie Frazell, Irene Grassi, Sarah Lyall-Combs, and Amy Tegeder for all of the various ways that they have offered me support. I am also grateful for the work of Kaylan Connally, Burk Gerstenschlager, and the staff at Palgrave who helped steer this book to press.

I wrote this book quickly (at least by my standards) and at a particularly intense moment in my life. At the same time, I had the benefit of a group of friends who helped me in too many ways to fully recount. Matthew Restall and Amara Solari have been both lifesavers and life-enhancers. Robert Denby has also been a great source of good wit and good cheer. Friends like Garrett Fagen, Khusro Kidwai, Michael Kuliakowski, On Cho Ng, and Dave Skipper also made the writing experience much more enjoyable. Thanks to Nancy Chiswick and Daniel Greenberg who literally kept me together during this process. I also had the good fortune during this time to learn from and share thoughts with Bryn and Devyn Spielvogel. They helped provide balance and offered opportunities for distraction and fun when I needed it most.

Finally (I hope!) I have written a book that my family might read. I am especially looking forward to hearing from my brother, Peter, his wife, Michelene, and, one day, from Ryan too. I also look forward to the thoughts of Jamie, Stephania, Mim, Susu, Edgar, Doug, Amy, Andrew, Michelle, Peter, Kathy, and LeAnn. Big thanks to Krystyana

Chelminski and James Czeiner for their extra enthusiasm for this project. I can never be grateful enough for my mom's support, but her help this past year has been truly monumental. She has offered me a space within which to live and breathe, she has given me more kinds of help than I can fully mention, and she has encouraged me throughout this process. Isabel and Sebastian remain my constant reminders of why I write books—especially one like this one. Every day they teach me how to be curious and to question the status quo while having fun in the process.

This book is also for Eric, *mein Liebster,* who walked across a room and changed my world. His undying confidence in this project moved me along when I couldn't see forward. He created the cover image and helped coax the words inside.

INTRODUCTION

Echoing a common worldwide opinion of post-9/11 political discourse in the United States, George Monbiot of London's *The Guardian* asked days before the 2008 U.S. presidential election: "How did politics in the U.S. come to be dominated by people who make a virtue of ignorance?"[1] What Monbiot's claim missed though, was the significant presence within the United States of those who have made a virtue of *mocking* those who make a virtue of ignorance. Almost immediately following the attacks of 9/11, a series of comedians emerged on the national scene who used satire, irony, mockery, and parody to offer the public an alternative to the ignorance, militarism, and hubris that dominated much public discourse. And their massive fan base demonstrated that their combination of comedy and social critique resonated with a population hungry to vent their frustrations, share a laugh, and lampoon those in power.

Without question, the most visible comedian to occupy such a space has been Stephen Colbert, who had been a cast member on Jon Stewart's *The Daily Show* prior to 9/11. In 2005, he acquired his own show, *The Colbert Report,* which satirizes personality-driven political shows like *The O'Reilly Factor.* Comprised of parodies of current news and simulated right-wing punditry, Colbert's program offers its audience a way to combine entertainment with political reflection. When Colbert began his program in 2005, dissent was cast by President George W. Bush's government and its supporters as highly unpatriotic, even, at times, criminal. Many members of the media, educators, and pubic intellectuals came under attack in the years after 9/11, some losing their jobs or worse, when they dared to question the decisions made by the Bush government.[2] Satire became one of the few means through which the public could express resistance to reigning political policies and social attitudes.

Satire serves as a comedic and pedagogic form uniquely suited to provoking critical reflection. Its ability to underscore the absurdity, ignorance, and prejudice of commonly accepted behavior by means of comedic critical reflection offers an especially potent form of public critique, one that was much needed in the post-9/11 environment. But can comedy really be that politically powerful? Satire is not commonly considered to be as potent a form of critical intervention as, say, the work of a public intellectual like Noam Chomsky, who offers incisive critical commentaries, social theories, and political editorials all in a serious tone aimed at agitating his audience to care about unjust, unfair, and unreasonable social practices. If you're laughing, even if the laugh is more an uncomfortable chuckle than a guffaw, then you're having way too much fun to be engaging in dissent, right? Wrong. My argument is that Colbert's satire has been one of the, if not THE, primary source of social critique in the United States since his show launched. Against claims that would suggest that satire is merely negative criticism that at best encourages cynicism and at worst provokes political apathy and narcissistic diversion, I would argue that Colbert has not only offered his fans ways to productively engage in contemporary politics, but that he has also redefined the parameters of political dissent.

When I refer to Colbert's satire as "public pedagogy," I am describing it as an educational force that takes place on a large, public scale. Henry Giroux, the theorist who developed the idea of "public pedagogy," has argued that education occurs more and more often outside of the space of the classroom.[3] He has been especially interested in the way that youth, and the population in general, increasingly learn modes of thought via the spectacle of mass media. Key to his argument is the idea that, if most learning happens outside of the classroom, then we need to pay even greater attention to those cultural interactions and social processes that are the source of learning and thinking. This means being more fully aware of the ways that the news media, political discourse, and forms of entertainment teach us how to think about the world. What Giroux argues is that the public pedagogies of any given moment are typically complex. While public pedagogies tend to simply reinforce the status quo, these reductive, repressive, and often reactionary pedagogies are always confronted by other practices that encourage critical thinking, civic engagement, and moral imagination. There is a difference between pedagogies that ask the pubic to be passive, distracted, and obedient and those that suggest that the public should be active, attentive, and progressive. This difference is one with high stakes, since, according to Giroux, democracy depends on a public with a sense of civic agency and with a dedication to working to achieve the goals of a democratic, egalitarian society.

This book argues, following Giroux's line of thinking, that Colbert's program emerged in a moment when the reigning public pedagogy was especially repressive. Any questioning of the government's practices after 9/11 became virtually tantamount to treason. With hindsight, it is now relatively easy to see that the public during the period of 9/11/2001 to the election of Barack Obama in 2008 was given very little room within which to question the decisions to go to war in Iraq and Afghanistan, to pass legislation that radically reduced civil rights, and to practice torture and illegal detention. The public pedagogy of the news media in that period mainly reinforced the government's practices, with few exceptions. This is why the work of Colbert, and comedians like him, was particularly important, since, via parody and satire, they were able to open a space for critical reflection and public questioning of the status quo. And, even more importantly, they did this through the very same media force—cable television—that was itself the source of some of the worst forms of public pedagogy. What is most noteworthy, then, is that Colbert's satire served as both a public pedagogy and a critical pedagogy combined. Giroux calls pedagogies that encourage reflection, the development of democratic sensibilities, and social commitment "critical pedagogies." Colbert's work is significant because it uses a wide-reaching media forum to foster public debate of major issues. And it does that in a way that energizes and amuses its audience.

There is little doubt as to Colbert's public visibility. He has been named one of *Time*'s 100 Most Influential People for three consecutive years (2006–2008). He has won Emmys, Grammys, Peabodys, and The Golden Tweet for the most forwarded tweet of 2010, an honorary doctorate, and the key to Columbia, South Carolina. Colbert has appeared on the covers of several major magazines, including *Wired, Rolling Stone, Esquire, Sports Illustrated,* and *Newsweek,* for which he was a guest editor. He is a cult phenomenon and his range of influence is extremely wide. After the Saginaw Spirit defeated the Oshawa Generals in Ontario Junior League Hockey, Mayor John Gray declared March 20, 2007, "Stephen Colbert Day." He was knighted by Queen Noor of Jordan in exchange for his support of the Global Zero Campaign to eliminate nuclear weapons.[4] NASA named a treadmill after him and Virgin Air named one of its airplanes "Air Colbert" in his honor. He almost had a Hungarian bridge named after him, but lost out to a rule that only allowed the bridge to carry the name of a Hungarian. He has a species of spider named after him, a bald eagle born at the San Francisco Zoo named after him, and he has his own flavor of Ben and Jerry's ice cream, Stephen Colbert's Americone Dream. Colbert was honored for the Gutsiest Move on the Spike TV Guys' Choice Awards on June 13, 2007, for his performance at the 2006 White House Correspondents' Association Dinner, and in 2006 he was named one of *GQ*'s "Men of the Year." And that doesn't even include all the awards he has won for being sexy. His fan base, to use a Colbertism, is "superstantial." Even before the premiere airing of *The Colbert Report*, it was enjoying significant media coverage. It was featured in articles in *The New Yorker*, NPR's *All Things Considered* and *Fresh Air*, CNN, and *The Washington Post*. *The New York Times* ran three articles on the *Report* before its first airing. The show drew 1.13 million viewers for its premiere episode, 47 percent more than the average for that time slot over the previous four weeks.[5] *The Report* averaged 1.2 million viewers per episode in its first week, more than double the average for the same time the previous year. Colbert has 1.9 million followers on Twitter, he logged more than 1 million members within one week of starting his Facebook page to support his short-lived 2008 presidential campaign, and he is also a digital-media icon with clips of his show posted on YouTube (they are now all archived on ColbertNation.com), green-screen challenges, iPhone apps, and fan blogs.

Those facts only prove that he has a huge fan base, but, you might say, it pales in comparison to media moguls like Oprah Winfrey, whose "Oprah Effect" rivals the "Colbert Bump" and whose viewers number at least five times more than Colbert's. Colbert's force as a public intellectual, though, is not limited to the public scope of his visibility. One thing that makes his work especially powerful is the way that he combines entertainment with social critique. This is what happens when he takes his show to Iraq and he blends silly bits of himself undergoing basic training or getting his head shaved with more significant commentary on the war and the crises facing the troops. But Colbert does much more than make critical refection and political awareness palatable enough for prime time. He has actually shaped public discourse in significant ways.

Probably one of the most obvious ways that his satire has influenced public ways of thinking is his coining of neologisms that have become part of our common lexicon. The most significant of these is *truthiness*, the term that he used to open his very first show on "The Wørd" segment, and which later became the Word of the Year in 2005 for the American Dialect Society and in 2006 for Merriam-Webster. *Truthiness* was a direct reference to the discourse of President George W. Bush, who often spoke of using his gut to make decisions on matters as important as whether or not to go to war, who to nominate for major government positions, and what to do about natural disasters like Hurricane Katrina. Colbert defines *truthiness* as a truth that you know from your gut without reference to facts, intellect, or reason. If the term doesn't seem that funny, it is only because its reference to the realities of the Bush administration's decision-making strategy is more disturbing than comedic. What Colbert did with the word, though, was call attention to an ongoing practice by U.S. leaders that had been taken for granted by the public as a whole. His word was both funny and immensely critical. It sounded silly while simultaneously describing a belief system that was extremely dangerous. One of the most chilling examples of *truthiness* can be found in the arguments the public heard about why we should invade Iraq. We had no proof that there were weapons of mass destruction (WMDs) in Iraq, but Bush and Vice President Dick Cheney felt in their guts that they were there and that was enough, not just for them but also for the U.S. public, who, at the time, supported the decision to invade. Nine years, thousands of lives, and billions of dollars later, no WMDs were ever found. And while many of us knew that the decision to invade was not based on the truth, Colbert's naming of such practices as *truthiness* gave us all a common vocabulary through which to talk about these issues that was both biting and witty.

Since then Colbert has coined other terms like *wikiality,* a reference to Wikipedia, the encyclopedia that gives users the ability to edit entries. *Wikiality* is the idea that "together we can create a reality that we all agree on—the reality we just agreed on."[6] And while the term is less sharp in its social critique than *truthiness,* it, too, questions what happens in a world where facts are less important than consensus. And then more recently he coined *freem,* which he explained as "freedom without the do, because I do it all for you." Here he pokes fun at the idea of what it means to fight for freedom in a culture that has become excessively passive in its commitment to civic agency and democratic values. If we let leaders make all our decisions, then how can we also define ourselves as "free"? Each of these terms offers viewers a smart, incisive, clever way to think about current social crises.

I have shown that Colbert has major public visibility, that his form of satire opened up a needed space for critical reflection in a time when public dissent was difficult and discouraged, and that he has also had a tremendous impact on the way that the public thinks, by coining terms that expose prevailing practices that damage our society. But his character and his show have done even more in terms of intervening well outside of the traditional parameters of satire. At the heart of satire is the exaggerated, parodic acceptance of the status quo, done in a way that serves to ridicule common practices and beliefs in order to provoke the audience to rethink its behavior and ideas. But Colbert's satire has often been taken as non-satirical, even at times becoming a news source, rather than a parody of the news. In one noteworthy example from his now infamous "Better Know a District" series, Colbert interviewed Robert Wexler, a candidate for the House of Representatives in Florida who was running unopposed, and therefore, guaranteed a win. Colbert convinced Wexler to say something that would otherwise cause him to lose the election, and the result was a silly statement about cocaine and prostitutes being fun. *Good Morning America*, *The Today Show*, and *Fox News* aired edited versions of the segment in an effort to discredit Wexler and question his judgment. In response, Colbert told viewers "vote Wexler, the man's got a sense of humor, unlike, evidently, journalists." But the problem went well beyond whether or not these news agencies had a sense of humor; what was even more revealing was that they were using footage from a Comedy Central-sponsored interview as news, rather than as comedy. Somehow the flow from reality to parody had been reversed and parody was now being taken as "fact."[7]

Programs like Colbert's *The Colbert Report* and Jon Stewart's *The Daily Show* consistently have served as a news source, rather than being simply a parody of the news. In one especially salient example, Colbert asked Representative Lynn Westmoreland, who had co-sponsored a bill to have the Ten Commandments on display in the U.S. House of Representatives and Senate, if he could think of a better place to display them. Westmoreland couldn't. The idea of a church, for instance, simply did not come to mind. Colbert went on to ask Westmoreland to name the Ten Commandments, which he could not do either. The irony was intense and the impact was immediate. Even beyond that, though, Colbert had made news. In a nation that is founded on the idea of separation of church and state, where that separation is always under fire, Colbert showed that one of the advocates for breaking down that separation was uneducated about the very same guiding principles he felt should guide the U.S. legislative branch. It was not the news media, but rather Colbert via his satire, that gave the public valuable information about important pending legislation. More importantly, Colbert pointed out that the information he provided viewers was absent from the mainstream media. In his rebuttal to the Wexler controversy, he provided clips of the media spending time wondering about the adverse effects of tanning beds and other equally mindless issues. He then asked viewers to compare what they learn on mainstream news shows and what he has brought to public attention. After interventions like these, viewers are unable to watch mainstream news media without being aware of the superficial and silly ways that they often cover stories. In effect, Colbert has not only added to public information, he has also radically changed the way his audience consumes news media.

That programs like Colbert's and Stewart's have a direct influence on viewers, encouraging them to better understand current issues at a level that exceeds viewers of typical mainstream media, was proven by a 2007 Pew Research Center study that asked viewers of a number of major news outlets a series of questions about current events.[8] They found that viewers of *The Daily Show* and *The Colbert Report* had the highest knowledge of national and international affairs. Meanwhile, Fox News viewers ranked nearly dead last. The Pew study merely reinforced the notion that satire has the ability to engage greater public awareness of significant issues. So, not only is Colbert hugely visible, not only does he reach a wide public, not only has he coined terms that satirically encapsulate troublesome social practices, not only has he turned around the flow of information from reality to parody, but he has also created a program that, along with *The Daily Show*, gives viewers greater awareness of current events than any other news source.

Colbert has also had the opportunity to use his satire to speak truth to power. There are at least four examples of key moments in Colbert's career where the lines between satire and direct political participation have been blurred. The first was his appearance at the White House Correspondents' Association (WHCA) Dinner in 2006, where he roasted President George W. Bush, while also taking shots at the media and other government officials. Even though it is common for the host of the correspondents' dinner to ridicule the President to his face, Colbert's satire was so close to the truth that he made even the President squirm. Second was his short-lived bid to run for President in the 2008 elections, which stirred substantial debate about whether he had gone too far, whether he ran the risk of taking votes away from other candidates, and whether his involvement threatened to increase public distrust of politics. Key debates circled around whether his campaign would engage the public or make them more cynical.[9] Few thought that Colbert would actually go through with the campaign, but it is worth remembering that in the same election cycle, Al Franken, a former member of *Saturday Night Live*, ran for and won a seat as a senator from Minnesota, a fact that again shows that post-9/11 satire had gone from parody to direct political action.[10]

Then on September 24, 2010, Colbert appeared in character before Congress as an expert witness before the House Judiciary

Subcommittee on Immigration, Citizenship, Refugees, Border Security, and International Law to describe his experience participating in the United Farm Workers' "Take Our Jobs" campaign, where he spent a day working alongside migrant workers in upstate New York. At the end of his satirical testimony about the challenges of migrant labor, Colbert broke character and explained why he cares about the plight of migrant workers: "I like talking about people who don't have any power, and it seems like one of the least powerful people in the United States are migrant workers who come and do our work, but don't have any rights as a result."[11] What was most fascinating about this exchange was Colbert's presence before Congress. Even though a number of congressmen suggested it was inappropriate for him to appear before them in this manner, the fact remains that Colbert's satire had moved beyond cynicism, mockery, and ridicule of people in power: he was engaged in direct political action. Lastly, there was his rally on the National Mall with Jon Stewart that gathered an audience of 250,000 people, with many others watching it via live streams. A total of 2.82 million watched the show either live or on the TV/Web.[12] While the goal of encouraging voter turnout for the midterm elections may not have been as successful as Colbert and Stewart hoped, it is clear that the rally showed the extent to which the two of them have transformed from being simply political satirists to being direct political actors themselves.

Similar to Jon Stewart's work in *The Daily Show*, Colbert's program critiques political discourse while equally satirizing the inanity of the mainstream news media. In contrast to the anti-intellectualism, sensationalism, and dogmatism that tend to govern most news media today, Colbert's program offers his audience the opportunity to understand the context through which most news is reported and to be critical of it. In so doing, Colbert's show further offers viewers an opportunity to reflect on the limited and narrow ways that political issues tend to be framed in public debate. Segments like "The Wørd" and "Formidable Opponent" are designed to expose the logical fallacies, the twisted reasoning, and the abuse of language that takes place both in politics and the media today. Recognizing that the political opinions of most U.S. citizens are shaped by an uncritical acceptance of the issues as provided by the mainstream media, Colbert uses the same venue to critique that process.

It is hard to separate the critical impact of Stewart's work and Colbert's since there is such synergy between their shows. But there are some key differences to Colbert's particular style. By impersonating a right-wing pundit, Colbert differs in significant ways from other critical comedians since his form of humor embodies that which it critiques. In contrast to Stewart and Bill Maher (whose use of irony clearly separates them from the object of their mockery), Colbert's particular form of parodic satire offers a scathing indictment of the cult of punditry, which positions itself as biased, unreflective, politically incendiary discourse. His show consistently suggests that the cult of personality and the passion for scandal that drive most news programs are inimical to democratic deliberation, but it does so via its own cult of personality and passion for scandal. Emphasizing the dangers of succumbing to the persuasive powers of punditry, Colbert asks viewers to question the very ways that political debate is staged in the mass media. This is tricky terrain, though, since in-character parody has both the potential to be more incisive in its critique and also more dangerous. When Colbert emulates the narcissism and egotism of right-wing pundits, creating a cult of personality, he runs the risk of merely mirroring the same passive viewing practices common to programs like *The O'Reilly Factor*.

This is why his show has elicited contradictory responses, with some viewers not recognizing his satire. This delicate balance will also be one of the topics further explored in this book, since it isn't always clear whether Colbert is simply creating a meta-pundit or whether he is effectively undercutting punditry. One of the main arguments in this book, though, will be to suggest that Colbert's satirical simulation of Bill O'Reilly-style punditry facilitates analysis of how his show engages with a series of right-wing ideologies, which include, but are not limited to, war on terror fundamentalisms, race relations, economic warfare, and masculinist patriotism. Consequently, I would suggest that his work should be read in conversation with public intellectuals and social theorists such as Noam Chomsky, Henry Giroux, and Slavoj Žižek, who theorize the connections between post-postmodern political apathy, neoliberal free-market ideologies, and other challenges facing progressive democratic politics. From their various perspectives, all of these public intellectuals call for considering ways to reinvigorate the public sphere through engaged and meaningful debate of social issues. My claim is that Colbert's satire is as intellectually powerful as other non-satirical intellectual projects, if not more.

This book also contributes to the ongoing conversation about how satire and humor post-9/11 have been able to effectively encourage critical perspectives on major social issues, thereby providing an important source of public pedagogy. Focusing on one of the leading figures of satire TV, *Colbert's America* claims that

Colbert's program incorporates a series of features that foster critical thinking and that encourage audiences to resist the status quo.[13] By analyzing the context within which the program emerged and the specific features of the program, this book offers readers insight into the powerful ways that Colbert's comedy challenges the cult of ignorance that has threatened meaningful public debate and social dialogue since 9/11.

In the following chapters, I provide a combination of historical context and critical analysis of Colbert's character and his program. Chapter 1 begins with his appearance at the White House Correspondents' Association Dinner, since that was the watershed moment that launched Colbert into international fame. His speech also encapsulated many of the core themes of his work. Chapter 2 explores the context within which his show emerged. It explores the status of democratic deliberation and public debate, especially as these were reduced in the post-9/11 era. At the time of Colbert's emergence as a public figure, a series of shifts influenced the possibilities for engaged public attention to pressing social issues. These included the transition to post-network television, the rise in right-wing fundamentalisms, the increasing influence of free-market-based neoliberal economics, and the culture of fear brought on by the war on terror. Chapter 2 analyzes how Colbert's work responded to that context and offered viewers an innovative way to practice critical thinking. Chapter 3 focuses on his use of satire and its connection to the legacy of U.S. satire. From Ben Franklin to Samuel Clemens to *Saturday Night Live*, the United States has a long history of using satire as a way of speaking truth to power. Situating his work in that tradition, the chapter considers Colbert's comedy as both unique and in conversation with a series of predecessors.

Chapter 4 delves into the particular details of his show and analyzes it according to main themes that have been an ongoing focus of the program. As mentioned above, Colbert has been especially concerned with the way that the idea of truth morphed to mean nothing more than one's own opinion, thus *truthiness* occupies one section. Other sections study his use of wordplay, his satire of identity issues, his association of himself with "America," and his development of a youth-oriented public sphere. The concluding chapter, chapter 5, returns to the question of the degree to which Colbert's satire is effective as a critical form of public pedagogy. While I hope to have shown the degree to which his show has had a measurable and positive impact on the U.S. public's ability to actively connect to vital social issues, such an impact is always difficult to prove. As the first book to trace the range of Colbert's satire and to analyze the various components of his show, I hope that *Colbert's America* will lead to more attention to Colbert's work.[14] In that spirit, I'll finish this introduction by posing a typical Colbertian query: Stephen Colbert, great satirist, or greatest satirist? Hopefully, after reading this book, you will have your own answers.

1

I STAND BY THIS MAN: COLBERT
SPEAKS TRUTHINESS TO POWER

"I stand by this man. I stand by this man, because he stands for things. Not only for things, he stands on things, things like aircraft carriers and rubble and recently flooded city squares. And that sends a strong message, that no matter what happens to America, she will always rebound with the most powerfully staged photo-ops in the world."[1]

Stephen Colbert's appearance at the White House Correspondents' Association Dinner on April 29, 2006, represents a watershed moment in the George W. Bush presidency. Colbert, in character as a Bill O'Reilly-esque conservative pundit, made satire history as he delivered a highly nuanced, extremely detailed critique of the president and the media that covered him while both the president and the media were in the room. When Colbert delivered his speech the government was awash in scandals—unjustified wars, suspension of civil liberties, wiretapping, extraordinary rendition, torture. Yet the mainstream media seemed incapable of offering the public any meaningful analysis of these events. Arguably, Colbert's speech marks the most aggressive public confrontation of the president made by anyone during Bush's period in office. Colbert's "balls-alicious" monologue coupled this act of dissent with a biting indictment of the media and with ancillary attacks on other equally spineless public figures.[2] He immediately became a legend.

This chapter begins with the White House Correspondents' Dinner since Colbert's particular form of political critique at this event dovetails with his rise in public visibility. Shortly after the speech, as video footage and a transcript of the presentation circulated globally, Colbert's television program, *The Colbert Report*, boomed in popularity. The event also sparked a vigorous debate in the media about whether or not Colbert's speech was an example of "one of the most patriotic acts ever seen" or was simply a mean-spirited, not-very-funny insult. In this chapter, I will analyze the speech's content and critical mode, the response from both the media and the general public, its role in launching Colbert's worldwide visibility, and the ways that Colbert's comedic intervention offered audiences a unique and valuable form of public pedagogy.

THE WHITE HOUSE CORRESPONDENTS' ASSOCIATION AND ITS ANNUAL DINNER

It would be safe to assume that even those of us who regularly consume cable news have given little thought to the White House press corps and its association, but some background on the White House Correspondents' Association (WHCA) is necessary to fully appreciate the context of Colbert's famous speech. The WHCA was founded "on Feb. 25, 1914, after the White House let it be known that President Woodrow Wilson was interested in having an unprecedented series of regularly scheduled press conferences but was unsure how to pick the reporters to invite to these sessions."[3] When it seemed that the Congressional Standing Committee of Correspondents would select the reporters, the WHCA was formed by eleven correspondents who regularly covered the president. They stated that their "primary object shall be the promotion of the interests of those reporters and correspondents assigned to cover the White House."[4]

Since 1920 the WHCA has hosted an annual dinner and it has been presided over by the president since 1924, when Calvin Coolidge became the first of fourteen presidents to attend the dinner. For the most part, the dinner was seen as an opportunity for White House press to enjoy an evening with the administration and staff and it included a heavy dose of entertainment. The idea behind the dinner was to reinforce collegiality between the press corps and the White House. In the pre–World War II years, for instance, there was singing and other entertainment between courses. Frank Sinatra and Danny Kaye performed along with other entertainers in 1945. However, as one might imagine, such palling around between journalists and government officials appeared problematic and the dinner increasingly became a source of controversy over whether or not the press had the necessary distance from the White House to accurately report news on it. The dinner seemed to stand in for all that was wrong with news media, and by 2007 Frank Rich of *The New York Times* had decided that *The New York Times* would no longer participate in the festivities.[5]

In addition to concerns that the dinner represented the worst sort of collusion between the press and politicians, there have been other controversies. Prior to 1962 the dinner excluded female members of the WHCA; the dinner was only open to men. According to the WHCA's own website: "That changed when, at the prodding of Helen Thomas of UPI, President John F. Kennedy said he would not attend the dinner unless the ban on women was dropped."[6] The role of Helen Thomas here is noteworthy since she is the correspondent featured in a video that Colbert shows at the end of his speech that will be discussed in more detail below. The WHCA has also been criticized because it is primarily a mainstream media organization that does not include alternative and smaller news sources.

In recent years, controversies have developed over the way that the dinner has turned into its own form of media spectacle. Justine Holcomb notes that the dinner has become an opportunity for news organizations to line up celebrity dates: she describes how pre-dinner blogs linked to media outlets brag about which rich and famous people will be part of their entourage.[7] Despite the fact that the dinner ostensibly exists to support journalism scholarships and to offer awards for good reporting, in some eyes, it has become nothing more than an extreme example of the ways that the media has become a self-serving spectacle that depicts journalists as an elite. Rem Rieder, in a piece posted days after Colbert's appearance, called to discontinue the event: "This dinner has been an embarrassment for years. It's well past time to shut it down. It's a vivid symbol, like we need another one, of what's so very wrong with elite Washington journalism."[8] He quotes *The New York Times* Washington Bureau Chief Michael Oreskes who decided that the *Times* would not participate in the dinner in 1999: "The purpose of honoring good journalism with awards and raising money for scholarships has become lost in the circus...The association each year is seen around the country as host to a Bacchanalia that confirms everyone's worst sense of Washington. We should not be a part of this."[9]

The idea of a frivolous dinner that showcases an elite media partying with government officials and celebrities might have been enough to suggest that the role of an independent press had given way to a banal media spectacle that was uninterested and unwilling to question the country's ruling class, but there is little doubt that the George W. Bush administration exacerbated these tensions. Alternative media outlets had repeatedly reported in the post-9/11 years on the culture of secrecy that shrouded the White House. Bush was notorious for avoiding reporter queries and Scott McClellan, who was White House Press Secretary from 2003 to 2006, resigning only days before Colbert's appearance, also had a reputation for deflecting difficult questions. As McClellan would later recount in his memoir *What Happened*, the Bush presidency was based on an aggressive "political propaganda campaign."[10] McClellan revealed that the Bush administration made "a decision to turn away from candor and honesty when those qualities were most needed."[11] Such secrecy in the face of a terrorist attack on U.S. soil followed by military interventions in two nations would have been cause enough to worry that the U.S. public was being denied important information central to a functioning democracy, but the secrecy of the administration was matched by the apathy of the press. Peter Daou, writing only two days before the 2006 WHCA Dinner, expressed irritation at the lack of serious reporting on the part of the media. "One of the hallmarks of the painfully-too-long Bush presidency has been the abject failure of the traditional media to adopt an interrogative or disputatious stance toward the administration. We've been treated to a half decade plus of stenography."[12]

This is the context within which Colbert prepared to deliver his speech on April 29, 2006. On that night the room was filled with over 2,600 guests, among them Hollywood celebrities; the White House press corps; President Bush and the First Lady; high-ranking administration officials, including Supreme Court Justice Antonin Scalia and U.S. Attorney General Alberto Gonzales; members of the military elite; and other media representatives. As Holcomb notes, there were also some fairly vocal critics of George W. Bush present including Jesse Jackson, New Orleans Mayor Ray Nagin, who had been very critical of the administration's response to Hurricane Katrina, and Valerie Plame, whose identity as a CIA undercover had been allegedly leaked by the White House.[13]

In the last two decades, the main dinner entertainment has been two comedic performances: first by the current president, followed by that of a comedian who typically roasts the president in good fun and to the hearty laughs of the crowd. The event on that night was filmed and broadcast live on C-SPAN. It would be safe to say that what followed went well beyond tradition.

COLBERT DROPS A BOMB

As mentioned, the format for the WHCA Dinner has traditionally been a presentation by the sitting president followed by his roast by a comedian. On the night of Colbert's performance, President Bush performed a ten-minute skit alongside Bush impersonator Steve Bridges. Following the dinner's typical format, the president poked light-hearted fun at himself to the delight of the crowd. Bush played his public self, reading straight, deadpan lines, typical of his public speeches. Bridges played his inner thoughts, highlighting Bush's malapropisms, his basic distaste for public life, and his generally unsophisticated attitudes. One bit spoofed Bush's well-known inability to correctly pronounce "nuclear." Another series of jokes was aimed at Vice President Dick Cheney, who had recently been involved with a scandal over a hunting accident where he shot a fellow hunter in the face. Bridges (impersonating Bush's inner thoughts) started with "where is the great white hunter? He shot the only trial lawyer in the country who supports me."[14] Bush then said, "I am sorry that Vice President Cheney couldn't be here tonight." The play between them was a very funny spoof of Bush and the audience responded with hearty laughter.

The bit also included partisan comments with Bush-Bridges joking about Bush's unease with "Hollywood liberals" and "media types." Bridges, speaking as the president's inner voice, sniped that "the only thing missing was Hillary Clinton sitting in the front row and rolling her eyes." Bush also made fun of his basic inability to do the job when he self-mockingly remarked: "I am continuing to spread our agenda globally and around the world, as well as internationally." He then mocked his own weak sense of logic when he stated: "I love America. 'Cause it's full of Americans." That was followed by a series of "I believe" statements, which not only satirized the gap between Bush and Martin Luther King Jr., but would also resonate with a series of "I believe" statements Colbert would later deliver in his own speech. Bush ended on a serious note, saying, "God bless the troops, God bless freedom, and God bless America." Bush had been a good sport, remarking that it was important to be able to make fun of his job, but he had closed by returning to his best presidential tone and repeating his signature slogans. That flow suggested that, while the skit might have been funny, Bush was still in control. Then he and Bridges hugged and waved at the crowd to loud applause. Next Mark Smith, president of the WHCA, introduced Colbert and the mood in the room quickly changed.

Even though much of the media would emphasize that Mark Smith admitted that he had not seen much of Colbert on Comedy Central before he booked him, *The New York Times* would later report that "he knew enough about Mr. Colbert—'He not only skewers politicians, he skewers those of us in the media'—to expect that he would cause some good-natured discomfort among the 2,600 guests, many of them politicians and reporters."[15] That said, though, it is likely that he had little sense of how uncomfortable the room would get.

Colbert took the podium and began with a stiff joke about fourteen black bulletproof SUVs blocking another fourteen black SUVs in the parking lot. It was a fairly clunky opening to his presentation and it certainly did not seem like it was written by a well-established comedian with years of experience in improv and satire. Clearly, at its surface, the opening lines are meant to be a parody of the type of announcements made by speakers before they begin their presentations. But such comments are typically reserved for convention speakers—not celebrity events. I mention this, because later, when I discuss the responses to Colbert, the question of his speech's funniness will be a topic of concern. While it is impossible to know Colbert's intentions with these opening lines, I want to suggest that this joke sets up the audience to recognize that the speech won't be funny in a conventional sense. Most significant, though, is to note that Colbert begins his speech with a flat joke.

The opening joke set the stage for the next awkward moment when Colbert said: "Wow, what an honor! The White House Correspondents' Dinner. To actually sit here, at the same table with my hero, George W. Bush, to be this close to the man. I feel like I'm dreaming. Somebody pinch me. You know what? I'm a pretty sound sleeper—that may not be enough. Somebody shoot me in the face."[16] What is interesting with this joke is its direct interplay with the almost identical joke referenced above that had been part of the president's own bit. The president had already made fun of Cheney's hunting accident. What differed in Colbert's version, though, was its set up with the over-the-top delight Colbert expresses at being close to Bush. The result was an edgy audience response. Colbert's fake enthusiasm for being near Bush created an immensely awkward reaction.

It just grew tenser. Colbert's next segment pointed at how the government's response to 9/11—via both the civil-rights-suspending legislation of the USA PATRIOT Act and covert operations—had led to an erosion of the right to privacy: "By the way, before I get started, if anybody needs anything else at their tables, just speak slowly and clearly into your table numbers. Somebody from the NSA will be right over with a cocktail."[17] While the joke about illegal wiretapping may appear to be about the NSA, it seems more likely that it was aimed at the press, politicians, and celebrities who had known for some time about these practices and done nothing about them. Colbert's point is that, as far as his audience is concerned, illegal wiretapping is about as innocuous as getting another drink. After these set-ups, Colbert begins in (satirical) earnest:

> Mark Smith, ladies and gentlemen of the press corps, Madame First Lady, Mr. President, my name is Stephen Colbert and tonight it's my privilege to celebrate this president. We're not so different, he and I. We get it. We're not brainiacs on the nerd patrol. We're not members of the factinista. We go straight from the gut, right, sir? That's where the truth lies, right down here in the gut. Do you know you have more nerve endings in your gut than you have in your head? You can look it up. I know some of you are going to say "I did look it up, and that's not true." That's 'cause you looked it up in a book. Next time, look it up in your gut. I did. My gut tells me that's how our nervous system works. Every night on my show, *The Colbert Report*, I speak straight from the gut, OK? I give people the truth, unfiltered by rational argument. I call it the "No Fact Zone."[18]

Fans accustomed to Colbert's routine would have been familiar with Colbert's line about thinking from the gut, since that is the definition he used to describe his signature word *truthiness,* which he used to open his first show. But even seasoned Colbert fans would have been a bit surprised by Colbert's direct and blunt association of himself with Bush. The audience had just watched Bush make fun of his unsophisticated intellect, and they had just watched another comedian identify with and impersonate Bush, but it was Colbert's delivery and his sharp tone that made the silly fun of the first bit evaporate into discomfort during his routine. What's more, what he said often seemed to be so subtly satirical that it simply appeared like non-satirical commentary. When Colbert says that, like Bush, he gives "people the truth, unfiltered by rational argument" there is practically no comedic distance, just as there was virtually no physical distance between Colbert and the object of his critique.

Some of the best images of the event emphasize that Colbert was literally next to Bush when he delivered these lines—a fact that surely played a significant role in the way that people responded to Colbert's words, since they were either angered at what seemed like disrespect or enthused by what seemed like extraordinary courage. While many of the early images that show both men indicate that Bush is a bit uneasy, those taken later in the presentation reveal Bush looking increasingly unhappy with Colbert.

These images contrast with those of Bush-Bridges, where Bush is comfortable, grinning, and in control.

Photo 1.1   Colbert gestures to the audience as he describes his similarities with Bush.

In the Colbert speech images, Bush seems visibly disturbed. A Bush aide later remarked in reference to Bush's facial expressions: "He's got that look that he's ready to blow."[19]

The next segment of Colbert's speech tropes on the phrase "I believe," which, as mentioned above, resonates uncannily with some of the same statements that Bush himself had made. Bush, only moments earlier in his own skit, had said, "I love America. 'Cause it's full of Americans," followed by "I believe" statements such as, "I believe we are an America that should come together, Republican, Democrat, and John McCain" and "I believe in bi-partisan bipartisanship."[20] The statements did poke fun at Bush's beliefs and they did make him seem simple-minded and a bit stupid, as though he were not capable of grasping what a good idea to believe in would actually be. They were presented tongue-in-cheek and were funny even though a second thought about these same jokes would have had to disturb anyone concerned about the leadership of the nation. Colbert's series would be similar in many ways, but blunter and edgier.

Colbert's "I believe" series begins with statements that emphasize Bush's simple thought process and his tendency to favor his gut over facts: "Number one, I believe in America. I believe it exists. My gut

Photos 1.2 and 1.3 The screen captures the proximity of Colbert to Bush and documents Bush's increasing discomfort.

Photo 1.4   Bush and Bridges embrace after their performance.

tells me I live there. I feel that it extends from the Atlantic to the Pacific, and I strongly believe it has 50 states."[21] Another series aimed at the distance between Bush administration rhetoric and the harsh realities in Iraq: "I believe the government that governs best is the government that governs least. And by these standards, we have set up a fabulous government in Iraq."[22] Next Colbert referenced the naïve belief among free-market Republicans that economic resources are determined solely by one's effort: "I believe in pulling yourself up by your own bootstraps. I believe it is possible—I saw this guy do it once in Cirque du Soleil. It was magical."[23] And lastly, he alluded to right-wing religious intolerance with specific reference to religions practiced in the Middle East and in Central and Southeast Asia: "And though I am a committed Christian, I believe that everyone has the right to their own religion, be you Hindu, Jewish or Muslim. I believe there are infinite paths to accepting Jesus Christ as your personal savior."[24] Next Colbert made another silly, flat joke that seemed incongruous in light of the politically charged ones he had uttered only moments before: "Ladies and gentlemen, I believe it's yogurt. But I refuse to believe it's not butter."[25] While at first blush the joke seems inconsistent and clunky, on closer examination it actually sets up a key moment in the speech. I would argue that this joke is highly significant since it suggests that Colbert refuses to suspend belief. It references two products (I Can't Believe It's Yogurt and I Can't Believe It's Not Butter) that suggest the notion that the public consumes ideas that are not true. Colbert, though, claims that he is not duped like the rest of the public, an interesting twist given his assertion that he is just like the president, who ignores facts at will in favor of his gut. The lines hint to a split between Colbert as an in-character right-wing, opinionated pundit, and Colbert out of character. If we reflect on it and unpack the mess of negatives in "I refuse to believe it's not butter," this part of the "I believe" series seems to come more from Colbert out of character, thereby functioning as a wink to his intended audience of Colbert fans (which, as I'll discuss below, is not the same as the audience in the room). Even more noteworthy is that the last silly joke is the set up for the final "I believe" statement. Colbert ends the "I believe" run with: "Most of all, I believe in this president."[26] Believing in the president is akin to believing in yogurt.

By now, if there had been any doubt, the audience in the room knows that this is not true, that Colbert truly opposes the president and everything he stands for. All of what follows is then coded by this blanket statement, which reads in opposite fashion to the literal meaning of the words uttered. This ability to speak truth through lies, parody, or mockery is at the heart of the work of political satire. Satire's aim is to offer social criticism by adopting an extreme or exaggerated version of commonly held beliefs that are in need of radical questioning. And, as is well known, political satire does not produce huge laughs: the humor in satire is subtle and discomforting since it almost always pokes a bit at the audience itself. Its funniest moments take place when the audience feels like they "get it," that they are in the know, and that they too see the folly in the behavior being lampooned. Colbert's audience at the dinner included few "it-getters," suggesting that Colbert's real target audience was the general public, especially his fan base, who already felt alienated and unrepresented by the power elite Colbert was directly addressing in his speech.

Next, Colbert went after the president's low approval rating: "Now, I know there are some polls out there saying this man has a 32 percent approval rating. But guys like us, we don't pay attention to the polls. We know that polls are just a collection of statistics that reflect what people are thinking in 'reality.' And reality has a well-known liberal bias." Colbert pokes fun at Bush's low approval rating, while also returning to the idea that Bush is totally disconnected from facts, since he ignores any information that is unpleasant for him. Again, the even greater irony is that Bush had also joked about his low approval rating, asking, "How come I can't have dinner with the 36 percent of the people who like me?"[27] Given the fact that many of Colbert's jokes had previously been referenced in the Bush-Bridges skit, it becomes curious that Colbert's version was so disturbing to Bush. One of the obvious explanations for this is the fact that in the Bush-Bridges skit, Bush had been in control. With Colbert, he was clearly the butt of a joke.

I would suggest that the difference goes even beyond that, since another key difference was that Colbert's thinly veiled satire often appeared as direct, unfiltered critique. Holcomb describes the difference as between a form of satire that is funny because it is "familiar" and one that presents a version of the truth rarely seen. She describes the Bush-Bridges bit as an example of tragic humor, which relies on rhetorical recognition. In contrast, she describes Colbert's speech as an example of "comic criticism," which is more generally disturbing. "Its laughter is born of the realization that what was said is closer to the truth than what is typically said in discourse."[28] Colbert, in the opening part of his speech, had gone after traditional Republican values, Puritanical religious intolerance, Bush's illogical decision-making and aversion to the facts, the president's low approval rating, the apathy of his audience, and the suspension of civil rights after 9/11. He was just getting warmed up.

Perhaps coincidentally or perhaps purposefully (if we recognize that much of the Bush-Bridges act spoofed on the typical barbs thrown at the president), the second part of Colbert's presentation moves increasingly away from jokes that show direct connections to the Bush-Bridges skit. In fact, they move more and more to the sort of "speaking truthiness to power" that would forever mark the speech as one of the most extraordinary moments of dissent during the Bush presidency. One of the most biting moments was when Colbert said: "The greatest thing about this man is he's steady. You know where he stands. He believes the same thing Wednesday that he believed on Monday, no matter what happened Tuesday. Events can change; this man's beliefs never will."[29] These lines are especially critical for two reasons. First, they were delivered satirically by someone posing as a right-wing pundit, or nut case. But this nut case LOVES Bush, which then implies, and convincingly so for critics of Bush, that one would have to be a nut case to support Bush at all. Second, these lines simply seem like a statement of the truth—one that frighteningly suggests that the most powerful nation in the world is being led by a stubborn, obstinate man incapable of grappling with a complex world. Colbert was not alone in thinking this, but there is little doubt that Bush rarely encountered such a bold critic to his face. In the span of a few seconds, Colbert had suggested that you'd have to be crazy to think Bush was "great" and that Bush was a bullheaded man incapable of learning anything from experience.

As if it had not been enough that Colbert was standing a few feet away from the president when he described him with full satirical affection as incapable of making a good decision, Colbert then shifted to his next major target: the media. The media had also been referenced by Bush-Bridges: "The media really ticks me off by not editing what I say."[30] Here the joke was that the media did report accurately and it was unfavorable to Bush. Colbert's remarks about the media were radically different. Bush and Bridges had also referred to the "liberal media." For years, the right had used phrases like the "liberal media," but as Colbert's speech would show, there was not much evidence of a liberal media during the Bush presidency, if by *liberal media* we mean a media that would be left-partisan and critical of a conservative president. Geoffrey Nunberg points out in *Talking Right* that the right had long captured the ability to set the tone and meaning for important words linked to public democracy. He argues that conservatives had "been able to establish the meanings of words in everyday usage without setting off any alarm bells" and that these partisan meanings had been almost totally adopted by the media with little questioning.[31] The word *liberal* had almost become equivalent to treason and *media* was often referred to as having a "liberal bias." Nunberg shows that this perception had become commonplace, even though it had not been substantiated: "The charges of liberal bias have been so widely and insistently repeated that conservatives have been able to allude to them as a truth that requires no defending."[32]

Colbert's own satire directly aims at these same practices. One of his primary targets has long been the public's acceptance of biased, illogical, unsubstantiated ideas as true. Colbert did not take aim at the general public, though. Instead he focused on the sources of these ideas: Bush, his administration, right-wing pundits, and inane media were all under fire that night. Colbert's access point to critiquing the media during his WHCA speech is very clever, though. He actually hints that the media in 2006 had become more critical of Bush and less passive (which arguably *was* true). "As excited as I am to be here with the president, I am appalled to be surrounded by the liberal media that is destroying America, with the exception of Fox News. Fox News gives you both sides of every story: the president's side and the vice president's side."[33] By appearing to agree with Bush that the media is liberal and that it has been "unfair" to Bush, he then satirically barbs Fox News. This was the second direct reference to Fox News in his speech, a repetition that is noteworthy. The first was to suggest that Colbert had a copyright on the term "No Fact Zone"—a joke that Fox's news is all about catchphrases and hype, rather than about reality. However, in the second reference, Colbert praises Fox's tendency to frame all information in the form of an opposition, which often is set up in a way that is presented as extremely important, but actually remains totally illogical. The construction of false binaries, where two pundits with extreme views face off, is standard Fox fare. As Colbert stated during an interview at Harvard's John F. Kennedy School of Government, the turn to 24-hour news has often meant very little actual news reporting in relation to commentary on those few real news pieces.[34] Colbert critiques the way that commentary has come to overshadow the presentation of information to viewers. Instead of news, viewers get pundits who shout their unsubstantiated, vitriolic, divisive opinions at their audience. Their goal is not to encourage reasoned debate and civic engagement. Instead they aim to create cult followers. Colbert's goal, in contrast, is to expose the damaging consequences of this "news" process. And he does it by exaggeratedly embodying it.

Key to recall is that the moment of Colbert's speech was one of immense tension in the United States, when one might say that the role of the media had never been more important. Not only were we at war in Iraq and Afghanistan, not only was it increasingly obvious that the wars had been waged for unjustifiable reasons, but the War on Terror was unbounded, and was greatly affecting the lives of U.S. citizens, whose rights were ever more diminished by the demands of the so-called War on Terror. This was a moment in U.S. history when the public was beginning to get a series of reports from courageous reporters like Seymour Hirsh, who had brought to public attention the mistreatment of detainees in Guantánamo in 2004. It was becoming progressively clearer that the United States had violated almost all of its own values, principles, and actual agreements (like the Geneva Conventions) in the course of the War on Terror.

In 2004, the torture memos leaked to the public, revealing that the Bush administration had attempted to find legal loopholes to the United States' own prohibitions against torture. And in December of 2005, only months before Colbert's appearance at the WHCA, *The New York Times,* one of the few mainstream media outlets that had held the Bush administration accountable in the years following

9/11, reported on the government's crackdown on "whistle-blowers" and leaks. *The New York Times* article focuses on the government's investigation of the National Security Agency (NSA) wiretapping leak, which had revealed how the U.S. government was illegally spying on its own citizens, but it also referenced other similar conflicts between the press and the administration: "The case is the latest in a series of clashes between the Fourth Estate [the news media] and the Bush administration, which has aggressively enforced restrictions on classified information and has frequently complained about press disclosures related to terrorism or the war in Iraq."[35] *The New York Times* piece focuses on the tension between a secretive White House, the public's right to know, and the press's responsibility to report on these issues. In addition, it comments on dishonest, manipulative reporters like Judith Miller, who was accused of colluding with the government to leak the identity of CIA operative Valerie Plame, wife of Ambassador Joe Wilson, who had been a public critic of Bush. The inference based on *The New York Times* piece is that the news media has two major problems: partisan reporters and the White House's culture of secrecy and deception.

Colbert builds on these ideas and presents the barb that one reason the press is unlikely to pursue facts is that such news simply is not fun and entertaining: "But the rest of you, what are you thinking, reporting on NSA wiretapping or secret prisons in Eastern Europe? Those things are secret for a very important reason: they're super-depressing. And if that's your goal, well, misery accomplished."[36] Here Colbert tropes on the by then infamous appearance of Bush landing in flight gear on the USS *Abraham Lincoln* (CVN-72) aircraft carrier on May 1, 2003, when he addressed the United States and announced the end of major combat operations in the Iraq War, while an enormous banner reading "Mission Accomplished" hung in the background. Much would later be made of Bush's assertion that the mission was accomplished, when there were no other visible signs of any sort of drawdown of the U.S. military. It is worth recalling that it was after Bush's announcement that he later called for a troop surge. But Colbert's point focuses on the media, which had enthusiastically covered the "Mission Accomplished" speech, and its tendency to avoid difficult (i.e., depressing) news. As Colbert puts it: "Over the last five years you people were so good— over tax cuts, WMD intelligence, the effects of global warming. We Americans didn't want to know, and you had the courtesy not to try to find out. Those were good times, as far as we knew."[37]

Colbert suggests that it is the media's responsibility to make information available to the public, even when that information may be disturbing and might lead people to look away in discomfort. He suggests, along with most critics who believe that a vital democracy depends on an informed citizenry, that a news media driven by ratings and revenue can never adequately serve the public. News media that functions as entertainment media harms democracy by distracting the public rather than informing and educating it. This problem, though, enters into new realms of civic disaster when a democratic nation is at war and when that war seems to carry none of the sorts of checks and balances of previous ones. Such conditions call for an even more active investigative press that can demand that the public be given access to key information regarding government activities, especially when these threaten the civil rights of the citizenry and they violate domestic and international law. Instead, Colbert argues, the public had to contend with an authoritarian administration shrouded in secrecy that was covered by a passive media that had abandoned the journalistic ideals that had previously characterized the United States' free press.

In one of his boldest moments during the speech, Colbert spoke directly to the press and called them out for their complacency. Of course, he did this by stating the opposite, by suggesting that the press had become too bold, and that it needed to go back to an earlier, more docile time: "But, listen, let's review the rules. Here's how it works: the president makes decisions. He's the Decider. The press secretary announces those decisions, and you people of the press type those decisions down. Make, announce, type. Just put 'em through a spell-check and go home. Get to know your family again. Make love to your wife. Write that novel you got kicking around in your head. You know, the one about the intrepid Washington reporter with the courage to stand up to the administration. You know - fiction!"[38] The room responded with silence.

Colbert followed by shouting out to a few "journalists" he called heroes: Christopher Buckley, editorial writer famous for his political satire and son of William F. Buckley, Jr., who appeared on *The Colbert Report* to talk about *Thank You for Smoking* (March 13, 2006); economist Jeffrey Sachs[39], who appeared on Colbert's show (March 2, 2006) to talk about his book *The End of Poverty*; Ken Burns, a documentary filmmaker with work on the Civil War, baseball, and jazz and who has worked with PBS (appeared on November 1, 2005); and Bob Schieffer, host of *Face the Nation*, who Colbert contrasted against cable news hosts who shout at their guests and ignore facts. What is most noteworthy from this list is that only Schieffer falls into the typical category of journalist.[40] Schieffer proves, for Colbert, that there are some journalists with integrity and that not all of them have been drawn into the trap of ratings-driven, spectacle-heavy news. What we can learn from this list is that Colbert clearly imagines that a publicly committed media capable of supporting democracy will include a variety of media types, only some of whom will look like traditional journalists. Colbert jokingly asked Schieffer, when he had him on his show only one month prior to his appearance at the WHCA: "What advice do you give to guys like me, who are just starting out and changing the face of news?"[41] And while this caused Schieffer to giggle, it seems clear that Colbert is actually serious: he does consider himself to be someone who is out to change the face of news. Even more significant for the context of the WHCA was the idea that anyone working in media, anyone who has access to the public, has the opportunity to speak truth to power. And this was especially important in an era when those that should have been seeking facts and exposing truth, like the members of the WHCA, were not.

Next Colbert referenced a number of the people present in the room: Jesse Jackson, Mayor Nagin, Justice Scalia, Senator John McCain, and White House Press Secretary Tony Snow. His last bit focuses on the post of White House press secretary and how he would have liked to have gotten Tony Snow's job. Scott McClellan had resigned only shortly before the dinner, giving Colbert a chance to make a silly audition video for the post of White House press secretary. In it, he begins by appearing disinterested in the questions directed to him by the press, but then Helen Thomas begins to question him:

> *Thomas*: Your decision to invade Iraq has caused the deaths of thousands (Colbert's smile fades) of Americans and Iraqis, wounds of Americans and Iraqis for a lifetime.
> *Colbert*: OK, hold on Helen, look—
> *Thomas*: Every reason given, publicly at least, has turned out not to be true. My question is why did you really want to go to war?
> *Colbert*: Helen, I'm going to stop you right there. (Thomas keeps talking.) That's enough! No! Sorry, Helen, I'm moving on. (Colbert tries to turn her volume off, but the knob falls off his controls.)[42]

The rest of the video spoofs a B-horror film, with Thomas bearing down on an increasingly agitated Colbert, who assumes the position of the fleeing damsel (stumbling, dropping keys, running scared) to Thomas's "monster." It closes with Colbert thinking he has escaped her by leaving Washington, D.C., to be picked up in New York, only to discover that his car is being driven by none other than Helen Thomas. The skit is a silly play on the relentless journalist who transforms into a frightening monster for the poor, terrified press secretary. The choice of Helen Thomas was crucial, since she had a long history as an intrepid reporter. She also had been a vocal critic of the Bush administration, especially with regard to the culture of secrecy that loomed over the White House in those years. After screening the video, Colbert pointed to Thomas and thanked her, mentioned that it had "been a true honor" and thanked the audience.[43] As he describes it in his book: "I am happy to say my speech was met with respectful silence. You could hear a pin drop. Or a sphincter clamp."[44] Indeed. It would be safe to say that the people in the room had little idea that they had just witnessed a legend being made. It would not be long before the speech became one of the most famous examples of political satire in history.

THE RESPONSE

"Numerous attendees said that Colbert had 'bombed' with an excessively harsh routine; commentators, mostly on the left, countered that anyone who panned his performance was a toady of the administration."[45]

The silence of the audience foreshadowed the silence on the part of the mainstream media and the White House, which attempted to downplay or criticize the event. As Holcomb notes, one of the most telling aspects of the speech comes from the "divergent responses from the mainstream media versus the alternative media and the viewing public."[46] Most initial coverage in the mainstream media focused on the Bush-Bridges skit. As *Media Matters* reported on May 1, 2006: "Following the annual awards dinner of the White House Correspondents' Association held on April 29, numerous news outlets trumpeted President Bush's performance at the event. But in turn, many outlets entirely ignored the scathing routine delivered by the night's featured entertainer, Stephen Colbert."[47] Here is *Media Matters'* breakdown of the mainstream media coverage immediately following the dinner:

• April 29: C-SPAN broadcast the event live and aired the event in its entirety several times in the following 24 hours. It then aired an abridged version of the dinner that featured only Bush's performance. On April 30, C-SPAN broadcast a 25-minute segment (7:35 P.M.—8:00 P.M. ET), which featured approximately ten minutes of footage of guests entering the event, followed by the full 15-minute Bush-Bridges routine.[48]

- April 30: ABC's *This Week* host George Stephanopoulos played an excerpt of Bush's act and remarked that the dinner "gets more inventive every year."
- April 30: NBC's *Sunday Today* co-host Lester Holt introduced clips of the Bush-Bridges routine by noting that the "relationship between the White House press corps and the president can be a contentious one, but last night it was all laughs."
- April 30: Footage of Bush's performance also aired on NBC's *Nightly News*. They showed no footage of Colbert.
- May 1: All three major networks played clips of Bush's routine on their morning shows, but ignored Colbert entirely. CNN's *American Morning* did the same.
- May 1: *The New York Times* article on the event detailed the Bush and Bridges performance. The article reported, "With his approval ratings in the mid-30's and a White House beset by troubles, there is some evidence that Mr. Bush worked harder on his performance this year than in the past." They omitted mention of Colbert or the fact that he had highlighted the White House's current problems at the dinner.[49]

The nearly complete removal of Colbert's performance from reports on the WHCA Dinner by the very media sources that had been the brunt of much of his satire seems to require little explanation. Clearly, he had touched a nerve, and the media had retaliated by refusing to cover him. It is noteworthy that they spent so much time covering the Bush-Bridges skit—a move that again suggests their tacit approval of that form of humor, but not of Colbert's. On the face of it, the Bush-Bridges skit was pretty biting satire of the president, and it covered many of the criticisms that had been regularly leveled at him: he was inarticulate, uneducated, unprepared, uninterested, unsophisticated, disliked, and illogical. Responses by both the mainstream media and the blogosphere were positive about the skit, since it was generally perceived that Bush had done a good job making fun of himself.[50] Comments on the YouTube site that posted the video remarked that, even though some viewers didn't like or vote for Bush, they thought that the bit showed Bush's ability to be playful.[51] But, as Holcomb explains, what made the Bush-Bridges skit fall within the accepted bounds of humor was that it was "familiar"; it did not transcend the sorts of prodding and critiquing of the administration that were standard fare in the mainstream media. While on close examination, it was pretty biting—sitting just within the bounds of typical roasts— it did not raise any issues that were not already familiar to the public. In contrast, Colbert went for the jugular, and he did it while pretending to be an avid fan of the president. Thus, I would add to Holcomb's assessment of the familiarity/novelty distinction between the events that one of the major differences was the position of the comedian vis-à-vis Bush. Bridges had gotten to many of the topics Colbert also covered, but he had done so with camaraderie and within acceptable bounds, ultimately deferring to the power of the president. Colbert, in contrast, had feigned adoration of the president in a way that made his disapproval obvious, and on top of that, he had dared to directly address such touchy subjects as the loss of innocent life for an unjust war, the unwavering idiocy of the president, and the criminal complicity of the mainstream press that had been busy having a good time while the nation was in crisis. Clearly, he needed to be punished.

One form of punishment came via assertions that his performance had not been covered by the mainstream press was because it simply was not funny. *The Washington Post* reported on May 2: "The reviews from the White House Correspondents' Association Dinner are in, and the consensus is that *President Bush* and Bush impersonator *Steve Bridges* stole Saturday's show—and Comedy Central host *Stephen Colbert's* cutting satire fell flat because he ignored the cardinal rule of Washington humor: Make fun of yourself, not the other guy."[52] The question of whether or not Colbert had been funny appeared in a variety of news outlets, but what is most significant is that its lack of success as humor was repeatedly used to explain lack of coverage. Stephen Spruiell, writing for *The National Review* on May 1, 2006, claimed that the lack of coverage of the speech was not to protect Bush, but rather to protect Colbert: "The primary reason the press has downplayed Colbert's performance—other than deadline pressure the night of the dinner—is that members of the media *like* Stephen Colbert. Rather than shielding Bush from negative publicity, it is the other way around."[53] He suggested that Colbert simply fell flat, wasn't funny, and didn't deliver effective satire either.

Of course, explaining the lack of coverage for his speech on its degree of humor makes sense if one assumes that making the audience laugh was Colbert's goal. As I pointed out in my analysis of the speech, though, Colbert seems to signal to the audience with his opening announcement about fourteen black SUVs blocking another fourteen black SUVs that his speech will not be funny in a conventional way. What's more, Colbert has repeatedly satirized the press's tendency to frame issues in false binaries, making the funny/ not funny debate seem rather silly and misplaced. As Holcomb notes: "Rather than realize Colbert's criticism as a catalyst to transcend the problematic 'truthiness' of their punditry, many commentators simply positioned Colbert as a conventional comedian and thus focused on his (in)ability to get laughs. Thus, it appears to many viewers that the mainstream media—even some of those who proclaimed it funny—did not get the joke."[54] There is little doubt that Colbert's performance did not focus on any sort of traditional comedic humor. Rather than make the room comfortable, it was designed to make them squirm. By that standard, Colbert's speech was a huge success.

Beyond the blackout and accusations of not being funny, the other series of negative coverage came from those who accused Colbert of crossing the line. *U.S. News & World Report* took that angle in their story: "Comedy Central star Stephen Colbert's biting routine at the White House Correspondents' Association Dinner won a rare silent protest from Bush aides and supporters Saturday when several independently left before he finished."[55] They focused on the negative reaction of Bush supporters: "'Colbert crossed the line,' said one top Bush aide, who rushed out of the hotel as soon as Colbert finished. Another said that the President was visibly angered by the sharp lines that kept coming."[56] As they described the features of Colbert's speech, they returned to the idea that it was not as entertaining as Bush's skit: "Aides and reporters, however, said that it did not overshadow Bush's own funny routine."[57]

While the mainstream media was not covering, panning, and critiquing Colbert, an entirely different response was taking place in the alternative media, the blogosphere, and via other forms of alternative media. On May 3, *The New York Times* covered the other side of the story—the one where Colbert's speech was quickly becoming a media phenomenon: "What Mr. Smith [president of the WHCA] did not anticipate, he said, was that Mr. Colbert's nearly 20-minute address would become one of the most hotly debated topics in the politically charged blogosphere. Mr. Colbert delivered his remarks in character as the Bill O'Reilly-esque commentator he plays on 'The Colbert Report,' although this time his principal foil, President Bush, was just a few feet away."[58] As Noam Cohen reported almost three weeks later on May 22, 2006, also for *The New York Times*: "The after-dinner speech that refuses to go away has scored another distinction: top of the charts."[59]

Colbert's speech registered in alternative media in a number of ways: video views and downloads, blogs, comments posted, and coverage in alternative press venues were a lively sign of the disconnect between mainstream news media and alternative venues. The circulation of the video of his speech was repeatedly referred to as "viral." The *Wikipedia* entry for the performance states: "Even though Colbert's performance 'landed with a thud' among the live audience, a clip of Colbert at the dinner became an overnight sensation, turning into a viral video that spread across numerous web sites in various forms, with the sites that offered the video seeing massive increases in their traffic."[60] While it is difficult to get full data on the extent of the popular consumption of the speech, here are some highlights.

As reported on Wikipedia's coverage of the speech [61]

- Three weeks after the dinner, audio of Colbert's performance went on sale at the iTunes Music Store and became the #1 album purchased, outselling new releases by the Red Hot Chili Peppers, Pearl Jam, and Paul Simon. The CEO of Audible.com, which provided the recording sold at iTunes, explained its success by saying, "You had to not be there to get it." It continued to be a top download at iTunes for the next five months and remains a top-selling audiobook on the service.
- According to CNET's News.com site, Colbert's speech became "one of the Internet's hottest acts," and searches for Colbert on Yahoo! were up 5,625 percent.
- During the days after the speech, Google saw twice as many searches for "C-SPAN" (the television network that broadcast the event) as for "Jennifer Aniston"—an uncommon occurrence—as well as a surge in Colbert-related searches.
- The blog "Crooks and Liars," one of the first places to host the video, not only recorded their busiest day on record, but Nielsen BuzzMetrics ranked their post of the video clip as the second most popular blog post for all of 2006.
- Clips of Colbert's comic tribute climbed to the #1, #2, and #3 spots atop YouTube's "Most Viewed" video list. Before YouTube took down the video under pressure from C-SPAN, the various clips of Colbert's speech had been viewed 2.7 million times in less than 48 hours. In an unprecedented move for the network, C-SPAN demanded that YouTube and iFilm remove unauthorized copies of the video from their sites.
- Google Video subsequently purchased the exclusive rights to retransmit the video and it remained at or near the top of Google's most popular videos for the next two weeks.

- Both *Editor & Publisher* and *Salon*, which published extensive and early coverage of the Colbert speech, drew record and near-record numbers of viewers to their websites.
- 70,000 articles were posted to blogs about Colbert's roast of Bush on the Thursday after the event, the most of any topic, and "Colbert" remained the top search term at Technorati for over a week.
- *Chicago Sun-Times* TV Critic Doug Elfman credited the Internet with promoting an event that would have otherwise been overlooked, stating that "Internet stables for liberals, like the behemoth dailykos.com, began rumbling as soon as the correspondents' dinner was reported in the mainstream press, with scant word of Colbert's combustive address."

Other media examples

- On May 5, 2006, a *Huffington Post* piece by Marty Kaplan used the verb *Colberted*.[62] Colbert's performance had led to the creation of a new verb.
- A website *ThankYouStephenColbert.org* had posted the video and opened up a place for visitors to post. By May 3, 2006, there were 32,000 thank yous posted.[63] Holcomb reported 56,000 posts (some of which were repeated, spam, or critical of Colbert) in 2009.[64]
- *Bloggersblog* reported that on May 3, 2006, Colbert references in blogs were running nearly 4,000 posts per day.[65]

Bloggersblog would later suggest that it was the intense coverage of Colbert via blogs that later accounted for more mainstream outlets, like *The New York Times,* picking up on the story: "It is possibly proof that if bloggers can post enough on a topic the mainstream media will eventually be forced to report on it."[66] What is most interesting to note from the coverage of Colbert at the WHCA dinner, is that the discrepancy between coverage by the mainstream media and that of the alternative media led to a sense of empowerment for bloggers. Ironically, Colbert's jabs at the media for their passive and non-confrontational coverage of the scandals linked to the Bush presidency led to an explosion of alternative media coverage that showed that the mainstream media was out of touch with a large segment of the population. It also demonstrated that the blogosphere had the power to set public debate and initiate stories that would later be covered in the mainstream media.

It further revealed that the casual, tongue-in-cheek, and sometimes downright silly nature of the blogosphere's coverage of issues was not only idle distraction, but that it was actually one of the prime ways that many young people engaged with the news. In one example, Gawker, one of the most well-trafficked blog sites, posted a poll on May 2, 2006, that asked whether Colbert's performance at the WHCA Dinner was "One of the most patriotic acts I've witnessed of any individual" or "Not really that funny?"[67] Twenty-four hours after posting the poll, Jesse from Gawker wrote: "After 24 hours and some 11,000 votes—by a long shot, Gawker's most popular poll ever—the answer is clear: Stephen Colbert's White House Correspondents' Dinner performance was one of the most patriotic acts you've witnessed of any individual. Naturally, that 75 percent margin of victory proves—*proves*, damn it—Colbert's patriotic genius. No chance of a selection bias among Gawker readers. No chance at all."[68] Certainly, the poll does not prove that Colbert is a patriotic genius. It does prove, however, that Gawker's constituency enthusiastically supported Colbert's performance. Below is just a highlight of some of the blogosphere coverage for Colbert's speech as reported via Bloggersblog.[69]

- Alternative Hippopotamus: "You'll notice that Colbert pretty much 'killed' at the WHC."
- Liquidmatrix: "I have to admit I was so-so on the humor of Stephen Colbert. But, after having seen the speech that he delivered at the White House Correspondents' Dinner I'm a HUGE fan. I was a little confused when the major print media failed to make any mention of this speech. It was like it had never happened."
- Irresponsible: "I've watched the video a few times now, and it gets more and more stunning with each viewing. Just the absolute guts it took for Stephen Colbert to stand up there and wail on pretty much everyone in the room. It's stunning, just stunning. Check the link for downloads to all the vids."
- BlogCritics: "Colbert told the media, rather blatantly, that they weren't doing their jobs. They weren't keeping America informed of rather important events, such as Bush's tax cuts to the rich, WMD intelligence and the effects of global warming. He sarcastically said, 'We Americans didn't want to know, and you had the courtesy not to try to find out.' He is dead on."
- Media Cynic: "Stephen Colbert has brought back the subtle and difficult art of irony. His performance was absolutely hilarious. And that's the Wørd."

- Popwatch: "If you enjoy a comic rapport with Stephen Colbert, you probably had a very satisfying weekend. If you don't, well, you're probably the President of the United States."
- Uneasy Silence: "I don't think he should be expecting another invite soon. I don't seem to understand why the politicians didn't seem to laugh, but I feel one killer of an IRS audit will be heading his way next year."
- PSoTD: "No, Colbert's comments have a life that will extend the remainder of Bush's life. When GB II dies (or goes to jail), think anyone will remember any of the lines of Steve Bridges last night? Hardly."
- The Superficial: "Everybody's going crazy over this, so if you haven't seen it by the end of the day you're officially a loser."
- The Moderate Voice: "Bush's performance will be rerun on some shows for the next few days due to its entertainment value; Colbert's will be rerun and discussed because of how it was received by some in the audience, because it's dagger-sharp message has some news value and because he was willing to take a risk at doing the kind of satire he did...where he did it."

Bloggersblog is quick to point out, though, that all was not love for Colbert: "The following bloggers didn't get and/or didn't like Colbert's performance: *Riehl World View*, *Protein Wisdom*, *The Bullwinkle Blog*, *RightWinged.com*, Michelle Malkin, *HotAir.com* and *Media Blog*." These naysayers aside, though, it is clear that the blogosphere opened up a space for supporters of the performance to respond to it. Holcomb notes in relation to *ThankYouStephenColbert. org*, a site created just to allow visitors to see the video and post a comment, that a review of the comments posted there suggested that many of the posters wanted "to continue the conversation, whether on sites like this, with friends and family members, or through other forms of communicative interaction."[70] The room may have been silent, the mainstream media might have been stiff, but the alternative media sphere embraced Colbert's performance, launching it into greater and greater visibility, proving that peer-to-peer media, alternative news websites, and blogs rivaled the mainstream news media as a source of information and political commentary.

THE ROOM NO LONGER MATTERS

In a number of ways, Colbert's performance indicated a radical shift in media consumption and a shift in the power of satire to speak truth to power in an era of virtually unprecedented government secrecy and deception. The speech points to these changes in three ways: the overshadowing of "the room" by the people, the changing face of media (especially news media), and the rise of Colbert as not just a critic of the news but as an actual news source.

One of the key features of the speech was that while it was delivered to the WHCA and their invited guests, it appears that the audience in the room was not Colbert's primary audience.[71] In fact, their witnessing of the speech only contributed to the actual performance itself. Arguably, Colbert knew well before he got to the podium that he was going to make the room uncomfortable and that, rather than laughs, he would illicit uneasy groans. He also may have known that his "balls-alicious" performance to that room would make the speech legendary, since his willingness to displease the local crowd in order to please his broader audience would resonate with the public at large.

James Poniewozik, television critic for the online version of *Time,* wrote on May 3, 2006, that those who thought that Colbert bombed did not understand contemporary media culture. Their criticism of him was not necessarily a product of their politics, as evidenced by the left-oriented critics who still thought Colbert flopped, it was a product of their misunderstanding that the audience was no longer comprised of the people in the room. If we judged Colbert by the response of those present, then he bombed. There were few laughs over the course of the speech and many present left the room unhappy. But, if we judge him based on the response to his speech from those not there, he was an extraordinary success. At one time, event coverage would have focused only on the audience response, since few would watch the speech on C-SPAN. "So Colbert would have lived and died on how well he entertained the room and how well the room spoke of him in the media the next day."[72]

Colbert's performance changed the stakes; it changed the way that the public engaged with the event, because rather than wait to learn what the mainstream media reported, they accessed the speech themselves, read about it on blogs, and formed a wider range of responses, most of which were in no way contingent on mainstream media outlets for information and opinion. "To the audience that would watch Colbert on Comedy Central, the pained, uncomfortable, perhaps-a-little-scared-to-laugh reaction shots were not signs of failure. They were the money shots. They were the whole point."[73] If Colbert was able to get Bush to look like he was going to blow, that just added to the force of his speech. That, quite simply, was part of his goal. Poniewozik explains this as a function of the changing shape of media, where the top-down authority of mainstream outlets have been displaced and fragmented:

> In other words, what anyone fails to get who said Colbert bombed because he didn't win over the room is: the room no longer matters. Not the way it used to. The room, which once would have received and filtered the ritual performance for the rest of us, is now just another subject to be dissected online…All of this, in other words, is yet another sign of how authority is fragmented and democratized in the Internet era—the top-down authority to assess and interpret for the masses that used to be much of the raison d'etre of the room. So if the room wasn't too amused by Colbert Saturday night, you'll have to excuse them. They don't have as much to laugh about anymore.[74]

Sophia Stone points at this shift as well when she writes that: "The complexity of Colbert's humor involves the ability to play on an audience's disapproving avowal for orchestrating an approving avowal for a much larger audience."[75] What Colbert managed to do was to set up the local audience so that their discomfort would satisfy his intended audience.

Not only was the "room" no longer synonymous with the intended audience, but the discrepancy between the mainstream coverage (its ignoring Colbert and critiquing him) and the alternative media coverage (that found his speech to be one of the "most patriotic" acts ever) was a significant sign of a new media era. The Colbert speech coverage revealed how the mainstream media no longer had the final word. Even though it might have initially attempted to avoid covering Colbert, the massive alternative media attention to the speech caused a shift in coverage and showed that alternative media was a powerful source of public debate and information setting. The coverage of the event by those supportive of Colbert's performance also ensured that Colbert's speech would be legendary. Supporters like these comprise what Colbert affectionately refers to as "The Colbert Nation." Sometimes, he just calls them "heroes."

These shifts point to a few ways that Colbert's show—and especially his performance that night—redefined satire in the post-9/11 era, a topic that will be discussed in chapter 3. For now, it is important to note that Colbert's speech went beyond merely lampooning a right-wing pundit's adoration of the president. It actually used satire as a source of direct, political dissent, and it served to energize and empower a segment of the public that had felt immensely disenfranchised during the Bush years. Not to be underestimated, either, is the fact that the appearance at the WHCA Dinner served to launch Colbert's fame to a whole new level. While the show had enjoyed significant viewers, the WHCA appearance significantly boosted Colbert's public image, even leading Spike TV to give him the Gutsiest Move on their Guys' Choice Awards in 2007.[76] The speech remains one of the main events in Colbert's career. He explains in his book that he is constantly asked about it: "Wherever I go, from P. Diddy's annual White Party to Hollywood premieres to the men's room at Sharper Image, I meet Heroes. And they all want to know the same thing: 'What was it like to be you, Stephen T. Colbert, at the 2006 White House Correspondents' Dinner?'"[77] Even more important, perhaps, is not to forget what it was like for those who saw his speech and were stunned and grateful to see him speaking truth to power.

2

THE PUBLIC AT RISK: DISSENT AND DEMOCRACY AFTER 9/11

It is common to mark a radical shift in U.S. democratic practices to the events of September 11, 2001, and the ensuing War on Terror. But public debate and democratic deliberation in the United States were already under threat prior to the terrorist attacks of 9/11. Well before that day, a series of ideological turns—among them the post-modern crisis of the left, the rise in right-wing fundamentalism, and the cult of individualism fostered by extreme free-market capitalism—coupled with material shifts in politics, economic policies, and media infrastructure had severely limited the possibilities for productive and vigorous public debate of key issues facing the nation. The pervasive state of fear, the hyper-patriotism, and the militarized response to the 9/11 attacks thus combined with the already existing weakened state of democracy in the United States to create what one might consider the perfect storm for the public sphere. After 9/11, the very idea that democracy depended on an active and engaged citizenry willing to struggle for social change was often seen to be in itself unpatriotic. The conditions for thinking about how to improve the nation's commitment to equality, access, rights, and justice were in crisis.

This chapter will briefly survey the ways in which a combination of factors existed pre-9/11 to threaten the possibilities for dissent and democracy. It then analyzes additional shifts that took place after 9/11. The third section traces changes in mass media that influenced the public's access to key information about U.S. politics and practices. The chapter closes by suggesting that comedy, especially satire, emerged after 9/11 as one of the few ways through which it was possible to encourage the public to reflect critically on these issues. Certainly, comedians were not immune to post-9/11 assaults on dissent, as evidenced by ABC-TV's decision to fire Bill Maher in 2002, but it remains the case that public figures like Jon Stewart, Maher (who later moved to HBO), and Stephen Colbert used satire, comedy, and irony to question political practices post-9/11 in ways that were less possible in traditional news venues.

THE PUBLIC IS A PROBLEM

Most advocates of democracy recognize that, for it to truly function, citizens need to be able to actively participate in making key decisions about government policy. Thus, central to a commitment to democracy is the idea of participatory democracy. However, research on democracy shows that decision-making authority tends to privilege an elite, or certain power blocs, at the expense of others, who are often minorities. So, theories of participatory democracy work on creating ways to reach all of the various groups within a democratic state so that each group can meaningfully participate in decision-making.

In order for these various groups to be brought together for meaningful debate of social issues, scholars have argued that there must be a "public sphere." The idea of the public sphere was developed by Jürgen Habermas in his well-known work: *The Structural Transformation of the Public Sphere*, published in German in 1962 and in an English edition in 1989.[1] Habermas explains that the public sphere is that space between individuals and government where people come together to debate important social issues. These exchanges typically occur in public places (coffee shops, plazas, restaurants, clubs) and via the media (newspapers, letters, and other forms of communication that are not face to face).[2] The public sphere was understood as a way through which people could develop their individual ideas into public opinion that could then transform into political action.

Now it should be clear that as essential as this concept may be for the ideals of democracy, it is difficult to achieve and maintain. States are never fully inclusive: historically, groups have always been left outside of the space of democratic participation (e.g., women, slaves, immigrants, criminals, the mentally infirm, the propertyless, racially targeted minorities, the disabled, and the lesbian-gay-bisexual-transgender community). The complication is that, from the perspective of the conservative right wing, the United States is a land of freedom and opportunity, whereas, from the perspective of the left, the United States needs to work harder to be a fully inclusive democracy and equitable society. These tensions were further exacerbated in response to the social movements of the 1960s that struggled for civil rights. While the United States did make major advances in terms of civil rights during that era, not all of those gains have held sway, and some would suggest that the nation has slid back into an era of intolerance and inequity.

This sense of a conservative backlash is generally linked to the era of the Reagan presidency and the rise of conservative values, the adoption of free-market economics at the expense of state protections, and a heightened militarization of U.S. public policy. As Douglas Kellner explains in *Media Culture,* after the liberal period of the Kennedy era of the 1960s, "intense struggles between liberals and conservatives broke out, capped by the victory of Ronald Reagan in 1980, which established over a decade of conservative hegemony."[3] The "common sense" of Reagan, carried into the Clinton era, was that "government must be limited and taxes reduced; business must be strengthened to create jobs and national wealth; government 'red tape' (and thus, regulatory policies) must be eliminated; individual entrepreneurialism is the best road to success and producing a strong society, therefore government should do everything possible to encourage such business enterprise; life is tough and only the fittest survive and prosper."[4] These policies hold no compassion for the disadvantaged and disenfranchised. If someone needs help, it must be that person's own fault, and it certainly is not the state's problem to aid him. He is on his own. The state's job, instead, is to protect the accumulation of wealth and the interests of business, since that is the way to build a strong nation.

It is precisely linked to this shift that scholars began to debate the demise of "the public sphere" in U.S. democracy. In 1998 Gerard Hauser, a leading theorist of rhetoric and the public sphere, stated: "In an era when special interests and the state have reduced politics to mass-media spectacle, and 'audience' has become an economic variable of spectators expected to applaud and purchase, current deliberations over the public sphere advance a critical antidote."[5] The worry about the public sphere revolved around the idea that the shift from state concern for the citizen to state support for business causes damage to the idea of democracy. If democracy depends on deliberation and civic participation, then it requires a public sphere or spheres through which constituents can debate ideas, form opinions, and influence policy. When that process is threatened, so too is democracy. By the Reagan era, it seemed to many that the public sphere had been replaced by a privatized, elitist power bloc of special interests that mainly advocated for corporations.

For those familiar with the comedy of Colbert, it seems clear that one of his goals is to reinvigorate the public sphere by (1) using satire to open up a space for debate and deliberation about the state of the nation and its practices, and (2) creating a sense of empowerment among his viewers by reaffirming their ability to shape public discourse and influence politics. As discussed in chapter 1, Colbert's performance at the White House Correspondents' Association Dinner could be viewed as an inversion of the elitist power structure that had previously defined that event and which held sway over most media information flows. His performance that night and the responses to it offered his viewers an opportunity to imagine a different public sphere, one where their views would matter.

But to fully appreciate the impact of that event, it is necessary to outline the various ways in which the U.S. public sphere had been compromised by a series of material and ideological changes that began in the Reagan-Bush era and intensified with the election of George W. Bush in 2000. Arguably, one of the most significant factors was the rise of extreme free-market capitalism, otherwise known as neoliberalism. Neoliberalism was the economic policy spearheaded by Reagan and Margaret Thatcher in the United States and England in the 1980s, but which had its origins in the economic policies of Chilean dictator Augusto Pinochet in 1973.[6] Neoliberalism, an economic theory designed by University of Chicago professor Milton Friedman in the 1970s, describes a market-oriented economic and social policy that is grounded on the belief that economies function best when they are deregulated and governed solely by the force of the market. The goal is to emphasize the private sector over the public in setting economic policy and practices. An example of a neoliberal policy would be the argument that we should not have public schools, but that we should use a voucher system instead. The logic is that schooling would improve if schools had to compete for students. The problem, though, is that such logic turns schools into corporations that must vie to attract students, and their success is measured by attracting students rather than by teaching them. That sort of competition is less likely to encourage the sort of foundational principles necessary for a public education linked to democratic ideals, such as a commitment to serve all groups evenly, to assist and aid students from disadvantaged backgrounds, to foster principles of democracy and civic education, etc. Indeed, for years, neoliberalism has been encroaching on all aspects of U.S. life, leading to changes in schooling, healthcare, social services, correctional facilities, militarization, and more. In the last decades, services previously provided by the government are increasingly run by private businesses. This has meant that corporate "rights" now regularly trump citizens' rights in setting public policy.

Neoliberalism leads to the erosion of public services, the substitution of market values for social values, the cult of privatization, and the progressive elimination of the concept of the common good. Neoliberalism is far more than a change in government practices, trade policies, and regulatory systems: it is also a set of beliefs. Henry Giroux explains that the ideology of neoliberalism "makes it difficult for many people either to imagine a notion of individual and social agency necessary for reclaiming a substantive democracy or to theorize the economic, cultural, and political conditions necessary for a viable global public sphere in which public institutions, spaces, and goods become valued as part of a larger democratic struggle for a sustainable future..."[7] His book, *The Terror of Neoliberalism*, analyzes how neoliberalism necessarily leads to the destruction of democracy.

Key to understanding the social influence of neoliberalism is appreciation of its pedagogical function, of the precise ways in which it teaches individuals to live, to understand their place in the world, and to imagine the future. To this end, Giroux casts neoliberalism as a destructive form of public pedagogy. Only by appreciating the way that neoliberalism depends on convincing the public that they have "little to hope for—and gain from—the government, nonprofit public spaces, democratic associations, public and higher education, and other nongovernmental social forces"[8] can we begin to analyze its power to influence all aspects of social life.

Another key shift that takes place under neoliberalism is the transformation of the idea of the public and of the common good. Because neoliberalism privileges the private sector over the public in terms of economic strategies, the idea of a common public mission that undergirds the commitment to democratic principles also suffers. Imagine it this way: the move to privatize prisons, to outsource many of the basic functions of national defense, to corporatize schooling, to deregulate banks, and to open markets translates into a belief system that discourages shared public commitments and favors individual competition. The hyper-privatization of social life under neoliberalism frustrates the possibility of translating between the private and the public: "Democracy begins to fail and political life becomes impoverished when society can no longer translate private problems into social issues."[9] Under neoliberalism, every problem, no matter how socially pervasive, is perceived as a private problem that must be dealt with on an individual basis.

Whereas "freedom" used to refer to the citizen, now it refers to the market. Any reference to the common good is quickly denounced as a threat to the "freedom" of business. The language of community is now the language of big business. Even those few social programs that remain functioning in the United States are described in market terms. In one extremely disturbing example of this shift, we no longer immunize children against disease; state-sponsored immunization is now described as "an investment in human capital."[10]

If neoliberalism signaled a devastating assault on the notion of the public good, then the public sphere—the arena through which citizens deliberate, debate, and dream—further suffered as a consequence of the increase in right-wing fundamentalisms, which were also on the rise in the Reagan-Bush era. It is important to note that the right is not one monolithic group. There are the secular conservatives that want a government that will defend traditional values, the free-market neoliberal right wing that wants a government that will not interfere with their efforts to make profits, and a fundamentalist Christian right that wants their government to further support their religious beliefs. These groups can, of course, overlap, but they are not identical. Each of them, though, practices fundamentalism—conservative fundamentalism, market fundamentalism, religious fundamentalism. Fundamentalism is characterized by a tenacious clinging to a set of beliefs that warrants no critique, dialogue, or chance of alteration. One's beliefs are acts of faith, rather than the result of reasoned deliberation. These are precisely the sorts of worldviews that Colbert regularly satirizes on his show.

One of the most visibly dogmatic fundamentalist groups is that of the Christian Right. As Markos Moulitsas explains, their groups are "filled with a moral certitude born of religious conviction."[11] For them, "freedom means being free to submit to their god."[12] He cites Gary Potter, President of Catholics for Christian Political Action, saying: "After the Christian majority takes control, pluralism will be seen as immoral and evil and the state will not permit anybody the right to practice evil."[13] We might recall Colbert's riff on Bush's claims that everyone is free to find their own path to Jesus at the Correspondents' Dinner. It is worth remembering that Colbert's rise to fame as a cast member on *The Daily Show* came in part from his segment "This Week in God."

While Colbert is a practicing Catholic, he has dedicated much of his satire to lampooning absurd (usually fundamentalist) religious practices. The "This Week in God" segment often took Colbert on the road to interview members of the fundamentalist religious right, exposing their illogical beliefs. On the March 9, 2005, segment he did for *The Daily Show,* he satirized groups that wanted to put the Ten Commandments in government buildings. After one clip showed

Photo 2.1   Colbert is about to activate the God Machine for his segment "This Week in God."

someone praying on the Capitol steps, claiming that "God was in their hearts," Colbert asked, "if God is in your heart, why do you need to make a monument to him?" Then he cites a group that states that they plan to pray hard enough to "penetrate the building's bricks and mortar."

Colbert mockingly jokes that they must be praying to the Kool-Aid guy and he asks them "To leave our third branch of government alone."[14] Colbert might be smiling, but he is also serious—such practices threaten democracy, and they are completely out of sync with the idea of the public sphere. In contrast, segments like "This Week in God" actually reinvigorate the public sphere, since they provide those who disagree with such practices an opportunity to see their bullying and irrationality on public display. While it is generally hard to challenge religious beliefs, this form of satire makes it possible to highlight their extremism and the ways they threatens democratic values.

Colbert has also done segments that link free-market, neoliberal fundamentalism with religious fundamentalism. One excellent example is his "The Wørd" segment from September 29, 2008: "Ye of Little Faith," a piece dealing with the House Republican vote to reject a government bailout.[15] He started by showing a series of clips

Photo 2.2 Colbert's "This Week in God" segment shows newspaper coverage of fundamentalists' suggestions that their prayers will penetrate the Capitol.

of politicians ranging from Bush to Obama stating that they "believe" in the free market. The comments serve to underscore how ridiculous it sounds to say that one "believes" in the market—as though it were a logical place in which to put one's faith. "So just why did a free-market president like Bush propose a government bailout in the first place?" asked Colbert. He then shows a recent clip of Bush saying: "The market is not functioning properly." Pretending to agree with the House Republicans who voted down the bailout, Colbert mockingly scoffs that "the free market is not just some economic theory we can abandon when things get rough. It requires faith." Colbert then expanded on the link between religious faith and free-market fundamentalism, saying, "It is a lot like believing in another all-powerful being—God. The market is all around us...It guides us with an invisible hand...Like God, if we have faith in it, the free market is the answer to all our problems—but if we doubt it, it will withhold its precious gifts."

He then went on, "Some out there, folks, are going to say that this financial meltdown shows the market is fallible—that it is, in fact, not God." Shouting at his audience, he insisted, "It does not mean that the market is not God. It means that the market is just a dangerous and destructive god...Maybe the market isn't like the Judeo-Christian god at all. It might be a blindly vengeful god, with a thousand hungry mouths." As the segment went on, he emulated more and more religious right-wing rhetoric: "We must believe even harder! Our god demands sacrifice! And I don't mean regulation, I mean human flesh!" Read against his counterpoints that reminded viewers, for instance, that the free market would not provide universal healthcare, Colbert exposed the connection between religious fundamentalism and market fundamentalism, all the while critiquing the closed sphere of political debate that denies the public a voice. "Thanks to the House Republicans we are in the market's hands. And it will take care of us. Only if we trust it. O Ye of little faith." As a counterpoint, "And littler savings" appeared on the right-hand screen.

Colbert had made his point: Free-market fundamentalism had become synonymous with religious hysteria, and it was destroying both the public sphere as well as the role of government.

The problems with the public sphere and the nation's commitment to a common good, however, cannot be blamed solely on the rise of right-wing fundamentalism and the material shifts of neoliberal economics; the left has played a role as well. To a certain extent the

Photo 2.3 Conclusion from "The Wørd" segment from September 29, 2008: Ye of Little Faith.

left, in a broad, general sense, has unwittingly facilitated the decline of the public sphere, because since the 1960s progressives have been increasingly hesitant to advocate a political vision. During the 1980s, as the Cold War came to an end and the domination of the United States and of capitalist economics no longer had the counterpoint of the Soviet Bloc, the left underwent a crisis. During this era, two major currents of left theory came to shape the connections between leftist thought and political action. These were poststructuralism and deconstruction. Both of these postmodern theories were extremely complex and varied, and what follows only briefly summarizes some of their main ideas.

Poststructuralism was a theory that sought to examine the production of meaning and especially of truths. One innovation of poststructuralism was its attention to how language influences identity in ways that are always confining. For instance, words like *woman* are understood to contrast the word *man*—thereby setting up an opposition that has tremendous material and ideological consequences. But on closer examination, it becomes clear that these words can easily be destabilized, since most qualities attributed to these words are socially constructed rather than innate. Thus, the structure that opposes *woman* and *man* can be dismantled and shown to be repressive. Deconstruction, a theory developed by Jacques Derrida, is closely linked to poststructuralism. It argues that the apparent stable meaning of words is actually based on contradictions and oppositions that feign stability as a way to impose meaning on the world. The goal of deconstruction is to reveal that these foundations are irreducibly multifaceted, unstable, and/or impossible, thereby deferring meaning as an endless process.

While these theories radically and productively challenged the regimes of meaning that had structured life, they were also self-perpetuating: any breakdown in a repressive form of meaning inevitably led to a new meaning that needed to be critiqued. Combined, these theories formed some of the core concepts of postmodernism, a leftist form of thought that questioned the idea of objective truth, of the ways that master narratives structure our ideas of the world, and of the basic premises of freedom, progress, and democracy, which underpinned Enlightenment ideals. The idea was that dominant concepts like the West, man, and Anglo society had shaped ideas of value in ways that were repressive and socially destructive. The goal was to break down the hold that these ideas had had, and, in some versions of postmodern theory, replace them with ideas of multiculturalism, diversity, and difference. The ideas of truth and value were considered inherently repressive, since they would inevitably construct a hierarchy of meaning that disadvantaged social segments deemed less valuable. While these ideas may seem extremely abstract, it is worth noting the extent to which they have influenced public opinion. For instance, it is not uncommon for people to question the idea of objective facts and absolute truths, arguing instead that we all have a "right" to our own opinion. While we do have a right to our opinions, all opinions are not equally valid. You can believe them, but that does not make them right. There certainly is a difference between opinions that have a basis in facts and ones that do not. But the theories of postmodernism do not tend to help one make that argument. Recall Bush's satisfied way of telling the public that he thought from his gut. Or his claim that the meaning of the Geneva Conventions was vague, making it hard to determine how best to uphold them. In a press conference on the subject, President Bush declared: "This debate is occurring because of the Supreme Court's ruling that said that we must conduct ourselves under the Common Article III of the Geneva Convention. And that Common Article III says that there will be no outrages upon human dignity. It's very vague. What does that mean, 'outrages upon human dignity'? That's a statement that is wide open to interpretation."[16] Like it or not, Bush's explanation that the terms used in the Geneva Conventions were "wide open to interpretation" was made possible by postmodern critiques of language. And while Bush's destabilizing of the meaning of phrases like "outrages upon human dignity" was not the intended use of these theories and may very well be a violation of them, there is little doubt that his ability to make such claims publicly—and to little resistance—was a consequence of the way that the idea that there is no clear truth had thoroughly pervaded public consciousness.

Consequently, the influence of poststructuralism and deconstruction on U.S. critical thought has led to a wariness, if not an outright disavowal, of any foundational ideas. What was missing from many of the left theories of the 1980s was a positive counter-argument that highlighted the important role that the public sphere plays in the construction of civil society. As Masao Miyoshi notes, U.S. intellectuals share "an undeniable common proclivity...to fundamentally reject such totalizing concepts as humanity, civilization, history, and justice, and such subtotalities as a region, a nation, a locality, or even any smallest group."[17] The consequence is that advocates of multiculturalism have often been unwilling to link their claims to an ethical, political grounding. Susan Searls Giroux notes that, "The limp endorsement and bland acceptance of principles such as 'nondiscrimination,' 'diversity,' and 'openness' *in the abstract* enabled the Right's ruth-less appropriation of the vision and language of multiculturalism."[18] Thus the left's hesitancy in advocating a political vision has made it easy for the right to appropriate the left's language at the service of the right's own agenda. Filling the gap and recognizing the massively self-destructive tendencies of these left critiques, the right promoted a neoliberal view of society that understood people in terms of the market and within a society that measured success based on purchasing potential. As will be discussed in chapter 4 in the section dedicated to Colbert's wordplay, it is clear that one goal of Colbert's satire has been to expose the flaws in the left's critique of the representational power of language. Much of his work is dedicated to rescuing the idea of the truth from the grips of a socially pervasive tendency to truthiness.

9/11: THE DAY THAT CHANGED EVERYTHING

As described in chapter 1, the events of 9/11 brought with them a culture of secrecy, a state of emergency that threatened civil rights, an environment of militarization, and a public state of fear. The nation went from a country that had a long tradition of advancing the ideals of civil rights to one where illegal surveillance (wiretapping), torture, secret prisons, and extraordinary rendition were not only practiced, but were publicly accepted. While there isn't sufficient space here to detail the extent to which the nation changed on that day, there are a number of key consequences to the events of 9/11 that directly influenced the public sphere and the possibilities for a democratic society. As Henry Giroux describes it in *Hearts of Darkness*:

> With democracy in retreat in a post-9/11 world saturated by a culture of fear and uncertainty, public life was more and more militarized, shredding all vestiges of civil liberties, civic agency, and compassion for those that deviated from normative expectations by religion, race, class, age, and ethnicity; meanwhile dissent was increasingly treated as un-American. Under the Bush administration, a seeping, sometimes galloping, authoritarianism began to reach into every corner of culture, giving free reign to those antidemocratic forces in which religious, market, military, and political fundamentalism thrived, casting an ominous shadow over the face of democracy.[19]

While it is true that there was a brief moment of post-9/11 national unity and international sympathy, those feelings quickly gave way to a national culture of division, anxiety, intolerance, and suspicion, and an international atmosphere of hostility and distrust.

In what follows, I will briefly trace a series of post-9/11 shifts that negatively influenced the public sphere and the democratic potential of the nation. Rather than trace all the myriad changes, I will focus on the post-9/11 issues that are most prominently featured in Colbert's satire. The first and most obvious of these is the way that the 9/11 attacks led to an immediate reduction in civil liberties for U.S. citizens. The USA PATRIOT Act, illegal wiretappings, the Military Commissions Act of 2006 (which rescinded habeas corpus), and other combinations of legislation and government practice converged to pose the most serious threat to democracy that the U.S. nation has ever faced. These national shifts signaled a frightening turn to authoritarianism and an expansion of presidential powers. They then combined with military actions in Iraq and Afghanistan, with torture programs, with the development of secret black-site prisons, extraordinary rendition, and the creation of the enemy combatant—who would not be given the Geneva Conventions protection of a prisoner of war. When the terrorists attacked the United States, rather than strengthen democracy and the nation's commitment to its ideals, the terrorists' actions led to an increased militarization of everyday U.S.

Photo 2.4 "Last week Obama's justice department released four more Bush administration torture memos. Collect the whole set, and you get this free coffee mug."[21]

life. It became common for U.S. citizens to cede their rights to privacy and unreasonable search as their email was routinely read and their library records were scrutinized (via the USA PATRIOT Act). What Colbert typically emphasizes on his show, though, is the public's lack of response to these infractions of their civil rights.

Even worse was the public's bland reaction to the revelations of torture. Colbert chose to highlight this topic on his April 21, 2009, segment of "The Wørd—*Stressed Position*," which covered the Obama administration's release of four more of the Bush administration's torture memos.[20] He starts the bit by playfully displaying a coffee cup with a cat on a tree branch pictured on it that says: "Mondays are Torture."

The joke is that the word *torture* here is clearly not the same as it is when referenced in the torture memos. Colbert suggests that the public has lost its ability to take seriously the idea of torture as a human-rights violation, preferring to think of it as nothing worse than a cat hanging off a branch. But the real focus of Colbert's bit was Obama's reluctance to say that the people who had perpetrated the acts would be punished, which he described as a "stressed position," playing on the phrase "stress position," used to describe a torture practice in which a victim is held in an uncomfortable position for a long period of time. To make his point, Colbert shows a clip of Obama saying that he does not want to "pre-judge" what happened. To which Colbert ironically responds, "Because that would be a tragic betrayal of everything America stands for." The irony is that torture itself is a betrayal of U.S. principles, but that hasn't bothered the government or the public. Colbert shows a clip of Obama saying that he does not think that the CIA torturers should be punished, since they were following orders. Colbert then goes on to present another common position: that those who drafted and supported the memos should not be punished since they didn't actually torture anyone—they weren't in the room. He next eliminates the third and last group that could feel responsible—U.S. citizens. We "can't really punish any Americans because we all basically approved the torture when we re-elected President Bush."

Now, Colbert goes after his even deeper focus—the public—that did not sufficiently protest these practices. He targets the well-worn argument that the public was not fully aware by saying: "Now sure, it was secret. But we had some hints." He then shows a clip of Bush saying he will defend America by doing "anything" it takes from one of his 2004 campaign ads. He closes by saying we can't punish the people who perpetrated the torture, or the people who approved the torture, or any Americans for that matter, leaving the torture victims themselves as the only people left who can be punished. "We will have our justice without having any of the 'good guys' pay the price." On the left the bullet point reads: "Enhanced Self-Justification Technique." An earlier bullet point that accompanied Colbert's claims that the victims were at fault read: "He who felt it, dealt it." The segment indirectly asks: what happens when a president like Obama, who finds torture morally reprehensible (unlike Bush), cannot find a way to prosecute these crimes? He closes by saying we have learned a valuable lesson: "That there are times that we can torture with no repercussions." And with that ending there is no irony at all. He is simply stating a fact. What he has tried to do with this piece is draw his audience's attention to the incongruity of believing that the United States stands for the ideals of democracy and rights when we do nothing in response to learning that laws and rights have been violated. And he has subtly suggested that the public has a choice: they can accept the status quo and allow the ideals of the nation to be hijacked, or they can demand justice for the torture victims.

Much of Colbert's attention to the state of the nation after 9/11 focuses on the way that the event has influenced public responses and ways of thinking. Channeling the posturing of Bush, who thinks from his gut, avoids consulting facts, and tolerates no dissent, Colbert often satirizes the U.S. post-9/11 shift to a society of illogical affect, where emotion has become more important than reason, and arguments have been drawn in stark black and white. As Lauren Berlant notes: "*Nuance* quickly became a moral buzzword of the George W. Bush administration: even to pursue nuanced thought was deemed a performance of antipatriotism."[22] She quotes an April 2002 interview with Bush where he stated: "Look, my job isn't to try to nuance. My job is to tell people what I think. And when I think there's an axis of evil, I say it. I think moral clarity is important, if you believe in freedom."[23] She explains that during the Bush era, any call for nuance was typically characterized by the administration as "pedantic nuisance" or "genuine treason."[24] This meant that, as the nation faced one of its most complex national crises in history, its leaders refused to consider complex solutions to complex problems. Everything had to be black and white, good or evil, us versus them. And the ways that arguments were made to support the government's actions were increasingly bereft of any connection to facts. Even more importantly, once one believes something, that belief should never change or waver.

Colbert took Bush's over-the-top commitment to moral clarity to task when he stated at the White House Correspondents' Association

Dinner that Bush believed the same thing on Wednesday that he believed on Monday no matter what happened on Tuesday. While Bush and his supporters saw this characteristic as positive, Colbert worked to point out how dangerous unyielding belief systems can be—especially when these are founded on what one feels in their gut and when events and experiences are unable to alter one's ideas. Such positions have been used to explain why the discovery that there were no weapons of mass destruction in Iraq—which had been used as the justification to go to war—did not lead to a change in the U.S. position on the Iraq War. We once thought it was true, and we once thought that justified war, so we still feel that the war is justified. This is why Colbert likes to use phrases that falsely suggest nuance and choice, like "George Bush: great president, or greatest president?" They reveal the extent to which unreasonable, un-nuanced arguments are often packaged as reasonable and nuanced.

One of the best examples of Colbert's critique of the retreat from nuance can be found in his segment "Formidable Opponent," which parodies the false types of debates that are often posed on news-media programs. As Steve Gimbel explains in his analysis of the segment, its main purpose is to highlight the need to have moral doubt—not moral clarity—because moral doubt means that you are willing to re-examine your convictions based on things you learn and experience.[25] In these segments, Colbert explains that the only opponent worthy of debating him is himself. He then appears in split screen with one version of himself wearing a red tie and the other wearing a blue one. Typically, one Stephen presents a mildly liberal position, while the other Stephen takes a more aggressively right-wing position. He then performs a false debate presented as a real one, during which the right-wing Stephen inevitably poses an extreme hypothetical by which he proves to the other Stephen that the right's position is the right one. In these segments, "Colbert portrays how pundits display over-exuberant confidence, not in reason but in their own authority."[26] In "Formidable Opponent," the debaters never are able to appreciate nuance, and arguments are made absent of reason or fact. Most arguments hinge on extreme hypotheticals (like the ticking time-bomb scenario as a justification for torture), twisted reasoning, appeals to emotion, and logical fallacies.

These false debates also demonstrate the way that public opinion and political practice after 9/11 favored affect over reason. Berlant calls this "visceral politics." It describes a political sphere whose "dominant rhetorical style is to recruit the public to see political attachments as an amalgam of reflexive opinion and visceral or 'gut' feeling."[27] It goes without saying that the feeling most commonly recruited after 9/11 has been fear. The events of 9/11 sparked a sense of vulnerability that accompanied the reality that even a great superpower can be harmed. In some ways, the fear that followed that day had some basis in fact—lives were lost, terrorists had succeeded, and the future was unclear. But whatever sort of ground that justified the sense of fear in the early days after the attacks quickly gave way to the hype, hysteria, and anxiety caused by a permanent war that has no boundaries, no clearly defined enemy, and no end in sight. As Austin Sarat explains: "Since September 11 'fear again threatens reason.' Aliens have been imprisoned for months on the flimsiest grounds. The attorney general of the United States moved to deport people on the basis of secret evidence. The president authorized military tribunals to hold trials under special rules, and Congress passed the USA PATRIOT Act."[28] Fear was mobilized after 9/11 to justify the most atrocious acts, to silence the public into an anxious stupor, and to convert the public sphere into a place where dissent was treated like treason.

If the government used public fear to quell dissent and gather support for illegal and immoral acts, then it would be the media that would mobilize fear for profit and ratings. I'll discuss post-9/11 media in more detail below, but it is important to recognize that both the media and the Bush administration worked to ramp up a constant state of public fear. The cult of fear has been a constant target of Colbert's show. Colbert regularly riffs on the ways that a culture based on fear leads to poor decision-making, intolerance, bigotry, prejudice, and injustice. A recurring segment that best exemplifies these practices is "The ThreatDown," where he lists the five biggest threats to America. These often include bears and robots, or robot bears, as the #1 threat, in an effort to lampoon the silliness of such lists. Items on the list are often of no threat to anyone other than Colbert. For instance, Colbert has often mentioned in interviews that he really is afraid of bears, but they appear as the #1 threat to America in "The ThreatDown," since—in true pundit form—if he is afraid of them, then the entire nation should be as well. At other times, Colbert actually focuses on something the public is being told to fear, by the media and/or the government, and which is an unreasonable thing to fear. In one "The ThreatDown" segment, he targets the 9/11 Commission as a threat because of its suggestion that the United States is still vulnerable to terrorist attack.

Of course, a prime example of Colbert's efforts to show the extent to which fear permeates the public sphere was his rally on the National Mall with Jon Stewart on October 30, 2010, in anticipation of the midterm elections. His call for the rally was to "March

Photo 2.5   "The ThreatDown" 12/7/05: The 9/11 Commission.[29]

to Keep Fear Alive" in response to Stewart's call to "Restore Sanity" and encourage reasonable thinking. When Colbert announced on his show on September 16, 2010, that he would offer a counter-rally to Stewart, he reminded viewers that "Reason" was only one letter short of "Treason."[30] He shouted to his viewers that "America can't afford a rally to restore sanity in the middle of a recession." Spinning off the idea that the nation is governed by a military-industrial complex, he claimed that supporting sanity would cost jobs in the "fear-industrial complex"—like his own. He then showed a series of clips from the mainstream news networks of commentators referring to the U.S. public as "afraid," "terrified," "scared," "scared silly," and "frightened." He closed the segment by saying, "Now is not the time to take it down a notch, now is the time to freak out for freedom." Colbert's point couldn't be clearer: the more we focus on fear, the more damage we do to the nation's commitment to freedom.

MEDIA MATTERS

The eleventh of September, 2001 introduced the United States to the experience of domestic terrorism as no other event has ever done. For most people, word of this event first arrived as live television news. We are at home, or work. We see images of disaster of an extraordinary magnitude. As the morning of September 11, 2001 unfolds, television news anchors interrupt regular programming to speak to us from their studio chambers as they report what eludes their comprehension. Their reports and images offer evidence of a catastrophic event but provide no context or perspective. It is as if live television coverage rips the flesh from the face of the world and hurls it into our living rooms. Shocking, grotesque, obscene—this should not be conceivable. And yet it occurs—as rippled relays of incomprehensible destruction, catastrophic ruin.—Bill Nichols[31]

It is difficult to recreate the intensity of the events of 9/11 in the wake of the culture of fear, the theater of cruelty, and the atmosphere of intolerance that has followed from the events that day. It would be a mistake, however, to forget the shock of that day and the very real ways that those events caused a sense of national vulnerability. As Bill Nichols explains above, the medium through which almost the entire nation received the information about that day was television. And while television news combined with other forms of media (websites, blogs, radio, etc.), it remained the primary media source in those days. Nichols explains: "As a tele-mediated crisis, September 11 was exceptional. The instantaneous transmission of its stupendous monumentality, its horrific trauma, coupled to profound initial uncertainty about its nature, extent or purpose collapsed a process that took infinitely longer for those who bore the brunt of the events that took place at Hiroshima or Nagasaki in 1945."[32]

Consequently, another characteristic of post-9/11 news media was its immediacy. Information came at viewers without context or explanation. As truly monumental as the event was, the news coverage of that day also quickly turned into the basest form of media spectacle. Images of the planes crashing into the Twin Towers repeated endlessly in a way that created a sense of panic, but also a sense of numbing. An image that should have borne a sense of gravity became almost a parody of itself. As Kellner explains: "The 9/11 terror spectacle unfolded in a city that was one of the most media-saturated in the world and that played out a deadly drama live on television. The images of the planes hitting the World Trade Center towers and their collapse were broadcast repeatedly, as if repetition were necessary to master a highly traumatic event."[33] This media coverage converged with the Bush administration's urgency to define, master, and categorize the event. Enemies were named, an axis of evil was created, and the media packaged that information with catchphrases, graphics, and special sound effects. Whether consciously organized or not, the media and the government joined together to give a frame to the event that discouraged critical reflection, public dialogue and debate, and consideration of how the United States might best respond to the attacks. Instead, the public was whipped up into a state of fear, hysteria, and thirst for revenge. According to Kellner, "the mainstream media in the United States privileged the 'clash of civilizations' model, established a binary dualism between Islamic terrorism and civilization, and largely circulated war fever and retaliatory feelings and discourses that called for and supported a form of military intervention."[34]

If the coverage of 9/11 is a paradigm of the mainstream media's inability to cover major, complex events with critical attention, balance, and thoughtful reflection, it was not without precedent. Kellner points out that "while Bush ascribed 'fear' to its symbolic Other and enemy, as Michael Moore's 2001 film *Bowling for Columbine* demonstrates, the U.S. corporate media have been exploiting fear for decades in their excessive presentation of murder and violence and dramatization of a wide range of threats from foreign enemies and within everyday life."[35] The trouble is that many viewers still hold onto network-era ideas of the value and integrity of the news. Geoffrey Baym in *From Cronkite to Colbert: The Evolution of Broadcast News* explains, though, that much has changed in broadcast news from the sort of serious reporting associated with a figure like Walter Cronkite. The transition from the network era to the multichannel/cable era brought a number of shifts. First, broadcast news had to compete with other non-news programming that offered alternative options for viewers with cable. This directly led to more efforts to make news entertaining. A direct consequence of this was the turn toward more visual displays and other graphic depictions and away from verbal information. Baym reports that coverage of Bill Clinton's affair with Monica Lewinsky "contained some 70 percent more visual images than those during Watergate."[36] He goes on to point out that "One story...contained thirty five different images in less than two and a half minutes, an average of less than four seconds per picture."[37] Not only were viewers barraged with sensationalist images, these flashed on the screen with no real time for analysis or reflection on what was shown. These images were then accompanied by "a variety of postproduction effects, such as slow motion or the altering of color and tone to complicate imagery, an approach virtually nonexistent in the Watergate coverage."[38] News media increasingly offered spectacle over information and analysis. The goal was no longer to present information to the public, but rather to "construct engaging, reality-based stories."[39]

Added to the barrage of special effects and images, another new development has shaped the news: the appearance of the analyst over the newsmaking participant. Baym explains that in place of participants in the political process, the networks have tended to turn increasingly to analysts. These are academics, lawyers, former government insiders, and other paid pundits who work for the network. Baym notes that in the coverage of the Clinton affair, "the analyst sound bite averages eleven seconds longer than those of lawmakers."[40] An even greater shift, though, is the time spent showing conversation between anchors, across commentators, and between pundits.

This sort of false dialogue that pretends to offer insight, but actually presents inane banter, is one of Colbert's common targets. His critique of this practice is especially evident in his recurring segment "Formidable Opponent." Colbert has further explained that the 24-hour news cycle has damaged the news media, since there simply is not enough "real" news to cover. Instead, the few news pieces of interest are presented and then commented on endlessly.[41] An example of this is his interest in showing the way that the media creates news out of reactions to its own coverage of stories. In one case he singled out the story of "Sarah Palin's reaction to the media's reaction to her reaction to the media's criticism of her rhetoric in the wake of the Tucson shootings." He then covered MSNBC journalist Mika Brzezinski's frustration at being asked to cover Sarah Palin's "re-re-re-reaction," a state he called "Palin Fatigue."[42] He shows a clip of Brzezinski offering a rare moment of critique of the way that mainstream news makes news out of un-newsworthy items. Brzezinski states: "At what point do you not become news? At what point do we just ignore her?" Colbert then turns to another camera and pretends to directly address Brzezinski. He tells her to buck up. "I know you think she has nothing to offer the national dialogue and that her speeches are just coded talking points mixed in with words picked at random from a thesaurus." He continued his Palin rant for several minutes by pretending to channel Brzezinski's ideas: "I know you think she's at best a self-promoting ignoramus and at worst a shameless media troll who'll abuse any platform to deliver dog-whistle encouragement to a far-right base that may include possible insurrectionists." But he closes, you might think those things, but your job is to "repeat what Sarah Palin said on Hannity last night, right into the lens. You know, news!"

In addition to pointing out the ways that the news media recycles stories and reports self-perpetuating coverage of its own stories, Colbert also goes after the presentation of supposed news items that he deems un-newsworthy. In his response to morning news show coverage of his "Better Know a District" segment with Robert Wexler

when Wexler made silly comments about having fun with cocaine
and prostitutes since his election was uncontested, Colbert criticized
those programs for questioning why politicians would want to appear
on his show. He stated in response to Matt Lauer's confusion about
why anyone would want to be his guest: "I can understand Matt's
confusion. This show is so complex...It's beyond some people, especially old news guys like Matt Lauer." He explains that people want
to come on his show because "this show is the news. Not only is it the
news. Evidently it is news. It's gotta be news because your morning
shows are the news and you're doing reports on it."[43] Congressmen
appear on *The Colbert Report*, he says, so that "you will use their
appearance on my show on your show." Here again, he points at the
problem of news media recycling stories, but he then gets in a dig
about the stupidity of many of the items that also appear on those
shows. He presents a series of clips: Matt Lauer announcing a segment
on a python that ate an electric blanket, a *Good Morning America*
piece on "tanorexia" (addiction to tanning), a piece on how sixty percent of women wear uncomfortable shoes, a story on women who do
not use diapers for their babies, and a closing clip of a morning-show
anchor playing poker with a chimpanzee.

Because Colbert's program is organized as a spoof of a right-wing
pundit show, an obvious additional line of Colbert's commentary is
the cult of punditry. As is well known, *The O'Reilly Factor* served
as the counterpoint for *The Colbert Show*'s initial design. Darrell M.
West explains in *The Rise and Fall of the Media Establishment* that the
1980s marks a substantial rise in punditry. It is worth noting that the
term *pundit* originally meant an expert. The early media pundits provided commentary and context that journalists were not expected, or
trained, to provide. Dan D. Nimmo and James E. Combs point out
in their book, *The Political Pundits*, that "one of the oldest and most
cherished public forums for punditry in the history of print journalism is the column."[44] Pundits expressed expert opinion about important issues, a practice that seems in keeping with Colbert's ideas of
what is useful information for the public. While he is always quick
in interviews to describe his own show as comedy and not news, it is
clear from stunts like the rally on the National Mall and his aborted
run for presidency that he fashions himself as someone who provides
insights into issues that he hopes will lead to public debate.

That sort of punditry, though, is a far cry from the right-wing
bloviating and fear-mongering punditry of figures like Bill O'Reilly,
Glenn Beck, Lou Dobbs, and Sean Hannity. These types of pundits
have played a major role in creating a post-9/11 media intent on

whipping up public hysteria, fostering intolerance and bigotry, and creating a sense of the United States as a nation at constant risk. According to François Debrix, "Since 9/11, the conservative, populist, loud-mouthed Fox News network talk-show host and pundit Bill O'Reilly has taken it upon himself to represent and protect American lives."[45] He explains that what makes these shows dangerous is that they are "intent on producing the impression of news reporting, information providing, facts revealing, and truth declaring," but what they really do is allow O'Reilly to "convince his audience of the moral superiority and greater commonsensical value of his punditry." The problem is that shows like these report unsubstantiated opinion and biased ideology as factual, true, and objective. Moreover, they are organized around a constant sense of crisis and a never-ending state of fear: "The shock-value of O'Reilly's interventions (or interpretations) is aimed at gathering popular support or triggering public scandal by unleashing waves after waves of fear among his audience members."[46]

Colbert's show has been particularly interested in parodying this type of so-called news media, and chapter 4 will analyze some of the ways that Colbert's work inter-texts specifically with O'Reilly's show. In addition to O'Reilly, Colbert's show targets a range of right-wing pundits. For instance, it was Glenn Beck's own "Restoring Honor to America" rally on the National Mall on August 28, 2010, that seemed to prompt Stewart and Colbert to host their rally.[47] In one especially entertaining clip, Colbert compares himself to Glenn Beck, whom he calls the "Pillsbury dough pundit," showing images of Beck against those of his own show.[48] He sets up the bit calling himself a huge fan of Beck's, a "Beckerhead." Then, in order to parody Beck's hubris, Colbert shows a series of clips of Beck, where Beck refers to the significance of his own show. In one part, Beck tells listeners that while at the Vatican, someone he met told him, "What you are doing is wildly important." Next Colbert comes to Beck's defense, complaining that the media was not being fair to Beck when they called him insincere. Of course Beck is sincere, says Colbert. Then he shows a clip of Beck in tears saying: "I just love my country, and I fear for it."[49] The clip works to point out the way that pundits link fear and hyper-patriotism.

To make the point that Colbert's show is commenting on the punditry of figures like Beck, while doing something completely different, and to show that the media often does not fully grasp the distinction between Colbert and Beck, Colbert next presents a series of clips from the mainstream media calling Beck a fake alongside a similar set of

Photo 2.6   Colbert compares himself to Glenn Beck.

images of the media declaring that Colbert, too, is a fake.[50] Colbert then addresses the audience, saying: "The it-getters out there know that for the past four years I have meant every word that I felt. So all we really need to do to gauge Glenn's sincerity is to compare him to me." What follows is a series of images of Beck pieces and Colbert's parodies of the same types of pieces. Next we see images of Glenn crying against images of Colbert parodying pundit crying. Colbert describes the montage as "looking into a mirror, after doing a ton of coke on it."

Colbert explains that it is refreshing to see how similar they are, "because if he and I don't believe what we say, and don't mean what we feel, then you, our viewers, aren't just being intellectually impoverished, you're being emotionally defrauded. And that would be a cynical manipulation of Americans' legitimate fears. In which case, we shouldn't be on TV at all. And I don't know about Glenn Beck [Colbert starts crying], but that idea makes me very sad." In a short segment, Colbert has parodied punditry, revealed its base fear-mongering and tendency to hysteria, and directly called it a mode of media that intellectually impoverishes its viewers.

As already noted, one of the central arenas for the development of a vibrant and engaged public sphere is the media. According to

Baym, "It is axiomatic that the vitality of democracy depends on an informed citizenry...Today, more than ever, news media serve as a primary link connecting individuals to the political process."⁵¹ But changes in media infrastructure, including deregulation, the 24-hour news cycle, the multichannel era, the cult of punditry, and more have influenced the quality, depth, and caliber of the material presented as news to the public. These shifts then combined with the post-9/11 environment of hostility to nuance, intolerance for critique, xenophobia, and militarism. These are precisely the sorts of social shifts that are the concern of *The Colbert Report*.

It would be a mistake, however, to describe post-9/11 media without attention to the growth of alternative media, the rise in participatory media, and the complexity of the post-network era, when media consumption is no longer contained within traditional formats. Viewers consume television, for instance, more and more often via the Internet, streaming video, cellular-phone applications, TIVO, and other devices than during standard programming times. As described in chapter 1, the blogosphere played a huge role in disseminating the video of Colbert's performance at the White House Correspondents' Association Dinner. The case can be made, as well, that it was the blogosphere's coverage of the event that later led to its greater attention in the mainstream media. This is simply to say that, just as the mainstream news has become more entertainment-based and more incapable of providing the public sphere with the information it needs to be actively engaged citizens, other forms of media have appeared to offer alternatives. Chapters 4 and 5 discuss the specific ways that Colbert has encouraged this sort of media, since it is clear that Colbert has not only been picked up by the alternative media as a source of content, but that he has also worked to encourage those types of connections. In that sense, his program lies at the intersection between two extremes—the public sphere threatening mainstream media and the participatory potential of alternative media. According to Baym, "it is clear that *The Daily Show* and its spin-off *The Colbert Report* have become central sites for news and political discussion in an increasingly complicated media environment."⁵²

9/11 AND DISSENT

While the network era of newscasters like Walter Cronkite is effectively gone forever, a new era has emerged with greater public choice for news-media consumption, and greater public risk, since most of the news media has been disinclined to offer the public the sort of information and critical commentary vital to fostering productive public debate. In the midst of these tensions, a series of comedians offered the public ways to reflect on social issues via satire, parody, and humor. While satire dates back to Antiquity, post-9/11 satire appeared in a complex moment for both the media and the state of the nation. A consequence of this was that satire became one of the few ways that the public could experience dissent.

The next chapter traces the role of satire in fostering dissent, especially in the United States, but here I want to point to the very real ways that a number of journalists and other public intellectuals came under fire after 9/11. In the period following the terrorist attacks, some journalists lost their jobs or were pressured for reporting news critical of the Bush administration. Anthony R. Dimaggio in *Mass Media, Mass Propaganda: Examining American News in the "War on Terror"* reports that: "As the stakes underlying the 'War on Terror' increased with the invasion of Iraq, the media remained intolerant of substantive anti-war dissent. Many prominent media figures were fired or encouraged to retire, including former *CBS News* anchor Dan Rather, former international correspondent for *NBC News* Peter Arnett, and Jon Lieberman, a former political reporter for Sinclair Broadcasting."[53] And these were some of the most visible members of the media. Many other less publicly powerful figures were fired, threatened, and harassed. Even more pernicious for public dissent, journalists regularly self-censored. DiMaggio explains that the practice of self-censorship after 9/11 was pervasive: "One study done by American University scholars surveying 210 journalists in the U.S. found that most of those interviewed chose to self-censor in their reporting of the Abu Ghraib scandal by refusing to run 'graphic' pictures, and by putting more grisly details regarding the abuses inside their papers, rather than on their covers."[54] At the same time, professors and public intellectuals like Norm Finkelstein, who was denied tenure at DePaul, or Ward Churchill, who was fired after years as a senior professor, also lost their jobs due to pressures from right-wing groups that claimed that anyone critical of the Bush administration was guilty of treason.

Comedians weren't safe either. The most well-known case is that of Bill Maher, who at the time of the 9/11 attacks hosted a show called *Politically Incorrect* on ABC. Shortly after the attacks, media critics wondered how the event would change media venues, which typically had thrived on a certain degree of critique of the government, like late-night talk shows, such as *The Daily Show, Jay Leno, David Letterman,* and *Politically Incorrect.* Paul Achter explains that

"For almost three weeks after the terrorist attacks of 2001, comedians in the U.S. embarked on an unusually serious assessment of comedy and its proper role in public life."[55] Leno and Letterman, true to form, "told fewer and safer jokes, mostly at the expense of easy targets like the Taliban and Osama bin Laden. *The Daily Show*'s Jon Stewart was so shaken he cried."[56] Not so with Bill Maher, who broke the ice and made bold claims that other comedians had yet to utter. On his first post-9/11 appearance on September 17, 2001, Maher stated: "I do not relinquish—nor should any of you—the right to criticize, even as we support, our government." He went on, "This is still a democracy and they're still politicians, so we need to let our government know that we can't afford a lot of things that we used to be able to afford. Like a missile shield that will never work for an enemy that doesn't exist. We can't afford to be fighting wrong and silly wars. The cold war. The drug war. The culture war."[57] Maher was one of the few comedians who took the chance to tell his audience to be critical of the government. As Robert Thompson, director of Syracuse University's Center for the Study of Popular Television, says, Maher's commentary offered a unique form of criticism of the U.S. government in that moment: "He was the only dissenting voice out there that week."[58] And that was only the beginning.

Maher was soon fired when ABC decided against renewing his contract in 2002, after he made a controversial on-air remark shortly after the September 11th attacks. The trouble started when he agreed with his guest, conservative pundit Dinesh D'Souza, that, whatever one might want to say about the attacks, the 9/11 terrorists did not act in a cowardly manner. Maher said, "We have been the cowards. Lobbing cruise missiles from two thousand miles away. That's cowardly. Staying in the airplane when it hits the building. Say what you want about it. Not cowardly. You're right." Even though Maher later explained that his comment was not meant to be anti-military in any way whatsoever, the damage was done. And his show was canceled.[59]

Despite Maher's setback, he re-emerged with another show, and it would not take long for him to be joined by other comedians, like Jon Stewart, who used comedy to foster critique. These comedians use irony, satire, and parody to ignite their audience's critical thinking. In addition to television satirists, another major source of satirical critique was *The Onion*. They issued a special edition of their magazine a week after the attacks, with the slogan: "Attack on America: Holy Fucking Shit."[60] In their next issue they ran a story: "Shattered Nation Longs to Care About Stupid Bullshit Again." Achter describes the post-9/11 pieces in *The Onion* as a "useful public deliberation over proper emotional responses to a news-saturated moment."[61] Satirical pieces like those in *The Onion* or those on programs with Stewart and Maher offered their audiences opportunities to think outside of the good versus evil paradigm and hyped-up hysteria that the public received in the days following the attacks. Baym explains that, "Unlike traditional news, which claims epistemological certainty, satire is a discourse of inquiry, a rhetoric of challenge that seeks through the asking of unanswered questions to clarify the underlying morality of a situation."[62] These comedians juxtapose images and sound bites that reveal the double-speak of the government. They call out a purposefully superficial news media for its inability to present the public with the information it needs to make sound judgments, and they joke that while they are comedy programs, they are providing the nation's news. Within this cohort of dissent-encouraging comedians, Colbert has become renowned for the variety of ways that he seeks to engage viewer participation and critical thinking. While Colbert's show was spared the direct post-9/11 climate of censorship and intolerance for debate, there is little doubt that his appearance at the White House Correspondents' Dinner stands as one of the, if not THE most aggressive critiques of the Bush administration. Without question, Colbert has been a key figure in promoting dissent in the post-9/11 era. Along with other comedians, he has worked to reinvigorate democratic deliberation and an active public sphere in a moment when the spaces for public debate have suffered both crisis and opportunity.

3

PROUD TO BE AN AMERICAN SATIRIST

While much was made after 9/11 over the question of whether or not comedy was an appropriate response to the attacks and over whether or not such comedy was un-American, those familiar with U.S. history know well that political comedy—especially satire—has a long tradition in this country.[1] Beginning with the founding fathers, satire and fake news were used to encourage the public to support the goals of the Revolution. Colin Wells writes that during the Revolutionary period, satire was "the most popular and politically important literary form in American political life."[2] Rather than think of Colbert's satire as an anti-American, treasonous practice that threatens the nation, my argument is that Colbert's comedy both participates in and furthers the legacy of U.S. satire.

It is important to note that ideas about humor after 9/11 were mixed. Shortly after the 9/11 attacks, some suggested that humor was a necessary balm, a therapeutic act that could help heal a wounded nation. This view of humor was at play when Lorne Michaels, producer of *Saturday Night Live*, asked New York City Mayor Rudy Giuliani at the beginning of their season, on September 29, 2001: "Is it OK to be funny again?" To which Giuliani sarcastically replied: "Why start now?" Paul Achter notes that Giuliani's blessing of the show was revealing: "Paralleling his mobilization of America's first city—its firefighters, police officers, and victims of the attacks—Giuliani had now mobilized a comic institution in the service of the country's need to laugh."[3] This view of humor was not radically different from Bush's urging of U.S. citizens to travel, support the economy, and live the way that they did before the attacks. This was humor to have fun and enjoy life, not to ask questions or challenge the status quo.

In considering the role of humor after 9/11, it is also worth remembering another current of U.S. humor that was pervasive, even if it was rarely acknowledged in major public ways. In his book *Cracking Up*, Paul Lewis calls attention to the post-9/11 rise in sadistic humor,

and uses as evidence the smiling images of the prison guards torturing Iraqis at Abu Ghraib. He references testimony by U.S. Army
Specialist Sabrina Harman who explained that she attached electrical
wires to an Iraqi detainee's fingers, toes, and penis because she was
"just playing with him."[4] The kind of humor that allows one to "play"
in such a way with another human being is a clear demonstration of
the dehumanizing effects that sadistic humor can have. In addition,
Lewis points to the damage done by jokes that tend to dismiss troubling subjects through amusement and silliness, downplaying real
pain and suffering, and threatening compassion and concern for others. He further points to the negative impact of right-wing jokes that
mock progressive issues, such as jokes that refer to environmentalists
as tree huggers or to feminists as femi-nazis. Here the line between
a joke and outright name-calling begins to blur. Lewis says, though,
that humor has been a way of seeing how we are divided: "The purpo-
sive and embattled state of American humor comes into focus as soon
as we attend to conflicts between the attempt to amuse and resistance
to it—between ridicule and resentment, satire and outrage."[5] He contrasts a restorative and healing humor that is fun, but distracting,
with a prejudicial, spiteful, sadistic humor that desensitizes humans
to the humanity of others. Both forms, he suggests, are a threat to
democracy and critical thinking: "Over the past twenty-five years, the
yearning for detachment from seemingly unsolvable and yet inescap-
able problems, seen in the popularity of both killing jokes and healing
laughter, has contributed to a politics of denial."[6]

Politically progressive satire, such as that practiced by Colbert,
though, is a particular form of humor and, while it always requires a
"butt" of the joke, the target in politically progressive satire is understood to be a threat to society. The goal of such jokes is not just negative critique. Instead, this is a form of humor meant to cause change.
David Marc explains: "In its long development from ancient Greek
theater to the inky page, satire was a term reserved for a particular
kind of humor that makes fun of human folly and vice by holding
people accountable for their public actions."[7] And, as discussed in
chapter 2, the post-9/11 context demanded a form of humor that
could foster an audience's interest in seeking accountability for public
actions, since this was a moment when, in response to a terrible attack
on U.S. soil, the President made decisions based on feelings he had in
his "gut." It was also a moment when U.S. society had increasingly
lost access to and interest in a public sphere for debate, dialogue,
and deliberation about vital social issues. Satire is a form of humor

that does more than encourage the public to laugh at the expense of others, making it of particular value in the post-9/11 context.

I begin this chapter with an introduction to the notion of satire as public pedagogy. This idea draws on Henry Giroux's theory of public pedagogy, which argues that most learning takes place outside the traditional classroom and that public culture is often the primary means through which society acquires knowledge and learns to model social interaction. Giroux claims that pedagogical spaces are contentious, however, and they can be equally used to facilitate solidarity, dialogue, and critical thinking or to support rigid, unequal, and unjust social practices. My position is that Colbert offered a specific form of satire as public pedagogy after 9/11 that provided a much-needed opportunity for U.S. citizens to laugh at, reflect on, and engage with a series of social crises. After explaining certain key features of satire as a critical mode and a form of public pedagogy, I briefly trace Colbert's links to icons of satire like Jonathan Swift, Ben Franklin, and Samuel Clemens. Then I provide background on Colbert's more recent predecessors, such as *Saturday Night Live* and, of course, *The Daily Show*. The chapter closes by situating Colbert's form of satire within this legacy while also explaining some of its innovations.

SATIRE AS PUBLIC PEDAGOGY

"Public pedagogies...bridge the gap between private and public discourses, while simultaneously putting into play particular ideologies and values that resonate with broader public conversations regarding how society views itself and the world of power, events, and politics." –Henry Giroux[8]

How do we come to form opinions about the world in which we live, our roles and responsibilities as citizens, and what democracy can and should be? Where do we learn to ask questions, think about our social roles, and reflect on our community's challenges? For some time, the answer to those questions seemed to be the classroom, and to a lesser extent the home. But, as Henry Giroux has argued, education increasingly takes place via the mass media, the movie theater, and other forms of public culture: "While John Dewey, Paulo Freire, and various other leading educational theorists in the last century understood the important connection between education and democracy, they had no way in their time of recognizing that the larger culture would extend beyond, if not supersede, institutionalized education, particularly schools, as the most important educational force over developed societies."[9] This larger culture performs what Giroux calls public pedagogy. What he suggests is that, even though formal education sites still hold an important value in schooling, a range of other knowledge and meaning-producing spheres, such as advertising, television, film, the Internet, video-game culture, and the popular press, are increasingly becoming more powerful sources of ideas about the world than schools. Giroux suggests, following Raymond Williams, that public culture has become a form of "permanent education."[10]

But what do we learn from public culture? Giroux claims that, more often than not, what is learned simply reinforces commercial interests, supports the status quo, and justifies existing inequities. This has been especially true in the era of neoliberalism and in the post-9/11 context of a culture of fear and permanent war. Giroux explains that "Under neoliberalism, pedagogy has become thoroughly reactionary as it operates from a variety of education sites producing forms of pedagogical address in which matters of personal agency, social freedom, and the obligations of citizenship conceive of political and social democracy as a burden, an unfortunate constraint on market relations, profit making, and a consumer democracy."[11] Neoliberalism produces a corporate-driven public pedagogy that teaches individuals to compete, to devalue the troubles of others, and to privatize all forms of inequity. Gone is the idea that social crises require collective commitment for change. Poverty is a personal problem, just as racism no longer explains major disparities in social opportunity. The rising racially-based prison population does not indicate a national crisis, but rather a greater threat to the country's security, thereby justifying even more investment of public funds into prisons instead of schools. These commonly held beliefs are the public pedagogy of neoliberalism and, as explained in chapter 2, they were exacerbated by the hyper-patriotism, militarization, and xenophobia that followed the 9/11 attacks.

Giroux's call to address the negative, cynical, corporate-minded, and pro-war effects of these public pedagogies has tended to focus on the democratic potential of what he calls "critical pedagogy," which teaches the public to practice critical thinking. Throughout his recent work, his goal has been to provide "a new language for politics, justice, and freedom in the global public sphere."[12] He explains further: "We need a new vocabulary for talking about what educational institutions should accomplish in a democracy and why they fail; we need a new understanding of public pedagogy for analyzing what kind of notions of agency and structural conditions can bring a meaningful democracy into being. Most important, we need to make pedagogy and hope central to any viable form of politics engaged in the process of creating alternative public spheres and forms of collective resistance."[13]

In keeping with Giroux's line of thought, my argument is that post-9/11 satire has been a very particular form of public pedagogy, one that is relatively unique since it communicates via the same media outlet that tends to offer reactionary and reductive public pedagogies—that of cable television. I'll discuss the venue of cable television in the Internet era in more detail in chapter 5, but for now, it is worth noting that the same media source that offers viewers the political invective of Fox News has also offered alternative information sources like *The Daily Show*, *Real Time*, and *The Colbert Report*. Each of these comedy shows is undeniably committed to fostering public debate and political engagement with current events. My contention is that satire deserves greater attention as one of the most significant forms of critical public pedagogy in operation today. Russell Petersen explains that "Genuine satire can give us information and insight that enhances our ability to fulfill our role as citizens in a democracy."[14] If democracy is at risk, if the public sphere has been undermined, and if corporate mentalities have overshadowed civic responsibility, then satire has become one of the prime ways to challenge these developments. And its impact is not merely theoretical. A Pew Research Center for the People & the Press survey in 2004 found that 61 percent of people under the age of thirty got some of their political "news" from late-night comedy shows. Their research shows that "young people, by far the hardest to reach segment of the political news audience, are abandoning mainstream sources of election news and increasingly citing alternative outlets, including comedy shows such as *The Daily Show* and *Saturday Night Live*, as their source for election news."[15] In another Pew Research Center poll, Jon Stewart was ranked eighth on a list of most admired journalists, with scores slightly below Brian Williams and Anderson Cooper, a fact that suggests that today's political satire does not just comment on the news, but is seen by many to be a source of it.[16]

All contemporary forms of satire are not equal, though, and programs that are primarily focused on politics, like *The Daily Show*, should not be confused with other late-night comedy aimed more at apolitical irony than actual political satire. Petersen describes a difference between satire and what he calls pseudo-satire. One version may be silly and fun, but is ultimately committed to providing conditions for critical thought, while the other stops short of delivering a message: "Satire nourishes our democracy, while the other stuff—let's call it pseudo-satire, since it bears a superficial resemblance to the real thing—is like fast food: popular, readily available, cheap; tasty in its way, but ultimately unhealthy."[17] We might think of it as the difference between the Bush-Bridges skit at the White House Correspondents' Association Dinner, which was biting and made some jabs at the president, but didn't appear threatening to the status quo, versus Colbert's speech, which led to intense reactions among his supporters and critics.

Other examples of satire and irony that do not lead to productive political debate are shows like *South Park* or *The Simpsons*, which have been accused of being "willing to attack 'everything,' thereby not amounting to any form of 'meaningful' political discourse."[18] These are programs that are intensely critical, but they provide a negative critique that offers little, if any, of the hope and radical imagination Giroux describes as necessary for an effective public pedagogy. Negative, merely sarcastic satire, then, should not be confused with politically productive satire. Both forms play with social norms and both lead to critical reactions, making it often difficult to discern between the two, but the difference is that politically productive satire is not satisfied with cynicism as a response.

Jonathan Gray, Jeffrey J. Jones, and Ethan Thompson offer a breakdown of the central components of satire in their essay "The State of Satire, the Satire of the State." They explain that one of the prime elements of satire is that, through the performance of scrutiny and critique, the audience is asked to perform their own scrutiny and critique. Thus, one significant feature of satire is its call for an active audience. News may seem to offer viewers information, but satire does more. Satire asks the audience to take a piece of news and play with it, test it, reflect on it, and question it, "rather than simply consume it as information or 'truth' from authoritative sources."[19] Key, then, to satire's pedagogical function is the way that it encourages critical reflection on supposed sources of authority and truth. Unlike intense political commentary or abstract critical theory, satire can reach a general, educated public, and it can show, in a way that can combine silliness with seriousness, that commonly accepted truths require reconsideration and resistance. While political satire always has ethical goals, these come in a playful package that allows the audience a chance to "get it" without feeling demeaned. This form of comedy creates a sense of community among those who get the joke, thereby playing a crucial role in reinvigorating a sense of the public sphere.

Critics of satire suggest that it tends to encourage cynicism, that it can devalue the public's commitment to important social issues by belittling them. While these reactions are also possible, I would suggest that they are more common with Peterson's pseudo-satire or what I've called cynical, apolitical satire. As Gray, Jones, and Thompson explain, "Satire is provocative, not dismissive—a crucial point that critics typically ignore when assessing its role in public discourse."[20] One of the reasons that television satire has often been less politically incisive, they contend, is that satire tends to be a negative form, even if it has positive intentions, and runs the risk of alienating the audience, a fact that generally means a smaller potential market.[21] Consequently, television satire has often opted for blander, more audience-friendly forms of comedy that are safer and more predictable.

George Test argues that satire is at once "an act of judgment, aggression, play, and laughter."[22] He explains that, "The playfulness of satire, especially when yoked with serious questions, may disconcert some."[23] But these risks of alienating an audience are necessary if satire is to elicit critical reflection. It can't be easy or palatable or just plain fun. It needs to be uncomfortable and a bit disconcerting. It can't offer easy answers and simple jokes. Gray, Jones, and Thompson further point out that it requires a certain level of sophistication from its audience, since this is humor that requires "work" and will not offer "clear-cut or easily digestible meanings."[24] This process asks the audience to interrogate power, to use reason and critical thinking to understand social processes, and to question the status quo. Thus the laughter, silliness, and ridicule of satire are meant to lead to positive change.

When satire is combined with parody, as is the case with *The Colbert Report* or *The Daily Show*, the combination is especially powerful. Parody mocks or makes fun of an "original." If satire aims at human folly, vices, and abuses, then parody packs an extra punch as the comedian embodies that which is being lampooned. When Colbert presents himself as a right-wing, bloviating, political pundit who thinks with his gut and believes that his fears should be those of the nation, he adds an additional layer of critique to his satire. In Colbert's case, his parody of O'Reilly-style punditry always overlays his remarks against the object of his parody. Such a technique teaches his viewers how to detach from the type of information that O'Reilly offers on his show. Jon Stewart parodies a mainstream news show, allowing him to mock television news anchors while also performing a level of critical questioning rarely seen on regular news shows. As Gray, Jones, and Thompson explain, "parody aims to provoke reflection *and re-evaluation* of how the targeted texts or genre works."[25] This means that satirical parody has the potential to be an even more effective source of public pedagogy, since it adds additional layers of critique and asks the audience to work even harder to make sense of the joke as well as of the world.

BETTER KNOW A FOUNDER: COLBERT'S SATIRICAL PRECEDENTS

As a sign of Colbert's awareness of some of his satirical predecessors, he presented a segment on December 13, 2010, that served as a shout out to one of history's most famous satirists: Jonathan Swift.[26] That night "The Wørd" segment was entitled, "Swift Payment," in response to legislation that would continue the Bush tax cuts for the wealthiest Americans. Colbert opened with a bit on how the tax cuts would lead to a zero to one tenth of a percent chance of less unemployment, and he then covered Congressional debates on trickle-down economics. He went on to explain, though, that Ted Turner had recently come up with a plan for redistributing wealth that he could endorse. Turner had suggested that the United States institute a one-child policy, thereby allowing the poor to sell their fertility rights to the rich. He shows a quote from Turner that reads: "Poor people could profit from their decision not to reproduce." Colbert responds, "Some people see life, liberty, and the pursuit of happiness as constitutional rights, but visionaries like Ted Turner see them as menu options." Colbert then remarks that Turner's proposition does raise some troubling questions, "like what other rights of the poor can we treat as fungible commodities?" Next he mentions Turner's thoughts on global warming, where he claims that in thirty years there will be no crops and that the surviving humans will become cannibals. This leads Colbert to elaborate that, in that situation, the rich will buy poor children to eat for food, allowing him to pull out an old copy of Jonathan Swift's "A Modest Proposal" and read a quote from it about the delicacy of eating babies: "A young healthy child well-nursed, is, at a year old, a most delicious nourishing and wholesome food, whether stewed, roasted, baked, or boiled."

Colbert's segment makes a brilliant link between his satire and that of Swift. Swift, who also wrote *Gulliver's Travels*, was an Anglo-Irish satirist who produced a number of well-known satirical texts in the early eighteenth century. One of his most famous works was the essay "A Modest Proposal for Preventing the Children of Poor People in Ireland From Being a Burden to Their Parents or Country, and

for Making Them Beneficial to the Public," commonly referred to as
"A Modest Proposal," written and published anonymously by Swift
in 1729. "A Modest Proposal" is considered by many to be one of
the best examples of satirical writing in history. Swift suggests in his
essay that the impoverished Irish might ease their economic troubles
by selling their children as food for rich gentlemen and ladies. The
essay's satirical hyperbole is heightened by the format, where Swift
slowly paints the picture of Irish suffering only to shock readers with
his solution. Just like Colbert's satire of Turner, "A Modest Proposal"
mocks heartless attitudes toward the poor.

It seems hardly a coincidence that Colbert referenced Swift.
Despite the centuries that separate them and despite the difference
between publishing pamphlets and appearing on television, the two
satirists clearly have much in common. Both Swift and Colbert critique economic policies that render the poor nothing more than
commodities. And both created their satire in a moment when the
wealthy increasingly offered more and more illogical schemes for
dealing with the misfortunes of the poor. As George Wittkowsky
explains, Swift's "A Modest Proposal" was "a burlesque of projects
concerning the poor," that were commonly circulating during the
early eighteenth century.[27] In similar fashion, Colbert has repeatedly done segments on his show that call attention to insensitive
and insane arguments made about what the nation's commitment
should be to those living in poverty. In one segment, he critiqued a
Tea Party mission to undo an economically and racially integrated
school where 94.5 percent of all children's families were happy with
the system.[28] In another he went after Andre Bauer, Lieutenant
Governor of South Carolina, who suggested that the poor should
not be given "ample food," since that would allow them to "reproduce," a stance Bauer said came from his grandmother's advice not
to feed stray animals. Colbert defends Bauer, saying that he only
said that it is bad to feed "strays": "I am sure that he wouldn't
mind taking the poor to a farm upstate where they can be happy
and chase rabbits." In another connection to Swift, Colbert points
to the link Bauer is making between the poor and animals. In "A
Modest Proposal," Swift has his narrator use language ordinarily
reserved for animals to refer to the Irish in order to further degrade
them. Colbert, though, doesn't have to create that language since
Bauer has done it for him. Near the end of the segment, Colbert
explains that Bauer defended himself by claiming that his analogy
was being taken as a metaphor. Bauer clearly doesn't really appreciate the difference between an analogy and a metaphor, giving

wordanista Colbert an excellent opportunity for satirical wit: "A metaphor is poor people are animals. An analogy is poor people are to animals as Andre Bauer is to douche bags."[29]

Jonathan Swift may have been writing from Ireland and England, but his work had a strong influence on many of the pro-Revolutionary colonists that became the founders of U.S. satire. As Linda Morris points out, satire has been an ongoing feature of Colonial and post-Independence (U.S.) American culture, appearing most vigorously in moments of crisis and conflict:

> From the beginning, conditions were ripe for political, social, and religious satire. Satirists poked fun at the Puritans, rude country people, and people who aspired to lives of fashion, as well as at the British, who fought to keep the colonies under their legal and economic control, and at the democratic institutions that arose after the Revolution. Political abuses were frequently the targets of satire, whether in the eighteenth or nineteenth century, no matter the party in power. Writers used their biting humor to attack the institution of slavery as early as 1797 and as late as 1865.[30]

There is not sufficient space here to trace the full complexity of this history and how it relates to Colbert's work, but I want to offer a few key points of connection that show how Colbert has a number of significant U.S. predecessors. Colbert fans might recall that one of the spin-offs of the recurring segment "Better Know a District" is "Better Know a Founder," one segment of which featured Ben Franklin. Franklin then reappeared on the show on a number of occasions, most notably during the week of April 14–17, 2008, when Colbert moved the show to Philadelphia to broadcast from the same location where the Democratic Party was holding the primary debates.

While Ben Franklin may appear on the show as rather stiff and silly, his satirical work has a direct connection to some of Colbert's techniques, and Colbert references one of Franklin's masterpieces of satire, *Poor Richard's Almanack,* in his "Better Know a Founder" segment.[31] *Poor Richard's Almanack* appeared yearly from 1732 to 1758 under the pseudonym of "Poor Richard" or "Richard Saunders." The almanac was a best seller for a pamphlet published in the U.S. colonies with print runs that reached ten thousand per year. One of the direct links to Colbert is that the text was known for its wordplay and aphorisms, many of which remain in use today. In a similar vein, Colbert, unlike any other modern-day comedian, has focused much of his satire on creating neologisms, many of which, like *truthiness, wikiality,* and *freem,* have entered the larger U.S. lexicon, appearing in dictionaries and in printed texts with frequency.[32]

Probably the most well-known examples of Franklin's ability to produce biting satire are "An Edict by the King of Prussia" and "The Sale of the Hessians," which according to Bruce Granger are "illustrative of the situational mask, wherein personae are created 'who embody and illustrate the ironic contradictions between what *seems* to them and what, as the reader knows, actually *is.*'"[33] This basic element of satire, where the audience is presented with the disconnect between the object of satire's arrogant ignorance and their own awareness of that absurdity, produces a critical effect that allows the audience to see the folly of a public figure and take distance from their actions while also judging them. Many of the Colonial-era satirists used masks, personae, and noms de plume as does Colbert, who not only masquerades as a right-wing pundit, but also takes on other personalities, such as that of Tek Jensen, where he appears as a sci-fi comic-book hero, or Esteban Colberto, where he appears as a Latin American emcee of a variety show, *El Colberto Reporto Gigante,* similar to *Sábado Gigante.* Morris also comments on how frequently masks/personas are used in U.S. satire: "American satire of the eighteenth, and especially of the nineteenth century, often relies upon the creation of a naïve persona who inadvertently, and in an understated manner, reveals social truths. Yet, American satire also frequently relies on comic exaggeration."[34] Colbert, in keeping with his early American predecessors, combines the naïve persona with comic exaggeration. He often refers to his character as a "well-intentioned, high-status idiot."

According to Wells, during the Revolutionary period satire was "the most popular and politically important literary form" in American political life. "In fiction, drama, and particularly poetry, satire emerged during this time as a crucial means for shaping American social and political discourse, intervening in virtually every major controversy from the Stamp Act crisis to the War of 1812."[35] The link between Franklin and Colbert highlights the way that satire has always played an important role in public discourse in the United States, especially in response to political decisions and trends. But the connection between Franklin and other colonial satirists and Colbert also derives from the fact that their satire appeared during a period of war and military conflict. Wells and other scholars emphasize the analogy of satire as a weapon of war: "Befitting the political turbulence and fervor that characterized the era, early American satirists envisioned their works as weapons in a literary and ideological war to decide the future of the new Republic. During the Revolution, anti-British satires appeared regularly in newspapers or as broadsides, responding to specific events and depicting King George III and his supporters as villains or buffoons."[36] In a similar vein, Colbert and Stewart have used their satire to discredit the policies of the Bush administration and to intervene directly in politics, exemplified by their rally on the National Mall right before the midterm elections of 2010. In times of war and conflict, satire erupts as a form of critical discourse that asks the public to question the status quo, make public figures accountable, and engage in political actions themselves.

Satire can also play a crucial role in pointing to a society's injustices, as evidenced in the work of another Colbert influence: Samuel Clemens, who published under the pseudonym Mark Twain. On January 5, 2011, Colbert had an opportunity to connect his work with that of Twain. Colbert began his bit by saying: "Nation, I am on record as being a huge fan of censorship. Of course, you won't actually find it in the record—I had it taken out."[37] Colbert used these comments to preface his thoughts on the fact that the new edition of Mark Twain's classic novel *The Adventures of Huckleberry Finn,* published by New South Books, had been edited, replacing each instance of the "N-word" with the word *slave.* Colbert points to the ridiculousness of the censorship, but his comments also resonate more deeply, since he too, has taken risks in his satirical work that have led him to come under fire.

Colbert claims, during the segment, that one of his favorite books was *Huckleberry Finn.* Revealing that as a child, he thought that the slave character Jim was "so great I wanted one of my own." Unlike Twain's Huck, who represented the voice of a less-educated southern child, Colbert's in-character voice comes from the position of the high-status hypocrite and bigot. What they have in common, though, is the presentation of an extreme social position that then allows the public to draw conclusions about the injustice of common practices. In Twain's *Huckleberry Finn,* it was slavery. For Colbert, here, it is censorship. As Colbert closes the segment, having pushed the so-called logic of the censors to the extreme, he charges that the changes to *Huckleberry Finn* do not go far enough. "Who knows," Colbert asks, "what other words it contains that are OK now that someday might be offensive?" Beyond suggesting that censorship, once justified, knows no limits, Colbert is also asking how it has come to be that the nation is not capable of contextualizing a word used satirically. This issue has particular weight for Colbert, who also uses words in ways that demand critical sensitivity.

Twain's legacy to modern day satire has been noted by Robert Miller, publisher of *HarperStudio*, who suggests that "Twain is the grandfather of Stephen Colbert, Jon Stewart, and Steve Martin. He has such a dry, subversive wit that you feel like he's invented modern humor."[38] In another example of a modern-day link, a reader's letter to *The Washington Post*, responding to Colbert's appearance before Congress to talk as an "expert" on immigration, suggested that he was following in Twain's footsteps.[39] Don Bliss wrote: "Loosen up, Republicans. Stephen Colbert's testimony on migrant labor before the House Judiciary Committee was in a great American tradition."[40] He explains that, "On a wintry Dec. 7, 1906, Mark Twain... had the Senate patents committee rolling in laughter as he argued for the extension of copyright protection. Midst the quips and humorous stories was a compelling logic that persuaded Congress to act."[41] Rather than see Colbert's appearance on the Hill as an insult to the political process, Bliss asks, what if it were understood as an effort to use wit to urge lawmakers to find a solution for a serious social problem? "Perhaps a little more humor would help the polarized political parties to find common ground and act in the national interest."[42] Similar to Twain, Colbert's satire may mock the political process, but this is in the service of asking more from it, demanding that it be publicly accountable, and pushing it to base decisions on rational judgment. When Colbert appeared in Congress that day, he may have made silly jokes about his doctor telling him that he needed to protect undocumented workers because he needs roughage and they are the ones that pick our fruits and vegetables, but he also made a reasoned argument for why Congress should consider immigration reform: "Now I'm not a fan of the government doing anything, but I've gotta ask, why isn't the government doing anything?"[43] In these lines Colbert is only tenuously holding onto his character, visible primarily in the phrase "I'm not a fan of the government doing anything." Otherwise, the statement more closely represents Colbert out-of-character. So, in a twist from Twain, and more similar to Franklin, Colbert used his satire to gain access to the public sphere and used his celebrity to further a political cause. At the end of his testimony he closed by saying: "I thank you for your time. Again, it is an honor, a privilege and a responsibility to be here. I trust that following my testimony, both sides will work together on this issue in the best interest of the American people, as you always do."[44] His emphasis on his role there as a "responsibility" reveals his commitment to use his satire toward political impact. It makes his last mocking words about an ineffective and partisan Congress even more powerful, since he clearly fashions himself as someone who, while an entertainer, does indeed work "in the best interest of the American people."[45] What is most useful to draw from this brief survey is Colbert's own self-conscious link to icons of satire like Swift, Franklin, and Twain. When we recognize how much of his satire is aimed directly at the "nation" (understood here as a play between the United States and the Colbert Nation), then we can begin to recognize that his work has direct parallels to satirists who hoped to use their work to change political ideas and actions. Unlike satirists who fashion softball critiques of society at large and lampoon everyday customs, the majority of Colbert's satire goes directly to larger political issues. His merging of his own identity with that of the nation will be discussed in more detail in chapter 4, but it's worth pausing to reflect on how something as simple as the opening credits to his show emphasize his role as an American satirist. When the show first aired, the opening title sequence began with an eagle soaring past Colbert, followed by images of Americana, stock footage of Colbert, and words describing Colbert passing by him. Some of the first words included the neologisms *Megamerican, Lincolnish,* and *flagaphile*—all clear signs of his association with Americanness. Through his wordplay, masquerades, witty satire, bitingly critical look at injustices and inequalities, and parodic public appearances, Colbert's comedy has built on a long legacy of satirists who used their work to provoke critical reflection and public engagement.

SATIRE TV

Let's fast-forward through this history lesson and enter the mid-twentieth century when satire became more prevalent on U.S. television. While fans of Colbert may have been less aware of his efforts to draw connections between his satire and that of other early satirists, they are probably well aware of some his more recent predecessors—*The Smothers Brothers, Saturday Night Live,* etc. The presence of satire as a televisual force is relatively new and has been fairly complex, with a range of modalities and issues at stake. Gray, Jones, and Thompson point out that while satire has long been understood as a source of social and political criticism in literature, television satire has a more tenuous history.[46]

David Marc explains that the sitcom became the dominant format for humor on television during the 1950s. Sitcoms, though, are a form of humor vastly different from satire. They tend to ridicule personal behavior, and they are not invested in critiques of power per se. They do not ask the audience to act or think, just to mock or deride. One well-known example of this trend was *All in the Family*, whose main character, Archie Bunker, was meant to satirize opinionated bigots. Instead, though, the sitcom format allowed the audience to uncritically love him.[47] Shows like *Seinfeld* or *Cheers* offer bland, localized, personal mocking absent the bite and impact of satire. Comedic skirmishes with characters like *Seinfeld*'s mail-carrier nemesis, Newman, do not link to a broader social category, and the contours of the conflicts they depict do not have a political angle. Marc explains that in the pre-cable era, "television was more reliable as an object of satirists than a medium for the presentation of their work."[48]

The first full-on television satire program was *That Was the Week That Was* (hosted on NBC from 1964 to 1965). It centered on a "news-of-the-week-in-comic-review" format that predated *Saturday Night Live*'s recurring segment "Weekend Update" by more than a decade.[49] The next major television satire show was *The Smothers Brothers Comedy Hour* (CBS, 1967 to 1969). The Smothers Brothers were musical performers and comedians, and the show started out as a typical comedy-variety show of its era. Soon after, though, it evolved into a show that extended the boundaries of what was considered permissible in television satire, leading eventually to its cancellation.

The Smothers Brothers offers two important precursors to Colbert's work. First, it attracted a youth audience in a moment of protest against the Vietnam War, which led it to take on more and more aggressive satirical topics. In a manner familiar to viewers of Colbert, the bulk of the program's satire was aimed at three targets: racism, the president of the United States, and the Vietnam War. (Colbert's three might be the media and especially punditry; the right-wing government, particularly the Bush administration; and neoliberal free-market capitalism.) Unsurprisingly, *The Smothers Brothers* was soon the object of CBS censorship. "At the start of the 1968–69 season, the network ordered that the Smothers deliver their shows finished and ready to air ten days before airdate so that the censors could edit the shows as necessary."[50] The show had touched a nerve by regularly featuring entertainers that were openly against the war, like Joan Baez, who tried to dedicate a song to her husband, David Harris, who was about to go to jail for avoiding the draft. Her dedication was later censored when the show eventually aired.

Not only did *The Smothers Brothers* offer an example of the sort of satire TV that challenges the government, but one of its cast members, Pat Paulsen, also launched a fake presidential campaign, previewing a future Colbert move. Thus, the second link between the shows was the use of satire to spill beyond the TV screen and directly into the realm of politics. Again, in resemblance to later Colbert work, Paulsen had regularly appeared on the show as a stone-faced, deadpan news commentator, who appeared awkward before the camera and incapable of understanding complex social issues. As Heather Osborne Thompson notes, Paulsen's "deadpan delivery, odd facial ticks [sic], and seeming unease before the camera radiated a lack of both sophistication and sincerity that linked him to many of the politicians his commentaries took aim at on the show." Sound familiar? He would "espouse earnest-sounding but inept positions" on key issues facing the nation, such as a new draft lottery based entirely on hat size.[51]

Paulsen ran six times between 1968 and 1996, and each time gained in polls. The context for Paulsen's first fake presidential bid was 1968, an extremely volatile moment in U.S. history. This was an era of student protests, civil-rights activism, and anti-war marches. It was Nixon and Vietnam. Paulsen's campaigns were grounded in comedy, but seriously satirical comedy. His campaign slogan was "Just a common, ordinary, simple savior of America's destiny," and one can imagine Colbert using something almost identical. Paulsen responded to all criticism with his catchphrase "Picky, picky, picky." One of the key elements of Paulsen's campaign, relevant for Colbert, is the way that it took place on and off television, pressing on the boundaries of satire TV in ways that would happen again in the post-9/11 moment with Stewart, Colbert, and also with the successful Senate run of satirical comedian Al Franken.

Following *The Smothers Brothers* and its incisive commentary on 1960s social and political issues, the 1970s saw the launch of *Saturday Night Live (SNL)*, whose satire waned as its audience grew. Much the same took place in the 1980s as well, when social satire on *SNL* "was often subsumed into silly characters with little or no rebuke."[52] Of course, the segment "Weekend Update" offered an early example of news parody, but it was mostly after cheap laughs and silly banter, rather than powerful comedic punch. Much would change in the 1990s as television entered the cable era more fully and stations like Comedy Central (originally called Comedy TV) were founded, and programs like *Politically Incorrect* took the air. Gray, Jones, and Thompson note that since "the introduction of *Politically Incorrect*, Comedy Central has recognized that satirical treatments of politics are central to its identity."[53] Another important parody show that emerged in the same period on Comedy Central was *The Daily Show*, which was hosted by Craig Kilborn until Jon Stewart took over in 1999.

There is not sufficient space here to draw out all of the links between Stewart and Colbert; their shows are clearly inextricably linked. Beyond offering Colbert the chance to develop the persona that now hosts his spin-off show, Stewart's satire effectively provides the critical base from which Colbert's program took off. The format for *The Daily Show* is a combination of talk show (interviews), news parody, and news itself. One of the key features of Stewart's satire that is also evident in Colbert's (and often directly linked to it) is its hybrid news nature. It is at one and the same time a parody of the news and a source of it. Similarly, the interviews are often exceptionally intense, completely unlike the soft-ball chitchat on other late-night comedy shows like the *Late Show with David Letterman*. The difference, of course, is that Colbert's interviews are performed from the position of a high-status, right-wing idiot, whereas Stewart often interviews with little ironic distance, if any.

As Don J. Waisanen explains, "Stewart typically uses his own voice, which is inflected by a tone of disbelief and tongue-in-cheek awe."[54] In interviews, he often follows that mode with a sharp, unexpected question that takes interviewees off guard and calls for them to respond absent the layers of performative rhetoric that they typically use. In those moments, he is engaged directly in deliberative debate and critical dialogue with his guest. That sort of directness is almost totally absent from Colbert's style, although it can appear from time to time as well. Waisanen points out that Stewart delivers his jokes in his own left-leaning, astounded-but-amused persona, whereas Colbert's character and show are "formal, stylistic appropriations of generally right-wing news reporting."[55]

Colbert's tongue-in-cheek moments often come from the perspective of a smug Republican who thinks liberals are idiots. This means that Colbert's satire always has an extra layer, since he has to couple those performative remarks with ironic gestures that wink at his audience. Waisanen explains that Colbert does this with facial expressions and other "I'm jesting" gestures to indicate his irony and play. Stewart also uses facial expressions effectively to indicate his irony, but these are expressions of awe, shock, and bewilderment, as opposed to Colbert's winks and sardonic grins. What is most important to recognize, though, is that the two programs have created entirely complementary satire. Stewart's openly left-leaning persona allows him to push interviews in specific ways that directly intersect with Colbert's taking of extreme right-wing views.

Stewart's intense confrontation with major social issues has led Geoffrey Baym to conclude that his show "represents something altogether different, an emergent paradigm of hybrid media that blends news and entertainment in unprecedented ways."[56] Thus, like Colbert, Stewart's show combines entertainment and news in a wholly new way, meaning that the satirical components of his work serve not just as commentary, but also as information. This shift has taken place, in part, as discussed in chapter 2, due to changes in news media in the post-network era that have made television news a "scattered profession that increasingly has become part informational resource, part circus sideshow, and entirely (and often crassly) self-promotional."[57] When the "real" news offers pieces on tanning addiction and snakes that eat electric blankets, then it is hard to separate it from the "fake" news that satirically, yet poignantly, covers such issues as the Iraq War or the Egyptian protests.

Another direct link between the satire of Stewart and Colbert is the target of their satire. While both shows occasionally have silly, non-socially-relevant bits, their goal is political satire. One difference, though, is that the bite of Stewart's political satire is unmediated through the character of a pundit as is Colbert's. As cited above, a Pew Research Center study tried to situate Stewart among journalists and found that viewers (especially young ones) considered him alongside anchors like Brian Williams and Anderson Cooper. Clearly, this is a transitional moment for news, as the mainstream moves more toward infotainment and spectacle, and alternative news sources have become the only place where one finds a combination of information and critical reflection.

While the history of satire reveals other times when satire itself created news, the era of satire TV has radically altered the stakes, regularly becoming a news source. One key to Stewart's angle, though, is his tendency to skewer, to call out, and to aggressively confront those in power, even as they sit in the hot-seat during interviews. The Pew study found that "The program's clearest focus is politics, especially in Washington. U.S. foreign affairs, largely dominated by the Bush administration's policies in Iraq, Washington politics and government accounted for nearly half (47 percent) of the time spent on the program. Overall, 'The Daily Show' news agenda is quite close to those of cable news talk shows."[58] Another ongoing topic is the press itself, and segments about the media accounted for eight percent of program time. The Pew study also found, though, that a major portion of news is not presented on *The Daily Show*, pointing out that the program did not cover events such as the tragic 2007 Minneapolis bridge collapse.[59] What this study shows, then, is that *The Daily Show* is not meant to replace the news, a point that has been made by

PROUD TO BE AN AMERICAN SATIRIST

Stewart himself on numerous occasions, most notably in his infamous interview with Tucker Carlson and Paul Begala on *Crossfire* in 2004. Stewart criticized them for acting like entertainers rather than news journalists, which then led them to ask him to "be funny."

> *Carlson*: Wait. I thought you were going to be funny. Come on. Be funny.
> *Stewart*: No. No. I'm not going to be your monkey.[60]

From there, Stewart pushed the news-media men even further, and they became more and more hostile toward him.

> *Carlson*: We're talking to Jon Stewart, who was just lecturing us on our moral inferiority.
> Jon, you're bumming us out. Tell us, what do you think about the Bill O'Reilly vibrator story?
> *Stewart*: I'm sorry. I don't.
> *Carlson*: Oh, OK.
> *Stewart*: What do you think?
> *Begala*: Let me change the subject.
> *Stewart*: Where's your moral outrage on this?
> *Carlson*: I don't have any.
> *Stewart*: I know.[61]

This last exchange returns us to one of the central features of satire evident in both the work of Colbert and Stewart: the encouragement of moral outrage. The development of moral outrage signifies the difference between apolitical pseudo-satire and politically effective satire. While it is always hard to measure the success of such a project, it is clear that both Colbert and Stewart follow their predecessors Swift, Franklin, Twain, and Paulsen in creating a satirical mode meant to make a difference. In particular, as examples of U.S. satire, we can note an effort on their parts to reinvigorate the ideals and promise of democracy, equality, and justice. It is no coincidence that each of these satirists has emerged during moments of intense social upheaval and diminished opportunities for the public sphere.

COLBERT, GREAT AMERICAN SATIRIST, OR THE GREATEST AMERICAN SATIRIST?

On his first show, Colbert began one of the last segments by saying that the first thing every news journalist needs is "humility": "the story is not about you, you are a vessel of communication"—an ironic comment, given Colbert's well-known hubris on his show and his constant emphasis on other media figures' egos. The second thing TV journalists need, he says, is "gravitas": "It is the weight, the authority, the soup bone in the stew of television news."[62] He then introduced his guest for that night: Stone Phillips, who was co-anchor of *Dateline NBC* at the time, and who was known for his clear delivery and gravitas in his reading of the news. Colbert then engages Stone Phillips in a "gravitas off" where they each read random snippets of purported news copy with their best gravitas, "to show you that if you possess sufficient gravitas, what you are saying doesn't have to mean anything at all." They then read inane headlines that sounded like they very well might have been read on television:

> *Phillips*: If you have ever sat naked on a hotel bedspread, we have a chilling report you won't want to miss.
> *Colbert*: Raheed and MC Fresh James were dropping mad beats at the house party when tragedy struck.
> *Phillips*: We invited Mother Teresa to respond to these charges.
> *Colbert*: Thankfully, alert gauchos were able to save the llama before it was swept into the blades of the turbine.

They ended the "gravitas off" with two difficult tongue-twisters. Each line that had been read had gotten increasingly more ridiculous, but they had all been delivered with the typical weight of anchor-speak. It was an extremely successful parody of the way that TV news media turns stories that are not news into stories that appear to be of tantamount importance to the viewer. It worked so effectively because Colbert's performance of gravitas alongside a real-life master of it made Philips simply seem like a performer as well: after Colbert's tongue-in-cheek use of the speaking style, Philips's use of it appeared like a mockery of itself.

One of the most brilliant features of Colbert's media parody is the way that he has been able to get major media figures to play along with him on his show. Exemplified by the persona that he takes in "Better Know a District," Colbert is able to use a tone and manner that can convince people to do what he says, even when it is clear that his goal is to mock them. In an interview that appeared that night before the "Gravitas Off" with Phillips, Colbert presented himself as a colleague of Phillips, as someone who wanted to learn from the master, but also as someone who was competing with Phillips. Phillips has been recognized as an excellent interviewer, and he had won an Emmy for his 1996 interview with New York subway gunman Bernard Goetz, leading Colbert to ask him for tips. In one interesting moment, Colbert asked Phillips what question he would ask himself if he were Colbert. Phillips responds: "Why are you here?"[63] Clearly, that is the key question. Why would a media figure appear on a show that mocks them? Even though this was Colbert's first show, its connection to *The Daily Show* likely meant that it, too, would parody media figures. Philips then explained that if he responded to his own interview question that he would say that he would have to check with his producer to get the answer, suggesting that he had not been the one who decided that he should be a guest on *The Colbert Report*.

The exchange was telling since it showed a major shift in the connection between the satirist and the object of satire. Whereas before, the "butt" of the joke might appear to play along and be a good sport, in most cases the object of ridicule did not aid the satirist. This has changed in the post-network era of satire TV as Colbert and Stewart have drawn such a large market. And Colbert has been especially successful at getting major public figures, especially from the media and politics, to help him make fun of them. Baym explains that, "the interview segments on both shows have become near-mandatory bookings for authors selling works of political nonfiction as well as for politicians hoping to influence the national conversation."[64] In addition, media figures have also been a staple on the show. This process has created a new form of satirical parody that has given satirists more power than ever. It is worth recalling that most early satirists published under pseudonyms or anonymously in order to avoid censure, lawsuits, and other blowback for their work. Recall also the cancellations of *The Smothers Brothers* and of *Politically Incorrect*. Colbert and Stewart operate in a different mode, because their shows have become extremely powerful and because we live in an era where ratings largely outweigh worries over sensitive content.

Also noteworthy is the fact that Colbert's performance at the White House Correspondents' Association Dinner was no less aggressive than Maher's comments about terrorists, but Colbert's show was not threatened afterwards: it actually gained more ground. These differences might be explained by three key differences between Maher's comments and Colbert's. First, Colbert's comments came with the distance of four years, no small amount of time when one recalls the post-9/11 hysteria that had gripped the country. Second, Colbert always performs his satire in character, whereas Maher's comments were delivered as his direct opinion. And third, both Colbert and Stewart tend to have an ease of manner where they offer sharp, biting satire, but then add self-mockery, silliness, and a softer tone than comedians like Maher, George Carlin, or Dennis Miller, for instance.

This tone allows them to have more leeway with their satire and to explore more topics more aggressively. But that does not soften their effectiveness when they soften their tone. I would suggest that they take their satire right to and only slightly over the edge of what the power elite will tolerate, which allows them to operate without constant fear of repercussions.

Baym argues that a key to Colbert's satire is his use of postmodern spectacle, where Colbert manipulates the reality of politics or the media in such a way that viewers question the very logic of representation itself.[65] The main targets of Colbert's satire are those public figures that "represent" the world to us. Politicians in a democratic society represent the people, or at least that is the idea. And the news media "represents" information important to the public, or at least that should be the goal. Following postmodern questioning on how those processes of representation work, Colbert exposes the degree to which the idea of representation itself is disconnected from reality, since these spheres only seem self-referential and self-serving. Rather than represent reality, the political process and the media that covers it construct an alternative "reality" that is damaging to the public sphere because it is no longer invested in the ideals of democracy, equality, or justice. When these representations are nothing but performance, farce, and folly, democracy suffers.

One of the best examples of this process in Colbert's satire is his recurring segment, "Better Know a District," which had its strongest presence from the debut of *The Colbert Report* until August 2006, when House members began avoiding the show, based on fears that it would lead to negative press and in response to comments from House Speaker Nancy Pelosi that representatives should not talk to him.

That caution, of course, was hugely ironic since in the 2006 midterm elections every one of the 27 sitting members of Congress Colbert had profiled won their seat.[66] The segment, as Baym points out, is an excellent illustration of Colbert's efforts to interject meaningful politics into an unlikely venue, that of late-night comedy. Colbert's segment was a brilliant effort to merge the goal of creating a public sphere with the goal of educating his audience about U.S. politics. By focusing on the House of Representatives, a body of government almost wholly ignored in the mainstream media, Colbert brought attention to an essential part of the federal government that drew little public attention. As Baym points out, almost all news is about the executive branch, with only a handful of senators and representatives getting major media time.[67] Just as the media ignores the House, so too do the voters, only 37.1 percent of whom voted in 2006.[68]

Consequently, Colbert's segments drew attention to political actors unknown to the public. The segment generally starts with a pre-taped introduction that appears like that of an educational video, followed by a highly edited interview segment with Colbert in typical right-wing,

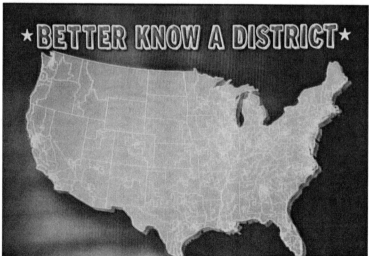

Photos 3.1 and 3.2 Colbert doesn't understand why Nancy Pelosi doesn't want representatives to appear in his "Better Know a District" segment.

ignorant, pundit-like form. Colbert's in-character performance places his work with the segment alongside that of Sacha Baron Cohen, who would take on identities like Ali G or Borat in order to conduct interviews that mocked his guests. But in contrast to the hilarious satire of Cohen, Colbert's comedy is less funny in a laugh-out-loud sense and more political. At the same time, though, the segment is highly effective in revealing the intellectual weaknesses of many of those who represent us in Congress. This is what happened when Colbert asked Lynn Westmoreland from the 3rd District of Georgia to name all ten of the Ten Commandments, since he was proposing that they be posted in courthouses. While the edited interview aired on *The Colbert Report* showed Westmoreland naming only three of the commandments, his press secretary said that he had named seven. Either way, the point was made.

Part of what makes the segment so successful is Colbert's interview style, which includes a certain kind of deadpan, matter-of-fact tone alongside outrageous comments. "Colbert's character lacks the *coherence* one might expect," Baym says, "he continuously shifts voices, intonations, and intimations. On its face, his performance seems to lack an underlying logic; it is irrational or deeply inconsistent, with claims, grounds, and warrants, hopelessly confused."[69] As discussed above in the analysis of his politically effective satirical components, Colbert's destabilizing discourse does more than simply produce cynical irony; it, in fact, provokes a viewer response.

Mixed with these efforts, however, Colbert's satire cannot be detached from his ever-present megalomania and ego-boosting, a feature of his satire that further differentiates him from Stewart. Emulating a highly egotistical pundit, Colbert takes ego-boosting to absurd levels, a move that mocks the self-aggrandizing of the media and of the power elite, while also feeding directly into Colbert's own urge to expand his fan base. In his coverage of the midterm elections of 2006, Colbert said that rather than focus on the elections as a whole, he wanted to focus on the elections that really mattered, those that showed his own power, those of the people whom he had profiled on his show as part of "Better Know a District."[70] When he presented the results of the election, each time one of the candidates who had won came up on the screen, Colbert superimposed an image of himself over them. "Their districts have become part of the Colbert Nation." After replaying Pelosi's comment that she "wouldn't recommend that anyone go on his show," Colbert pointed out that he had won, and that he expected something in return: "I'm not asking for anything big, folks, just the one thing that the nation desperately needs [pause]—a $315 million bridge to connect my desk to the interview table."[71] In the space of the pause, he gave his audience sufficient time to fill in the blank for themselves, likely imagining that what the nation desperately needs is a functioning democracy. After the pause, he then filled the gap with an exaggerated, but sadly not totally ludicrous, answer that only reinforced, through its satire of lobbying and cronyism, the need for participatory democracy and a viable public sphere.

In his analysis of "Better Know a District," Baym calls attention to Colbert's function as an educator and that there is little doubt that Colbert fashions his satire as a public pedagogy.[72] This gesture was especially visible in his efforts to regain awareness of the war in Iraq in June of 2009, when public attention had drifted from the war. In a move reminiscent of Bob Hope, he hosted his show from Iraq for a week in June of 2009, filming a segment where Obama orders his head shaved prior to departure. The on-air program held few surprises, but it did turn attention to the presence of troops in a country where we are supposedly no longer at war. The real art of Colbert's satire, nonetheless, came with an accompanying project, his guest editing of *Newsweek*, which was released upon his return.

In his editor's column Colbert started: "No, your eyes aren't deceiving you. You're reading Stephen Colbert. And for that I apologize. The last thing I want is to contribute to the corrosive influence of the print media. I prefer to yell my opinions at you in person."[73] It was a silly opening that just reiterated Colbert's long-standing rant against the printed word. Jon Meacham, editor of *Newsweek*, anticipated that readers might consider the guest editorship simply as a publicity stunt. He agreed that, of course, having Colbert guest editor would hopefully be good publicity for the magazine, but he wanted readers to avoid seeing this as purely a "stunt." "Colbert's involvement is an exercise not in silliness but in satire, and the two are very different things. His role means more attention for *Newsweek*, yes, and to me that is a good thing. It also brings more readers to a serious subject—and that heightened interest is a good thing, too. The test of whether the Colbert decision was a sound one, I think, is whether readers learn something from the following pages. I am confident they will."[74]

Meacham's decision is an example of using mainstream media for public pedagogy in the entertainment-saturated contemporary moment, when a satirical magazine issue edited by a comedian has a better chance of drawing public interest in the Iraq War than a serious issue would. As I explained in the introduction, it is this shift that indicates that satirists like Stewart and Colbert may be more powerful public intellectuals than those like Noam Chomsky, since they are able to effectively engage a much wider audience through a form of satire that teaches the public to ask politically meaningful questions. As an example, here is Colbert from his guest editor column: "I know what you're thinking: 'Isn't the Iraq War over?' That's what I thought, too. I hadn't seen it in the media for a while, and when I don't see something, I assume it's vanished forever, like in that terrifying game peekaboo. We stopped seeing much coverage of the Iraq War back in September when the economy tanked, and I just figured the insurgents were wiped out because they were heavily invested in Lehman Brothers."[75] He makes two major claims, that—like infants—the public forgets anything that does not appear in the media, and that the media has dropped a major social event off its radar. Colbert goes on: "Turns out there are still 135,000 troops in Iraq, which I don't understand because we've already won the war," again exposing the gap between the way that information is reported and the realities behind that information. Shown on the cover getting "IRAQ" shaved into the side of his head, Colbert helped to select the stories that were used, most of which were very serious—covering such things as the children of soldiers, the challenges to relationships separated by the battlefield, and Middle Eastern politics. Colbert's presence as guest editor was felt, too, as he published fake letters that his character had supposedly sent to the magazine over the years. The last page was a fun interweaving of Meacham's notes from his meeting to discuss the project with Colbert and Colbert's editing of Meacham. The *Newsweek* issue on Iraq blurred, yet again, the boundaries between news and satire, allowing Colbert to push his public pedagogy even further beyond the realm of his show.

There is little doubt of Stewart and Colbert's interest in having a public impact. Beyond their joint rally on the National Mall and the connections between the guests and topics they cover, Colbert's work stands out for its even greater blurring of boundaries. His broadcasts from Iraq and from Philadelphia during the primary debates, his run for president, his segment on the House of Representatives, and his guest editing of a major news magazine are only a few of the most visible examples of the ways that his satire is not meant to be cynical or apolitically negative. His show has made news and is no longer simply ancillary commentary on it. These interventions, beyond the space of his televised program, point to a degree of satirical intervention in the public sphere that is wholly unprecedented. While his work clearly has a debt to a number of major satirists, I've pointed to a number of extremely innovative ways that Colbert has changed the face of satire.

By taking conservative positions, agreeing with them, then pushing them to the ludicrous, Colbert exposes the folly in them. Similarly, by emulating a conservative pundit in an era when news media has come to be controlled more and more by a ratings-driven environment and has turned away from providing unbiased information and reasoned debate, Colbert emulates the current state in an excessively exaggerated way. Thus, his satire is a form of pedagogical provocation. He starts with playfulness, and then exaggerates it into ridiculous hyperbole. In so doing he reveals the degree to which play already dominates a realm—the political or the news media—that should be serious. Baym claims that what Colbert is doing is exposing the state of affairs in both the media and politics that poses a risk to the public sphere.[76] As the news media becomes more spectacle than news, satire television experiences an inversion and becomes more centrally the space for reasoned deliberation of major issues. In this way, Colbert's program is both playful and poignant, since it has become one of the primary spaces through which a mass public grapples with difficult questions. And like the influential satirists in whose footsteps he follows, Colbert's work has evolved in a moment of intense conflict—war, economic instability, rapacious free-market practices, climate change, rampant racism, and a disaffected and distracted public that is not helped by the ratings-driven frivolousness of the news media. This has been an era when it has been incredibly difficult to get people to take things seriously and when there have never been more serious things to consider. Colbert's satire, though, has taken comedy seriously, giving it a significant impact on the way his viewers perceive the world.

4

AMERICA ACCORDING TO *THE COLBERT REPORT*: OR HOW A TV SHOW CAN CHANGE THE WAY A NATION THINKS

> "Hosted by Stephen Colbert, the Emmy®-winning *The Colbert Report* features no-holds-barred discussions in which the important topics of our time and the daily news are treated with absolutely no seriousness whatsoever."[1]

The Colbert Report, according to its Facebook site description, treats "the important topics of our time and the daily news" "with absolutely no seriousness whatsoever." This statement gets at the heart of a central feature of political satire. Is it serious or not? Is it just entertainment, silliness, and mockery? Does it engage in negative critique, leaving the audience cynical and disaffected? Or is it a politically powerful way to change how people think? As I've argued thus far, satire is an extremely effective form of political critique, one that has a played a vital role in U.S. political debates. Building on this legacy, contemporary satire engages with the post-9/11 political context, the influence of market, right-wing fundamentalisms, and major changes in news and media consumption. Within that mix, however, Stephen Colbert's satire is unique: it has a huge fan base; it has had a measurable effect on the public psyche, visible, for example, in the presence of Colbert's neologisms in the U.S. lexicon; and it has radically transformed satire, making it no longer simply a lampooning of current events, but a news event itself. Colbert's satire has not only influenced our idea of public intellectuals, it has also made satire a more central form of political commentary than it has ever been in U.S. history. One could easily argue that Colbert and Jon Stewart combine to offer the most significant political critique available to the U.S. public today.

Don't expect them to make that argument, though. They both have repeatedly stated that their shows are not news programs, pointing out that they air on Comedy Central, and that it is not their responsibility to inform the public about anything.[2] Should we believe them, though? Avoiding naming one's goal as political is one of the hallmarks of satire. From Jonathan Swift to Samuel Clemens to the Smothers Brothers, satirists have consistently denied that they are trying to be political, using the cover of comedy to sidestep censorship and potential accusations of slander. On top of that, the satirist takes affront at being called a political agitator because that view misses the art of satire and its status as comedy. In an interview with *The New York Times Magazine* that appeared shortly before the first episode of *The Colbert Report*, Colbert played with the idea that what he and Stewart are doing is serious:

> *Will you continue the tradition of political satire that allowed* The Daily Show *to inject so much welcome gravity into the light, goofy realm of late-night TV?*
> Jon would be so happy as a comedian to hear that he injected gravity. Can I be the one to tell him?
> *Seriously, what do you have against gravity?*
> If we thought we added gravity to anything, we would feel that we had failed. We're just trying to ease the pain of people who feel the world is going insane and no one is noticing. We're like Cortaid, something not too heavy that is used for a rash or a bug bite. I wouldn't use it for a wound.
> *I think you're underestimating the influence the show has had. People might perceive it as substantive because the jokes happen to be political.*
> But I guarantee you that it has no political objective. I think it's dangerous for a comedian to say, "I have a political objective." Because then they stop being a comedian and they start being a politician. Or a lobbyist.[3]

The joke here is on the idea of politics, which Colbert opposes to comedy, but effective satire bridges these two realms in a way that is critically productive as well as artfully entertaining. As Colbert mentioned during the rundown of upcoming pieces during the show's premiere episode, "Finally, a new show premieres, and changes the world."[4] The thought of a television show changing the world seems unlikely, allowing Colbert to joke at the mere idea of it. Moreover, satirists can feign insult if their work is described as political, since that seems to ignore the skill of comedy. Politics is heavy and in no way funny, or so the story goes. The satirist, however, uses politics to poke fun, often doing nothing more than highlighting the inherent folly in particular political behaviors. Stewart will show a clip of an irrational political statement, shake his head, and look quizzically at his audience. Often that is all that is needed to make his point.

A key difference between "satire news" and news is that satire news is not meant to substitute for the news. It is meant to be consumed after or alongside non-satirical news. It is meant to prompt the viewer to challenge the ways that the news presents important social issues. In an interview in 2003 for *IGN* when Colbert worked with Stewart on *The Daily Show*, Colbert explained his view on the difference between news and "satire news."

> *IGNFF: How do you feel about the fact that* The Daily Show *has—especially in the last year—almost become a valid news source?*
> *Colbert:* I hear that. I hear people say that. It's a repackager of news. In that way, I suppose, it is in some ways a valid source. As long as people can understand when we're goofing and when we mean it. If they're not reading the normal news, I doubt that they can. People say, "Was that story real?" And I've thought, "Oh, you should really watch the real news before you watch our show, if you can't tell whether our stories are real." I wish people would watch the real news before they watch our show, because we have two games. Our game is we make fun of the newsmakers, but we also make fun of the news style. They're missing half our joke if they don't keep up with the day-to-day changes of mass media news.[5]

Colbert and Stewart don't envision their work as replacement for the news, but as a supplement or satirical addition, that can push conversations about current events into a more critical realm. As Colbert points out, if audiences are not aware of the current news, they cannot even appreciate the goofiness.

Because satire is always performative and always meant to bring a certain degree of pleasure to the audience, satirists can reject the idea that their work has the goal of influencing public opinion. This is even more so when the satirist assumes an identity—as in the case of Colbert's construction of an O'Reilly-like right-wing political pundit. As Colbert explained in an interview with Charlie Rose, "I get to hide behind a character face. And so I get away with a lot that maybe Jon wouldn't because they would judge Jon. And I have the layer. I have the protective mask."[6] During the same interview, Rose asked Colbert to comment on the *Rolling Stone* magazine cover that featured them in a piece on "America's Anchors": "Jon deconstructs the news and he's ironic and detached. I falsely construct the news and am ironically attached. I'm not detached at all. I'm passionate about what I'm talking about. Jon may point out the hypocrisy of a particular thing happening in the news; I illustrate the hypocrisy as a character. [He points at the cover] That's Jon being Jon and that's me being not me. That's me being the Stephen Colbert guy."[7]

The moral of the story is that you cannot trust the satirist to tell the unmediated truth about the political intentions of his work. Instead, you have to let the work speak for itself. And without question, as part of the description on *The Colbert Report*'s Facebook site claims, much of the show is dedicated to "the important topics of our time and the daily news." Lest there be any doubt that one of the primary topics on the show is the state of the nation, the Colbert Nation website, homepage for the show, hosted a series of clips of Colbert talking about Constitutional Amendments in March 2011 with the line: "Watch Stephen exercise his Constitutional right to talk about the Constitution."[8] The clips are all organized based on which amendment they refer to—functioning as civic lessons alongside satire of current issues.

But it's not all gravity on *The Colbert Report*. In fact, one reason why the show is so successful is because it makes political satire so much fun. Colbert's charisma, his winning smile, and his knowing winks to the audience meld with his performance of a high-status, conservative idiot to provide appealing entertainment to a large audience. In addition to combining effective political satire with a show that is highly entertaining, Colbert, much more so than Stewart, incorporates seemingly pure silliness on his show. Often this silliness is aimed at his youthful audience. In his Green Screen Challenges, for instance, he asks fans to take green-screen images and edit them with their own video content. But are these features of his show simply silly, with no seriousness?

Take for example the original Green Screen Challenge that formed part of a "Better Know a District" segment. On the August 10, 2006, episode, Colbert was shown wielding a light saber in front of a green screen that was precipitated by the fact that that night's "Better Know a District" segment took place in California's 6th congressional district, the home of *Star Wars* creator George Lucas.[9] Colbert's video was a parody of the "Star Wars Kid" Internet meme. (Years earlier a video of a Canadian high-school student swinging a golf-ball retriever as a weapon had gone viral, creating a pop culture stir.) In homage to the "Star Wars Kid," Colbert created green-screen footage that could be edited by fans and then posted on the Internet in a contest to create the best video. Lucas appeared on the show

Photo 4.1   Colbert announces the "Green Screen Challenge" in which viewers can create their own videos of him.

on October 11, 2006, to showcase his own entry and announce the winners.[10]

Totally silly, right? Yes and no. On the one hand, this seemed like nothing more than a game to get young tech-savvy viewers involved with the show, but, on the other hand, Colbert was also showing those viewers that their ability to work with digital media could be really powerful. In this case, the power was to make a fun video and gain airtime on *The Colbert Report*. The "Green-Screen Challenges" demonstrate to viewers that they have the resources to make public statements. If they can make videos of Colbert being attacked by aliens that get major media attention, they can make videos with more significant content. The point is that the silliness on *The Colbert Report* often has the possibility of suggesting something potentially more serious. Whether it actually does or not is another matter.

The show's silly features like the "Green Screen Challenges," Tek Jensen episodes (an animated sci-fi series where the hero is modeled on Colbert), or the "Wrist Watch" (a series where Colbert took up wrist injuries as a pet cause after injuring his own wrist in July 2007) all have subtle and complex ways that they comment on national issues. These are often linked to mass obsessions, most of which have been fabricated by the mainstream media. Thus, Colbert's "Wrist Watch" segment reveals how a pundit can get a fan base to pay attention to a "cause," turning a personal issue into a national concern. Similarly, "The Craziest F#?king Thing I've Ever Heard," where Colbert highlights a "bizarre" recent news item, riffs on *The O'Reilly Factor's* "The Most Ridiculous Item of the Day." In another example, "Colbert Platinum" is *The Colbert Report's* version of the show *High Net Worth (HNW)* on CNBC-TV. Colbert's segment profiles expensive and high-profile items, like personal submarines and $750,000 pens, that reveal grotesque excesses of wealth. The links between these segments and overt political satire varies in intensity. One example of a more direct link between silliness and political commentary was the segment "Sam Waterston Says Things You Should Never Believe in a Trustworthy Manner," which aired briefly when Waterston's costar from *Law and Order,* Fred Thompson, was running for president. The segment first aired in January 2008 with the specific goal of lampooning the "folksy" charms of Thompson, who had been described as a "Reagan figure" by the press.[11] The segment was discontinued after Thompson withdrew his campaign for the presidency.

The constant interplay between silliness and seriousness, then, is a hallmark of Colbert's satire. Another feature is that it has had an influence on the way that the nation thinks. It may do that through fun, and it may be tricky to determine Colbert's own motives, but either way, there is little doubt that one of the ongoing features of the show is the construction of an alternative public sphere through which viewers can imagine a different connection to their nation. A good example of this is the way that Colbert constantly addresses his viewers as the "nation" on his show. It is common for him to turn to a new camera and begin "Now, nation...". Following that address, Colbert typically speaks earnestly, but often irrationally, in ways that coax his viewers to question commonly held beliefs and current conceptions of the nation. Often he addresses the "nation" in order to take typical right-wing views an extra exaggerated step that helpfully reveals the basic logical flaws in much right-wing punditry.

This is what he did on the segment when he called Sarah Palin a "f—cking retard."[12] In that segment Colbert occupied the place of a staunch supporter of Palin much in the same way that he called Bush his hero during the White House Correspondents' Association Dinner. He started by suggesting that Palin nailed Obama when she asked an audience "how that hopey-changey stuff was going?" He then said he was proud of her for standing up for "the little guy— Rush Limbaugh" who had referred to liberals on his show as "f—king retards." He shows a clip of Palin explaining that Rush's use of the phrase was an example of satire, and that it was Rahm Emanuel who had originally used the term, and, according to Palin, when Emmanuel used the phrase, he was not being satirical. This leads Colbert to replay the Rush piece, which, given its vituperative tone and typical Rush spin, is obviously not an example of satire. Colbert, though, is on Palin's side, allowing him to mockingly say: "It is so subtle, see, so many layers. And Sarah Palin knows that it is OK to call someone a retard if, like Rush, you clearly don't mean it, which is why we should all come to her defense and say Sarah Palin is a 'f—cking retard.'" He then gives a wink-like gesture to the audience and says "get it?" Here he artfully exposes the flaws in Palin's logic, exposes the dangers of her position, calls attention to the damage such thinking is doing to the nation, and has a bunch of fun.

It is no coincidence that Colbert's fans are called the *Colbert Nation*, a term that plays on his demagoguery but also plays with the idea that his show is aimed at getting his audience to think differently about U.S. politics and the possibilities of using satire to reform democracy. In this chapter, I will outline and analyze these goals. The first section provides background on Colbert and his program and outlines the basic structure of his show. The next five sections analyze key themes that demonstrate the ways that he uses satire as social commentary. The first theme is that of *truthiness*, Colbert's signature term for truths that are generated from the gut. Next, I analyze his use of language, especially through his most significant recurring segment "The Wørd," in a section on wordplay. The third section focuses on Colbert's simulated punditry and the way that connects to his comments about the current state of prejudice and intolerance. Colbert has published a bestselling book, *I Am America (And So Can You!)*, which only enhances his self-identification with America. Consequently, the next section is dedicated to analyzing his self-construction as an all-American egomaniac. The last segment addresses his connection to youth culture with attention to how he creates a public sphere that is politically engaged as well as fun.

FROM COLBERT TO THE COLBEAR REPOR(T)

The Colbert Report first aired on October 17, 2005. The series won a prestigious George F. Peabody Award for Excellence in Broadcasting in 2008 and has had 15 Primetime Emmy nominations. Colbert and his writing team also won an Emmy for Outstanding Writing for a Variety, Music, or Comedy Program. *The Colbert Report* had an average of 1.2 million viewers per episode in its first week, and it has received countless signs of its public impact. As explained in my introduction to this book, the show had already attracted substantial media coverage before its first airing. Prior to the premiere, it was featured in articles in *The New Yorker*, NPR's *All Things Considered* and *Fresh Air*, CNN, and *The Washington Post*. *The New York Times* alone ran three articles on *The Colbert Report* before its debut.[13] The show has also repeatedly been covered in the media, often in reference to stories and events connected with the show, like the Stewart-Colbert Rally, the White House Correspondents' Association Dinner, or coverage of stories linked to the series "Better Know a District." Colbert's neologisms, like *truthiness*, have become common in the U.S. lexicon, and the show's influence on public thought is apparent in the variety of words, such as Colbert Bump, Colbertized, Colbertism, Colbertlicious, and Colbertocracy, that are variations of the Colbert name found in slang.[14] It's not only bloggers who reference Colbert in their work. For instance, Maureen Dowd, in a piece for *The New York Times* referred to Colbert's "Dead to Me" board as a metaphor in her column, saying that Oprah Winfrey "should take a page from Stephen Colbert and put the slippery James Frey on her 'Dead to me' list."[15] A significant difference between Colbert's show and that of other well-known political satirists is that *The Colbert Report* immediately became an Internet phenomenon, with fans posting a vast number of clips from the show on YouTube with an extensive presence in the blogosphere, and with the creation of the Colbert Nation, a dedicated fan base with digital media savvy. As a sign of his popularity, a Facebook page supporting his run for president had 1.5 million members within one month of the site's launch.

So how did the actor Stephen Colbert become the character Stephen Colbert? Colbert grew up in Charleston, South Carolina, and he originally studied philosophy at Hampden-Sydney College in Virginia before transferring to Northwestern to study performance in the School of Speech. When Colbert graduated in 1986, he found work at Second City in Chicago, even though he had originally shunned the sort of improv pieces performed there. While working at the box office, he was able to take classes and it wasn't long before he became a member of the touring company, performing as understudy to Steve Carrell. At the same time he met Amy Sedaris and Paul Dinello, with whom he worked on a short-lived HBO project called *Exit 57* (they also collaborated on later projects like *Strangers with Candy*). Then he worked for *The Dana Carvey Show*, again alongside Steve Carrell. After six months on that show, he worked as a writer for *Saturday Night Live*. Next he took a stint with *Good Morning America*, working on humorous news segments, but only one of these was ever aired. That last job, though, led him to get hired by *The Daily Show* in 1997, which was in its second season when Craig Kilborn was still the lead comedian. His early role on *The Daily Show* was as one of four on-location reporters. When Jon Stewart took over in 1999, the show became increasingly more political, attracting a larger and larger viewership. Among the changes Stewart initiated for the program, Colbert's role was expanded to include more in-studio segments and unlike Stewart, who plays himself, Colbert performed in-character. In an out-of-character interview about the Colbert character as it appeared on *The Daily Show*, Colbert explained "I'm essentially a very high status character, but my weakness is that I'm stupid."[16] He explained that a key part of the character was that he was a fool, or more specifically, "a fool who has spent a lot of his life playing not the fool."[17]

Actually, the version of Colbert's persona that he developed for *The Daily Show* had its beginning on *The Dana Carvey Show*, when he was on for seven episodes in 1996. A key feature of Colbert's persona he had developed at that time was the practice of "delivering sketch performances directly to the camera."[18] It was also with Carvey that he worked on "several sketches inspired by *The Onion* [that] had Colbert playing a deadpan anchor delivering the news."[19] Even though they did not air, they gave him a chance to work on his performance as a newsman—a role he would play on *The Daily Show*.

When Colbert first appeared on *The Daily Show* with Kilborn, he performed character-driven pieces as an on-location journalist. As he explained in an interview after he had begun working with Stewart: "The field pieces we did were character-driven pieces—like, you know, guys who believe in Bigfoot. Whereas now, everything is issue—and news-driven pieces, and a lot of editorializing at the desk. And a lot of use of the green screen to put us in false locations."[20] Under Stewart, *The Daily Show* shifted, adopting a more news-oriented tone. As Colbert explained: "We're more of a news show—we were more of a magazine show then."[21] According to Colbert, one of the big shifts was the idea that the show would be largely connected to recent headlines. If under Kilborn a piece might cover Clinton and the next piece might be on a Bigfoot hunter, with Stewart the pieces connected to current events: "The first thing I noticed, was that our field pieces were coming out of the news, and not in sort of opposition to them."[22]

As Colbert's character on *The Daily Show* transitioned into more in-studio pieces, he was often put in interview situations where he performed the role of the clueless fool up against a more knowledgeable interview subject. Colbert also tended to make arguments based on over-the-top logical fallacies and other flaws in reasoning. He was always quick to take an opinion on anything and to tenaciously stick to his view regardless of what other information he learned. The result was a humorous lampooning of common conservative arguments that media pundits made. This same style has been adopted by a number of *The Daily Show* correspondents.[23] In an interview with Terry Gross for National Public Radio, Rob Corddry explained that when he and Ed Helms first joined the show's cast in 2002, they "just imitated Stephen Colbert for a year or two."[24] Correspondent Aasif Mandvi also explained that his sharp, sarcastic tone had a readily identifiable source: "I just decided I was going to do my best Stephen Colbert impression."[25]

While on *The Daily Show* Colbert's character became well-known for a series of important segments. One of these, "Even Stevphen," placed Colbert alongside Steve Carrell. They would begin debating an important topic and then would end by lobbing insults at one another. In a retrospective series on the show entitled, "10 F#@king Years," Stewart explains: "In our ten years on the air we have tried hard to further the state of public discourse. Of course we have failed and never more nobly than when 'Even Stevphen' came along, a heated discussion on the issues of the day."[26] Next a clip of highlights from the recurring segment aired. Each time, Steve and Stephen took absolute opposing positions on current issues like stem-cell research. Often one of them would introduce the topic as a question, such as, "Should prostitutes have the protection of the state?" Then, before the cohost could answer, they would loudly shout, "yes or no?" The series was an entertaining spoof on simulated debates, exemplified by programs like *Hannity and Colmes*, that air on mainstream news channels. In these so-called debates, what actually happens is a lot of name-calling, yelling, and intransigence. Each "debater" more aggressively and less rationally defends his view regardless of what is said by his fellow "debater." These faux debates take up more and more air time on news shows these days as channels invite experts to debate current issues, some of which do not deserve much media prominence at all, instead of actually covering socially meaningful news.

In another example from his tenure on *The Daily Show*, from 2003–2005 Colbert hosted the segment "This Week in God." It began with Colbert starting the God Machine (typically a post that Colbert would hit[27]), and it was a satirical overview of "everything God did this week."[28] In one segment that aired post–Hurricane Katrina, Colbert showed a series of media clips, including one from Larry King, which suggested religious reasons for the natural disaster.[29] He closed the series by describing a "sect" known as meteorologists. He then gave the meteorological explanation of the hurricane, which spoofed the religious justifications of the event. As he ended the segment, he said: "The Lord may work in mysterious and sometimes painful ways but to paraphrase another theologian, Donald Rumsfeld, 'sometimes you have to worship the god you have, not the one you want.'"

While on *The Daily Show* Colbert filed reports from the floor of the Democratic National Convention and the Republican National Convention as part of show's award-winning coverage of the 2000 and 2004 U.S. Presidential elections. Some of these segments appeared on the DVD release *The Daily Show: Indecision 2004.* Colbert won three Emmys as a writer of *The Daily Show* in 2004, 2005, and 2006. He also worked with Stewart on some of the writing for *America: A Citizen's Guide to Democracy Inaction,* which was released in 2006. While working on the show, Colbert filled in as anchor for Jon Stewart, including the full week of March 3, 2002, when Stewart was scheduled to host *Saturday Night Live.* Later episodes of *The Daily Show* have reused older Colbert segments under the label "Klassic Kolbert" and his voice is still used for "The God Machine."

The day after the 2004 Emmys in L.A., when *The Daily Show* won the Best Writing and Best Variety Series awards, Colbert met with Doug Herzog, the head of Comedy Central.[30] At that time Herzog wanted to expand *The Daily Show* franchise, and Stewart and Ben Karlin, *The Daily Show*'s executive producer, were looking for a TV show for their production company, Busboy. That was when they decided to do their first project with Colbert. Steve Carrell had already left the program, and they did not want to lose Colbert's talent as well. So, at the meeting with Herzog, Stewart and colleagues made a one-line pitch: "Our version of the *O'Reilly Factor* with Stephen Colbert."[31] Herzog agreed to an eight-week tryout without a pilot.

The show's concept did have a precedent. In 2004, prior to the show's pitch to Herzog, a series of spoof commercials had appeared on *The Daily Show* announcing an "exciting new *Daily Show* spin-off." The ads showed an angry O'Reilly-like Colbert shouting at guests, threatening to cut their mics, and arguing that no matter what he was right. Thus the show's core concept was Colbert playing a bombastic pundit-like character that would be familiar to cable-news junkies. In an interview with *USA Today* before the first show aired, Colbert explained: "Shows like *O'Reilly* or *Scarborough* or even to some extent Aaron Brown's are more about the personality of the host and less about the headlines." He went on to say: "My show is really about opinions; it's about bluster and personality."[32] *The Colbert Report* would hinge on the development of his persona, which he had already honed on Stewart's show. It would be based on "'the manliness of Stone Phillips' and his 'thick lacrosse-player's neck' and Geraldo Rivera's 'sense of mission' as a 'crusading warrior' of journalism. But Bill O'Reilly, an 'admirable' talent—'I watch (him) with my mouth open,'" Colbert explained, would be "clearly the model for his satire."[33] Colbert's character for *The Report* presents himself as "right-wing, egomaniacal, fact-averse ('factose intolerant'), God-fearing, and super-patriotic. He claims to be an independent who is often mistaken for a Republican, but uniformly despises liberals and generally agrees with the actions and decisions of George W. Bush and the Republican Party. This is evidenced by one of the questions that he asks of many of his guests: 'George W. Bush: great President, or the *greatest* President?'"[34]

In true pundit fashion, Colbert is constantly engaged in self-promotion, frequently marketing fictional or real merchandise and other Colbert-connected products, including his own "man-seed." He often rallies his fans, "the Colbert Nation," to vote for him in various public-naming polls, such as that of a Hungarian bridge and one for

Photo 4.2   Colbert advertises his "man-seed."

NASA equipment. A further feature of his character is his decision to soften the final "t" on his name, a move that has led many to question whether he is sufficiently patriotic.

Is his decision to soften the last "t" on his name a move to eschew his Americanness and feign being French, as Bill O'Reilly has suggested? When Colbert appeared on *The O'Reilly Factor*, O'Reilly's first question to him was "Colbear, that's a French name isn't it?" To which Colbert replied "It's a French name just to get the cultural elites on my side, Bill. I'm as Irish as you."[35] Colbert's family is of Irish and distant German descent. Originally, the name was pronounced with a hard "t" in English. Stephen Colbert's father, James, wanted to pronounce the name with a soft "t" but used the hard "t" out of respect for his father. He then offered his children the option to pronounce the name whichever way they preferred. Stephen started pronouncing his name with a soft "t" in his twenties when he transferred to Northwestern University, taking advantage of the opportunity to reinvent himself in a new place where no one knew him.[36] Stephen's brother Ed, an intellectual-property attorney, appeared on the show on February 12, 2009. When his youngest brother asked him, "Colbear or ColberT," Ed responded "ColberT", after which Colbert jokingly responded, "See you in Hell."[37]

Even though Colbert had long lost the hard "t" to his name before he became a comedian, the choice has later had the ability to produce interesting meaning in connection with his show. The altered name pronunciation gave O'Reilly ammo to accuse Colbert of being Frenchified and his choice to soften the final "t" has other resonances as well. First, it makes his name end with "bear." Fans of *The Colbert Report* know about Colbert's longstanding fear of bears. He mentions it all the time in interviews and bears are typically listed as the #1 threat to America in his ongoing series the "Threat Down." He describes a recurring dream where a dancing bear is blocking him, and, even though it seems like a circus bear, he knows it is dangerous. Deciding to put bears as the #1 threat to America, when they are only an imagined threat of Colbert's, is an example of his efforts to play with the way that the media hypes up a state of fear in the public. Mainstream news programs are constantly pointing to new things for their audiences to worry about and fear.

Another interesting layer to Colbert's fear of bears and its tie in to his name is his repeated reference to Bill O'Reilly as "Papa Bear." During the same interview when O'Reilly grilled Colbert about his name pronunciation, O'Reilly stated, "It is hard to be me. Is it hard to be you?" To which Colbert responded, "It is hard for me to be you." He next answered O'Reilly's question about what he does on his show: "What I do every night is catch the world in the headlights of my justice," a phrase that sounds like only a slight exaggeration of the sort of thing O'Reilly would say about his own show. He went on to explain that his goal is to emulate O'Reilly and to use his show to bring O'Reilly's "message of love and peace to a younger audience—people in their 60s and 70s, people in their 50s, people who don't watch your show." Of course, that was a reference to the fact that O'Reilly had called all of Jon Stewart's fans "stoned slackers" when Stewart had appeared earlier on *The O'Reilly Factor*.[38]

These tidbits of exchange about bears and French pronunciations of Colbert's name point to another of the key features of *The Colbert Report*: language play. One of the best examples of this was the decision to have the show make the "t" silent on *Report*, a play that Colbertized the pronunciation of *report*. But Colbert noted another meaning in his interview with Terry Gross on NPR's *Fresh Air* on December 7, 2005. During his out-of-character interview, he explained that the pun on *Repor* was that it also meant "rapport": "One of sort of the unintentional puns of our show is that it is called the Colber(t) Repor(t), and it unintentionally plays on the word 'rapport'... which is a sense of understanding between the speaker and the listener. We're the same people you and me, we get it. The rest of the people out there they don't understand the things that we understand. The show is like an invitation to the audience to be part of the club."[39]

Gross then asked him about the connections between his character and Bill O'Reilly. Colbert began by saying that his take on him is that he is a "magnificent performer" and that a big part of *The Colbert Report* is dedicated to capturing the sort of confidence with which O'Reilly is able to talk about anything and make it seem important. Much of his massive ego on the show, then, is emulating O'Reilly's own performance of hubris. Another feature of O'Reilly that Colbert copies is his tendency to inform his audience that he is about to tell them something that no one else will be willing to tell them, but that he is doing it because he cares about them. O'Reilly presents himself as a victim and a conqueror at the same time. And we can see Colbert doing much of the same. His reference to his viewers as heroes is almost a direct paraphrase of the ways that O'Reilly addresses his viewers as well.

While O'Reilly serves as the "Papa Bear" for Colbert's persona, as mentioned above, other media figures, like Stone Phillips and Geraldo

Photo 4.3   Colbert celebrates O'Reilly's influence on him.

Rivera, have contributed to Colbert's persona as well. Colbert has compared himself on various occasions to Glenn Beck, and the decision to do the rally on the National Mall in 2010 appeared to be in response to Glenn Beck's own rally.[40] In the aforementioned interview with Terry Gross, Colbert also noted that he tries to emulate the crisp reporting of Anderson Cooper, that he loves how Lou Dobbs rides the same hobby horse, doing the same story over and over (especially because it cuts down on needing to think of new things), and that he admires how Hannity is bullheaded in ways that let him stampede his guests.[41]

All of these media figures provide inspiration for Colbert's persona, but how does he marshal that figure to lead a show? The show follows a fairly standard format, which also parodies much personality-driven television. Almost every segment offers the Colbert character another way to exercise his influence, stroke his ego, and attract viewer worship. And, while this is meant to be parody, it also simply works to stoke the power of the Colbert figure. The egocentric nature of the show is emphasized from the opening sequences. First, the show opens with Colbert announcing teasers for the show's topics and the evening's guest, and each teaser purposefully includes a pun. As he introduces each new segment, he addresses a different camera, shifting his body and turning his head. He then states, "This is *The Colbert Report*" as his theme music, "Baby Muggles" from Cheap Trick, begins to play. His announcement is often preceded by an aphorism, like "Open wide, baby bird, 'cause momma's got a big fat night crawler of Truth. Here comes *The Colbert Report!*" or "Put on the Sade and spritz on some musk! I'm going to truth you all night long! This is *The Colbert Report!*" or "I promise to deliver the truth in the next 30 minutes or it's free. This is *The Colbert Report!*"[42] Wikipedia reports that "The show's original opening title sequence began with an eagle diving past the host, followed by images of Americana, stock footage of Colbert, and words describing Colbert flying by (some of which have been used as The Wørd). The first word used was 'Grippy,' and has changed to include, among others, 'Megamerican,' 'Lincolnish,' 'Superstantial,' 'Flagaphile,' and 'Factose Intolerant.'"[43] The words swirl around an image of Colbert standing, running, and planting a flag. As the music plays, a computer-generated shrieking eagle, colored red, white, and blue, flies toward the foreground and exposes a live shot of the set. On January 4, 2010, a new opening debuted. The opening begins and ends with an eagle as before, but features new background renderings with new shots of Stephen Colbert and a more vividly colored American, red, white, and blue motif.[44]

After the opening sequence, Colbert generally begins with a rundown of recent headlines in a manner similar to *The Daily Show* with the difference that these headlines are reported via Colbert's unique pundit-like take on the news. Colbert then focuses on a specific topic, which usually leads him into introducing "The Wørd" segment. (I analyze "The Wørd" segment in the wordplay section later in this chapter.) Sometimes a short interview conducted at Colbert's main desk with someone connected to the featured topic follows "The Wørd" segment. The format for the show's middle varies; it tends to be a visual presentation or skit. The middle segment may include a recurring segment, like "Better Know a District"; "Formidable Opponent"; "The Threat Down"; "Tip of the Hat/Wag of the Finger," in which Colbert voices his approval or disapproval of prominent people and news items; "Cheating Death with Dr. Stephen T. Colbert, D.F.A.," a health segment; or "The Sport Report" with the "t" in both Sport and Report silent, a sports segment.[45]

The show's third part traditionally consists of an interview with a celebrity guest, such as an author showcasing a new book, a media figure, a government official, or, on occasion, a musical guest. A fun difference of Colbert's interview segment is the layout and staging. Unlike most late-night television shows where the host stays put and the interviewee enters and takes a seat by the host, Colbert leaves his main desk and jogs or walks to a table to his left on the set where the interviewee is already seated. The live audience applauds Colbert, and he sometimes works the crowd by giving the audience a high five, taking a bow, or doing a bit of a dance on his way over to his guest. In a parody of late-night talk shows, which seem to offer the guest a chance to talk, but often focus largely on the host, Colbert emphasizes his egocentric role as an interviewer by hamming it up and getting all the viewer attention as he approaches his guest.

Once he is seated at the interview table, the interview segment is characterized by Colbert's efforts to "nail" his guest. He asks seemingly well-intentioned but often inane questions that can disarm his interviewee. And he typically presents logical fallacies as absolute truths, asking his guests to agree or disagree with his statement. The flow of interviews varies according to the type of guest, and he tends to feign camaraderie with right-wing guests in an effort to get them to reveal their conservative views. As Geoffrey Baym notes, Colbert often tries to "out right-wing" his conservative interviewees, a move that has the potential to push the conservative guest more toward the center.[46] On occasion, however, it actually leads the conservative guest to reveal a position he or she might otherwise have not exposed on national television. For example, Colbert managed to get Harvard professor Harvey Mansfield, author of *Manliness*, to give him a high five in camaraderie when he joked that women were bad drivers.[47] Liberal or progressive guests get a slightly different structure with Colbert pretending to be opposed to everything they say, which can give the guest a chance to make their arguments. After the last commercial, Colbert closes the show by giving parting words to the audience or, if the interview has run long, he just ends with "Good night."

In a sign of the way that the show is closely tied to U.S.-American identity, the set for *The Colbert Report* is called the Eagle's Nest, and it was specifically designed to enhance Colbert's megalomaniacal style. As mentioned above, the set has two main areas: the main desk and the guest interview area to camera/viewer right. Graphics next to the interview desk tend to change, sometimes they display a New York skyline and sometimes church-like stained glass. These images are occasionally altered to reflect the interview topic. The main desk, in the shape of a C, stands for Colbert.

On the very first show, Colbert made a point of drawing his viewers' attention to the multiple times his name appears on the set: behind him, on the desk, on the floor. The set was redesigned on January 4, 2010, with enhanced digital graphics, vivid colors, and even more exaggerated Americana imagery. "The redesigned stage

Photos 4.4 and 4.5 Colbert shows viewers of his first show that the desk is shaped in a letter "C" for his name, and he points to the many times his name appears on the set.

features 41 MicroTiles arranged as three horizontal displays, in 1×4, 1×5, and 1×4 arrays underneath Colbert's desk; and four angled 1×7 vertical columns along the backdrop. The tiles display high-definition video and graphics created exclusively for the show."[48] These video and graphics in red, white, and blue are designed to center around Colbert's image to make him appear presidential, or even like a deity. For instance, in an opening sequence, as he turns toward a camera, a blue image of the Statue of Liberty may appear behind and next to him, and when he turns again, a red image of stars may appear behind him. The floor may also project stars that remind viewers of the U.S. flag. On the wall camera right, an artificial fireplace has an engraving *"Videri Quam Esse,"* meaning "to seem to be rather than to be," a play on the traditional Latin phrase *"esse quam videri"* or "to be, rather than to seem to be," a not-so-subtle reference to Colbert's simulated punditry.[49]

Above the fireplace is a portrait of Colbert, which has been altered each year to add another Colbert into it. The original version had Colbert standing in front of the same mantle on the set with another portrait of himself. Then on the anniversary of the first show, the portrait was replaced by one of Colbert standing in front of the mantle with the first portrait above it, adding another layer of reference to the picture of a picture. On October 17, 2007, the second portrait was removed and replaced with a new one that followed an identical pattern, but altered the newest representation of Colbert. When it was time to install a new version of his portrait, Colbert petitioned the Smithsonian to display his portrait, who agreed to "go along with the joke," though they stressed that it was only temporary, and on January 16, 2008, the "three-deep" Colbert portrait was placed on display "right between the bathrooms near the 'America's Presidents' exhibit" at the National Portrait Gallery in Washington, D.C.[50] When his portrait was first put on display, Colbert told fans, "I don't mean to brag, but as it contains three portraits, my portrait has more portraits than any other portrait in the National Portrait Gallery!" In the latest version unveiled on October 25, 2010, in honor of the show's fifth anniversary, Colbert goes six-deep and the newest addition of himself holds his newly won Grammy and sports a Roman laurel wreath made of gold.[51]

Clearly, the set design is not subtle in its efforts to boost Colbert's status as an American icon. While the set and graphics of the show work to create Colbert as an American icon, the nightly performances have focused, in large part, on the idea of the truth and how that has shifted in contemporary U.S. discourse. And that brings us to our next theme: truthiness.

ONE NATION UNITED UNDER TRUTHINESS

"I will speak to you in plain, simple English. And that brings us to tonight's word: truthiness."[52]

On the premiere episode of *The Colbert Report,* Colbert explained the basic rationale for the show, revealed a bit about his character, and then introduced what he later referred to as the show's "thesis statement" –the neologism *truthiness:*[53]

> Now I'm sure some of the Word Police, the wordanistas over at Webster's, are gonna say, "Hey, that's not a word." Well, anybody who knows me knows that I'm no fan of dictionaries or reference books. They're elitist. Constantly telling us what is or isn't true, or what did or didn't happen. Who's *Britannica* to tell me the Panama Canal was finished in 1914? If I wanna say it happened in 1941, that's my right. I don't trust books. They're all fact, no heart.[54]

While there would be later debates about whether or not Colbert actually invented the word *truthiness,* there is no doubt that his definition of the term became an immediate sensation.[55] After that first

Photo 4.6 Colbert celebrates the irony that his word *truthiness* is named "Word of the Year" by Merriam-Webster's, even after he told viewers he was sure the "wordanistas" at Webster's would say that it wasn't a word.

show, truthiness became visible in mass media, public discourse, and politics.[56] Scholars and linguists also immediately turned attention to Colbert's new word: A couple of months after the first show in January 2006, etymology professor Anatoly Liberman predicted that *truthiness* would be included in dictionaries in the next year or two.[57]

To prove him right, the very next day the American Dialect Society announced that *truthiness* was its 2005 Word of the Year. Their description of the word reads: "*Truthiness* refers to the quality of preferring concepts or facts one wishes to be true, rather than concepts or facts known to be true. As Stephen Colbert put it, 'I don't trust books. They're all fact, no heart.' Other meanings of the word date as far back as 1824."[58] The next year in 2006, the Merriam-Webster's Dictionary online announced that *truthiness* was its Word of the Year, based on a reader poll where it won by a 5–1 margin over *google*.[59] Their definition of the term was that used by the American Dialect Society with an addition: "truth that comes from the gut, not books."[60] John Morse, President of Merriam-Webster, later explained the significance of the word: "We're at a point where what constitutes truth is a question on a lot of people's minds, and truth has become up for grabs. 'Truthiness' is a playful way for us to think about a very important issue."[61]

The prominence of the term only spread: it has been used on *The Huffington Post,* in the writing of *New York Times* reporter Frank Rich, in *New York Times* crosswords, and it was even the topic of a speech by Ken Dryden at the Canadian Parliament.[62] The major impact of the word is ironic given that the segment was originally meant to feature the word *truth,* but at 3:30 P.M. the day of taping the first show, Colbert stopped his team and said that they needed a better word: "It's not stupid enough," Colbert stated. "We're not talking about truth, we're talking about something that seems like truth—the truth we want to exist." Then, as he explained in an interview with *New York Magazine,* he had an idea: "truthiness."[63]

This section analyzes the role of the "truth" and its connection to "truthiness" for the character of Colbert, especially in terms of its appearance on *The Colbert Report.* Similar to Stewart's critique of news reporting in the mass media, Colbert's program also opens with an ironic run down of the current headlines that inevitably reveals that the "truth" reported in the news is partial, biased, and distorted—that the news is more truthiness than truth. Perhaps more than any other comic satirist on cable, Colbert has placed the question of truth at the center of his program. His notion of truthiness—truth acquired from the gut and ignorant of fact—reveals the disturbing confluence of right-wing fundamentalist versions of truth and left-oriented postmodern relativism. Colbert's truthiness also takes aim at the way that the right-wing version of the truth, especially as evidenced by the rhetoric of George W. Bush, was anti-intellectual, anti-scientific, and anti-rational. In addition, the concept of truthiness reveals the absurdities of certain postmodern positions that question all sources of truth and that hesitate to advance any claims to truth. Clearly, Colbert's parody of truth derives from Bush and from figures like Bill O'Reilly, but as Geoffrey Baym points out, his use of irony also critiques postmodern ways of thinking that "reject reason and modernist knowledge claims."[64]

Colbert's choice of *truthiness* as the thesis statement for his show was meant to highlight what he perceived as a major national crisis. In an out-of-character interview on January 25, 2006, with Nathan Rabin, Colbert explained the seriousness of the problem:

> Truthiness is tearing apart our country, and I don't mean the argument over who came up with the word. I don't know whether it's a new thing, but it's certainly a current thing, in that it doesn't seem to matter what facts are. It used to be, everyone was entitled to their own opinion, but not their own facts. But that's not the case anymore. Facts matter not at all. Perception is everything. It's certainty. People love the President because he's certain of his choices as a leader, even if the facts that back him up don't seem to exist. It's the fact that he's certain that is very appealing to a certain section of the country. I really feel a dichotomy in the American populace. What is important? What you want to be true, or what *is* true?[65]

Colbert explains in the interview that despite the goofiness of the word "truthiness" and the silly, satirical way he introduced it on his show, the reality of truthiness as an influence on public thought is a serious problem. As explained in detail in chapters 1 and 2, Colbert's program emerged on the national scene when the nation was suffering a series of major crises: post-9/11 hysteria and an atmosphere of fear, curtailing of civil rights connected to the War on Terror, an expanded and increasingly secretive executive branch, transformations in news media that made it even more difficult for the public to stay informed about significant issues, and a culture of punditry that emphasized hubris and partisanship over democratic deliberation. All of these combined to threaten the public sphere and to limit the possibilities for collective, rational thought. And this happened at a time when the United States needed more than ever to exercise careful reasoning rather than emotional response. But, rather than reason, emotion—unhindered by facts—ruled the day. As Colbert put it on his first show: "If you think about the War in Iraq, maybe there a few missing pieces to the rationale for war, but doesn't taking Saddam out 'feel' like the right thing?"[66]

Colbert's satirical goal is to use comedy to call attention to this problem. What he does is exaggerate the role of truthiness in public discourse in order to encourage viewers to understand how pernicious the practice has become. Key to this has been to use the concept of truthiness to identify a series of ways in which truthiness has come to stand in for truth. These include:

Relativist truth. This is the idea that there is no universal truth. While in reality the philosophical arguments in favor of relativism over universalist truths are fairly complex, in everyday practice the idea tends to devolve into the theory that there is no universal truth that applies to everyone. Thus, each individual can make his own truth. And, not only that, truth is a right. We each have the right to our own truths, and we don't need to prove them, we just need to believe in them. Colbert exemplifies his satirically exaggerated version of truthiness as irrational relativism when he writes in the introduction to *I Am America (And So Can You!)*: "This book is Truth. My Truth."[67] He explains that the book "is not just some collection of reasoned arguments supported by facts. That's the coward's way out."[68] One key to the relativism of truthiness for Colbert, then, is the idea of it as a bullying relativism. Note that he uses a capital "T" for his individual truth. He further makes the point: "I deliver my Truth hot and hard. Fast and Furious. So either accept it without hesitation or get out of the way, because somebody might get hurt and it's not going to be me."[69] While there may not be universal truths and individuals may create their own truths, not all individual truths are equal. Those that come from positions of power are more "true" than others.[70] This leads directly to the next feature of truthiness.

Authoritative Truth. Colbert has repeatedly pointed out that news media has digressed to become nothing but pundits shouting at each other, seeming to present contrasting, reasonable positions, but often presenting false oppositions derived from emotion rather than fact. What makes a Bill O'Reilly or a Glenn Beck seem to be speaking the truth? Shouting. This idea of shouting and bullying as a way of falsely presenting the truth was satirized by Colbert and Steve Carrell on their recurring segment for *The Daily Show* "Even Stevphen," and it is also exemplified by Colbert's own recurring segment "Formidable

Opponent." But Colbert's concern with the way authority figures have
become sources of the truth that won't tolerate questions or accept
any opposing arguments is also connected to the authoritative view
of the truth that was the hallmark of the Bush presidency. As Colbert
explained in the Rabin interview, 9/11 created a context where U.S.
citizens looked to the president to be "daddy": "We wanted someone
to be daddy, to take decisions away from us."[71] According to Colbert
out-of-character, this sort of obedience to authoritative truth led the
U.S. public to forgo authority in favor of authoritarianism, allowing
bullying power to take over for reasoned thought. An authority would
be someone who actually has an adequate knowledge base to make
decisions, but an authoritarian is just powerful without a knowledge
base. He suggests that we now have:

> the idea that authoritarian is better than authority. Because authori-
> tarian means there's only one authority, and that authority has got
> to be the President, has got to be the government, and has got to
> be his allies. What the right-wing in the United States tries to do is
> undermine the press. They call the press "liberal," they call the press
> "biased," not necessarily because it is or because they have problems
> with the facts of the left—or even because of the bias for the left,
> because it's hard not to be biased in some way, everyone is always
> going to enter their editorial opinion—but because a press that
> has validity is a press that has authority. And as soon as there's any
> authority to what the press says, you question the authority of the
> government—it's like the existence of another authority. So that's
> another part of truthiness. Truthiness is "What I say is right, and
> [nothing] anyone else says could possibly be true." It's not only that
> I *feel* it to be true, but that *I* feel it to be true. There's not only an
> emotional quality, but there's a selfish quality.[72]

Thus, truth is not just relative, it has also been slanted to reinforce
existing power structures and disallow debate and consideration of
information that might contradict it. Certainly the rhetoric of Vice
President Dick Cheney during the Bush administration served as an
example of that notion of truth. David Corn explains that "the Bush
White House rigged the case for war by selectively embracing (without reviewing) convenient pieces of iffy intelligence and then presenting them to the public as hard-and-fast proof."[73] Consequently, a key
component to truthiness for Colbert is that it is a notion of truth that
lacks evidence but packs a punch. While Cheney was the master of
this sort of truthiness, Bush was the hallmark of a different version:
truthiness as thinking from the gut.

Intuitionist truth. As David Detmer points out, another key feature of Colbert's truthiness is that it is intuitionist.[74] Intuitionist truth is a truth that does not rely on facts, but unlike relativist truth, which is a personal truth, it is presented as universal. The reliance on the gut over reason as a source of knowledge is one of the most well-known features of Colbert's truthiness, but, as Detmer explains, Colbert's truthiness gives a very particular spin to the use of the gut as a source of knowledge. What Detmer makes clear is that philosophers have long held that there are some valid moments when we might use our intuition to arrive at an opinion. However, the problem that Colbert satirizes is the use of the gut in moments that are inappropriate. As Detmer explains, "The problem is not merely that politicians and pundits base their conclusions on gut feelings and unexamined prejudices, but rather that they do so in connection with precisely the kinds of claims where inferential reasoning and an appeal to evidence are most clearly necessary. What is perhaps even more disturbing is that the rest of our culture, for the most part, lets them get away with it."[75]

Again and again, over the course of the Bush administration, the public was told that government actions were not based on fact, but on feelings. In a moment of national panic and a culture of fear, such practices were especially destructive. To illustrate this on the evening that he introduced "truthiness" to the U.S. public, Colbert gave this example: "Consider Harriet Miers. If you think about Harriet Miers, of course her nomination is absurd. But the President didn't say he thought about his selection. He said this: 'I know her heart.' Notice how he said nothing about her brain? He didn't have to. He feels the truth about Harriet Miers."[76] He also made several references to this feature of Bush's decision-making during the White House Correspondents' Association Dinner. Colbert's character embodies just this sort of passionate commitment to unsubstantiated truths. He described thinking with your gut to Charlie Rose as "passionate emotion and certainty over information." A condition, he went on to explain, that he sees as more important "to the public at large and not just to the people who provide it in prime time cable."[77] The point is that it is not just politicians and the media, but U.S. citizens themselves who have allowed truthiness to overtake truth as the primary source of information in decision-making.

Fact-opposed truth. While the idea that truth is intuitionist and does not concern itself with evidence may seem to state the case that truthiness has little interest in facts, there is a further variation on the connection between truthiness and facts: bold disregard for the facts. This component of truthiness is obviously closely connected to intuitionism, but there is a slight, yet significant, difference. Colbert included this feature when he defined truthiness: "Well, anybody who knows me knows that I'm no fan of dictionaries or reference books. They're elitist. Constantly telling us what is or isn't true, or what did or didn't happen. Who's *Britannica* to tell me the Panama Canal was finished in 1914? If I wanna say it happened in 1941, that's my right. I don't trust books."[78] This was a direct reference to the anti-intellectualism of George W. Bush, who fashioned himself as an average Joe. The anti-elitism of Bush's rhetoric allowed him to make arguments that he didn't trust books or science and that he favored his heart over his head. This position was especially dangerous as the administration justified war in Iraq not only without evidence, but actually in opposition to evidence.

Colbert riffed on this problem when he highlighted Cheney's argument that all that was needed was a 1 percent chance that there were Weapons of Mass Destruction to justify the war in Iraq. In an interview with Ron Suskind, author of *The One Percent Doctrine*, a book critical of Cheney's altered notion of justifiable evidence for war, Colbert played the über-Cheney. Rather than agree with Suskind, Colbert's character suggested Cheney was soft on terror: "No offense to the V.P. but isn't that soft on terror? One percent? Shouldn't it be the zero-percent doctrine? I mean even if there's *no* chance that someone's a threat to the United States, and they just look at us funny, shouldn't we just [punches his hand] tag 'em?.... The problem with evidence is that it doesn't always support your opinion...That's what the Vice President was protecting us from. If we waited, we wouldn't have invaded. That's true because it rhymes."[79]

A similar bold disregard for existing facts and evidence is standard fare on much cable news. Recall, for example, Lou Dobbs's claim that Mexican immigrants had brought leprosy into the United States. Now Lou Dobbs was a major news source on CNN, and he was able to make an inflammatory claim with absolutely no facts to support it at all. Later, when Lesley Stahl of *60 Minutes* sat down to interview Dobbs on camera, she mentioned the report and told him that there didn't seem to be much evidence for it. "Well, I can tell you this," Dobbs replied. "If we reported it, it's a fact."[80] So, faced with evidence that a statement made on his program was untrue, Dobbs responded by saying that anything aired on his show had to be fact. This is what Colbert is getting at with fact-opposed truthiness. Or as his character put it during an interview with Tim Robbins: "I love the truth, it's facts I am not a fan of."[81]

Binary thinking or Truth knows no nuance. As explained in chapter 2, nuance became connected with dissent in the post-9/11 era, and it was often considered unpatriotic. Instead of nuance, the nation was typically given binaries in relation to the major concerns of the day. As Colbert explained on his first show, "We are divided between those who think with their head and those who know with their heart."[82] The presentation of the world as divided into two—friends versus enemies, red states versus blue states, patriots versus terrorists—was pervasive. Moreover, as Colbert exemplifies through the recurring segment "Formidable Opponent," audiences were commonly presented with what seemed like a debate between two views on a topic, only to be fed logical fallacies and emotive arguing rather than reasoned deliberation. The danger of seeking the truth based on binary thinking and without nuance is that it makes complex thinking about complex issues impossible. He illustrates this with a "Formidable Opponent" debate with himself on withdrawal of troops from Iraq.[83] He begins by explaining that the Iraqis are questioning whether they have been liberated or colonized and that, without a timetable for withdrawal, U.S. military presence in Iraq seems like an occupation—clearly a complex issue. But Colbert satirizes the way that this issue is discussed in the media by likening building a stable democracy to baking a cake. At the end of the segment, one Colbert tries to end the debate. The other, however, says that, if they end the debate there, he will just claim that he won. He then draws a gun and points it at his debate opponent. His opponent responds by also pulling a gun. The segment ends with both Colberts facing the screen, each holding a gun in the other's mouth.

On his first show, Colbert ended his discussion of truthiness by saying, "The truthiness is anyone can *read the news to you*. I promise *to feel the news at you*." His first on-air use of the term had highlighted a vast array of the features of truthiness that were plaguing the nation. He created a term that would later be used in the public sphere to identify a major social crisis, and perhaps most importantly, he had done it in a way that was so much fun that it got major public attention. He had identified truthiness as a problem in politics, the media, and the general public. Moreover, he had suggested that truthiness had severely limited the possibilities for truth based on evidence, reasoned consideration, and assessment of the facts. He certainly wasn't the first public figure of the post-9/11 era to suggest that truth had given way to gut feeling in making decisions, but he was the first to give such a practice a readily usable term. It was the specific way that Colbert packaged his satire that made his intervention so powerful. Do U.S. citizens demand more truth today as a consequence of Colbert's show? Do they themselves make better decisions based on facts rather than on feelings? Has Colbert's concept of truthiness changed the world or not? These questions do not have easy answers. What we do know, though, is that Colbert's concept of truthiness entered the public sphere and generated conversation, critique, and dialogue in connection with the term. Thus, what changed after Colbert was that a debate over truth had begun, and a term was coined that encapsulated a dangerous practice. And that is no small achievement.

AND THAT BRINGS US TO TONIGHT'S WORDPLAY

In an interview with Neil Strauss for *Rolling Stone,* Colbert drew a distinction between how he and Jon Stewart satirize the news: "Jon deconstructs the news in a really brilliant comedic style. I take the sausage backwards, and I restuff the sausage. We deconstruct, but then we don't show anybody our deconstruction. We reconstruct— we falsely construct the hypocrisy. And I embody the bullshit until hopefully you can smell it."[84] In the aforementioned interview with Charlie Rose where Rose asked him to comment on a *Rolling Stone* issue that featured him alongside Stewart on the cover, Colbert similarly suggested that "Jon deconstructs the news and he's ironic and detached. I falsely construct the news and am ironically attached . . . Jon may point out the hypocrisy of a particular thing happening in a news story or a behavior or somebody in the news. I illustrate the hypocrisy as a character."[85]

While much of this characterization of the differences between Colbert and Stewart rings true, it misses a central feature of Colbert's show that works as a counterpoint to his "constructions." Colbert may play a character, embodying a false construction, but elements of his show—like the bullet points of "The Wørd" segment—deconstruct that character as he performs it. Stewart and Colbert are the hosts, but the comedy of their shows is not limited to their individual performances. Thus, while Colbert's distinctions may be true in reference to the positions occupied by each comedian, the complexity of their shows adds further layers to the comedy presented each night. Just as Stewart's show includes the work of other comedians who perform in-character and provide the false constructions of parody that then allow Stewart even greater latitude for his comedic deconstructions, Colbert's show offers a variety of deconstructive moments that work with Colbert's character to add additional satirical meaning. An excellent example of this is his most significant recurring segment, "The Wørd."

The significance of the segment for the mission of the show cannot be overestimated. It was via "The Wørd" that Colbert presented the show's thesis statement that truthiness was causing a national crisis. "The Wørd" segment is a highly complex satirical exercise that largely keeps Colbert in character, but counterposes his verbal statements with textual bullet points that appear in the margin of the screen as he speaks. These bullet points often serve the purpose of deconstructing Colbert's statements, and they illustrate one way that *The Colbert Report* has put language—be it deconstructed, reconstructed, satirical, or silly—at the center of his show. In order to highlight the significance of critically purposeful wordplay to *The Colbert Report,* in this section I provide an overview of Colbert's use of language— his "The Wørd" segment, neologisms, puns, and other forms of wordplay—in order to analyze the specific ways that Colbert links language, politics, and social perception. My argument is that at the heart of these various practices is a sustained critique of the crisis of representation found in discourses of both the right and the left.

In order to fully appreciate the role of language for *The Colbert Report,* it is worth remembering the way that the post-9/11 era presented the U.S. public with a crisis in language. The Bush administration presented one of the most extreme examples of linguistic manipulation at the service of acquiring power in U.S. history. To cite merely a few of the most common tactics, the administration misrepresented, lied, obfuscated, named, renamed, refused to name, censored, and silenced.[86] Take, for example, the Abu Ghraib photo scandal, which demonstrated how the administration avoided words, re-semanticized words, and renamed places in a strategic effort to use language to preserve and expand social control. Responding to the administration's deployment of linguistic exploitation, Susan Sontag wrote: "Words alter, words add, words subtract.... To refuse to call what took place in Abu Ghraib—and what has taken place elsewhere in Iraq and in Afghanistan and at Guantánamo Bay—by its true name, torture, is as outrageous as the refusal to call the Rwandan genocide a genocide."[87] Sontag highlighted Donald Rumsfeld's evasion of the word, *torture,* but the refusal to link word and deed was not the only linguistic strategy used by the Bush White House. Shortly after the photos of torture were publicly circulating, Rumsfeld took a trip to Abu Ghraib. While there, he told soldiers "I am a survivor" in response to calls for his resignation.[88] If Rumsfeld was a survivor, then what were the torture victims? What linguistic conditions made it possible to call

Rumsfeld a "survivor" while denying the existence of the tortured prisoners? Consequently, not only did the administration refuse to name the torture as "torture," they also artfully began to reappropriate words that might have been used to describe the conditions at Abu Ghraib.[89] It was on that same trip that Rumsfeld renamed the prison "Camp Redemption." And this is only one small example of the way that the Bush administration manipulated language.

As described in chapter 2, these practices emerged at a historical moment when the mass media was especially ill-equipped to provide the U.S. public with news reporting vital to the creation of a public sphere and a deliberative democracy. In addition, these challenges to meaningful representation of social issues coincided with the rise of postmodern theory, some versions of which suggested that there was no way to actually represent reality, that reality itself was an elusive and misleading concept obfuscated by layers and layers of self-referential signs. Thus, some postmodern theories suggested that language was always deceptive, since it could never accurately represent the world; anytime a word stood in for a thing, some meaning was lost. Other postmodern theories focused on the way that symbolic systems had created master narratives of the world that repressed minority or contradictory views. And, even though much of the arguments for these theories has validity, these positions carried with them a significant distrust of language and representation overall. If words were always insufficient or repressive, then it was hard to argue against the way that the right misused them.

Add to that the atmosphere of fear after 9/11 when journalists, professors, and other public figures were threatened if they dared to critique the government. Recall that during this time, those who dared to ask questions about the way that the administration presented the public with information were often called traitors. For all these reasons, this was an especially dire moment for the use of transparent language, for productive debate, and for reasoned, informed, and inferential decision-making. And, while the election of Obama brought an end to the terror-speak of the Bush era, the need to call attention to representational flaws in the public domain remains relevant and necessary. Terror-speak may no longer come from the White House, but it is alive and well in the mainstream media. As I've argued throughout this book, since 9/11 satire has been one of the few ways through which the public has been offered an opportunity to question the status quo. Because satire takes an original object and then re-presents it ironically, it asks the audience to think critically about the way that those in power construct their versions of the world. Irony, puns, farce, and parody offer comedians the opportunity to get the public to reflect on these issues and, as a 2006 *New York Magazine* article put it, farce is a language "no one is speaking more fluently than Colbert."[90]

In that same article, Colbert explained how the role of language in the current political moment had inspired his own work: "Language has always been important in politics, but language is incredibly important to the present political struggle...Because if you can establish an atmosphere in which information doesn't mean anything, then there is no objective reality. The first show we did, a year ago, was our thesis statement: What you wish to be true is all that matters, regardless of the facts. Of course, at the time, we thought we were being farcical."[91] Colbert's point here is that the way in which the public is given false notions of the truth is through deliberate linguistic misrepresentation. A central goal of the show, then, is to highlight these practices and encourage the audience to think about them. But, rather, than offer a straightforward critique of language, Colbert uses a complex array of satirically funny wordplay techniques to point out the power of words as well as the ease with which they can be manipulated.

One of the clear ironic arguments of Colbert's show is that a huge difference exists between a politician purposefully using deceptive language and a comedian engaging in wordplay. When the U.S. government creates the term *enemy combatant* in order to avoid following the Geneva Conventions, that sort of neologizing is not the same as Colbert creating a word like *wikiality*. In the first instance, a new term was created in order to violate international law; whereas, in the second example, Colbert created a term that satirized a social condition in order to call for its scrutiny. It is worth noting that, since Colbert is the voice of a right-wing pundit who regularly spews "bullshit" to his audience, it makes sense that wordplay would be an especially central feature of his satire. He needs to be extremely careful to remind his viewer that he doesn't believe what he is saying; that, in fact, he thinks that what he is saying not only makes no sense, but that it is exactly the sort of communication practice that is damaging the nation.

To this end, each section of *The Colbert Report* showcases different forms of wordplay. The opening rundown of the highlights of the upcoming show is driven by the use of puns and malapropisms. Puns are a form of wordplay that points to a word's multiple meanings. This can happen through playing with homophones, words that sound similar; it can take the form of exploiting multiple meanings of words; or it can happen when a familiar word is altered or substituted by a word that sounds similar. Examples of puns from the opening rundown include: "It's not a recession, it's a correction. Correction, it's a recession. This Is *The Colbert Report!*"[92] And "Shave your head, strap yourself in, and throw the switch—you're about to get a truthocution."[93] Most of the opening rundown puns are fun plays on words, but these fun wordplays also hint at more serious political commentary as evidenced by the two examples above. At this moment in the show, Colbert is typically speaking energetically to the camera, turning his body and addressing a new camera with each new line. This is not a moment that encourages much viewer reflection, since the lines come quickly with no breaks. But, even so, these opening puns set the stage for a critical treatment of language.

The next part of the show is a veritable linguistic smorgasbord as animation of an American Eagle soars toward the viewer and a digital image of Colbert is surrounded by circling words. The words that are used in this sequence vary, but here are some examples, broken down into main categories:[94]

Puns and neologisms:

- Factose intolerant
- Colmes-free since 2009
- Lincolnish
- Libertease
- Fundit
- Überballed
- Heterosapien
- Grippy
- Megamerican
- Superstantial
- Freem
- Fearnix rising

Silly words:

- Batter fried
- Juice it!
- Purple-mounted

Flattering words:

- Star-spangled
- Patriotic
- Hell-bent

- Gung-ho
- Dogged
- Critically-acclaimed
- Courageous

Unflattering words:

- Cocksure
- Domineering
- Dogmatic
- Phlegmatic

I haven't listed all the terms, so this sampling is not meant to reflect the overall weighting of the types of words used in the opening credits. What I have listed favors the neologisms and puns. At the heart of this list is a parody of the types of ways that pundit shows are marketed on cable networks with increasingly absurd adjectives. Colbert's overuse of these terms is meant to underscore the exaggerated ways that pundits present themselves to the public. These terms also pack power, and that is another point driven home by their overuse. What does it mean to call Colbert "patriotic" and "courageous"?

Photo 4.7   A digitized Colbert is surrounded by swirling words that describe his persona.

When pundits are fashioned as exemplary patriots, those that disagree with them seem unpatriotic. To make this point, Colbert's opening includes specifically unflattering words like *dogmatic* and *domineering* that serve as a foil for the over-the-top array of flattering ones. These unflattering words might appropriately be applied to figures like Beck or Limbaugh who have a habit of shouting at those that don't agree with them, preferring to silence opposition rather than reasonably debate it.

Of course the most noteworthy and most entertaining part of the opening digitized sequence is the puns and neologisms. These words get at the heart of Colbert's signature wordplay. Words like *Lincolnish, Megamerican, Fearnix Rising,* and *Factose Intolerant* encapsulate much of the satirical qualities of the Colbert character. They highlight his exaggerated patriotism, his truthiness, and his pundit-like desire to create a culture of fear for his viewers. Their silliness immediately reveals the irony of these terms, making them function satirically and not literally, creating a critical layer of meaning between the term and what it represents. These are words that exaggerate and that, therefore, help Colbert advance his parody of the pundit identity. A key to these words, I would argue, is their placement alongside other puns and neologisms that technically are not ironic, but are simply pure comedy like *Fundit* and *Überballed*. These are words that seem to refer to Colbert out-of-character, to the nature of the work he is doing on the show. They may or may not be satire, offering the possibility to the audience to read them as comments on the character or on the man behind the character. Thus, the wordplay of these terms is simultaneously linguistic construction, reconstruction, and deconstruction.

Then, to add to all these layers of meaning and word uses, the sequence includes words that are simply silly, pure non-satirical goofiness, like *Batter fried* and *"Juice it!"* If we consider that the writing for this show has been done carefully, and that seems like a reasonable assumption, given that it is a satirical comedy show, then these words are also meant to provide important clues to the function of language on the show. I would argue that these words reveal the comedy—the fun for fun's sake—aspect of the program. They are meant to remind the viewer that while the satire functions as political commentary with a social purpose, this is still comedy, and it is meant to be fun. This is not Keith Olbermann or Rachel Maddow. This is a show on Comedy Central; it is not a news program or a straight editorial. Taken together, the words in the opening credit sequence offer viewers a blueprint to the various ways that language functions on the show: It is meaningful and powerful, it is deceptive, it is satirical, it is silly, and it is multilayered. Most importantly, these words circle the digitized image of Colbert, engaging in interplay and appearing in cross-reference. This technique allows these different types of language use to speak to each other and produce a critical space for the viewer to think about how language produces meaning, how it can be dangerously deceptive, and how it can be ironically and entertainingly deployed.

Now the viewer is prepared for the next major form of wordplay: "The Wørd." Clearly, this is the part of the show that most apparently comments on language, but as I've pointed out, two earlier features of the show provide an important linguistic context for the segment's language games. The segment is partially modeled on Bill O'Reilly's "The Talking Points Memo" where O'Reilly takes a position on a current issue. On *The O'Reilly Factor* viewers see a right side bar text identical to O'Reilly's words. Viewers thus can hear and read O'Reilly's words at the same time. On O'Reilly's show, there is no counterpoint: the textual mirrors the verbal. In contrast, Colbert's "The Wørd" segment uses the right side bar to parody, satirize, and pun on the words Colbert speaks. It creates a constant counterpoint to Colbert's purportedly right-wing, reactionary views and requires active and engaged viewer participation to follow. Much like the comments in the margin of his book *I Am America*, the bullet points offer another layer of commentary, and they create a complex linguistic play between what Colbert is saying and what the right side bar reads. The viewer literally has to do two things at once: listen and read. It is inherently constructed to ask the viewer to be more critically active than viewers of programs like *The O'Reilly Factor*, which include text and verbal presentations that are not dialectically interconnected.

The segment thus satirizes the ways that much right-wing discourse undercuts the possibility of critical thinking and functions instead as a constant drone, dictating to the audience what they should think on important social matters. But, just as the segment critiques O'Reilly-esque dogma, it also offers a critique of the limits of poststructuralist positions that suggest that fixing any meaning to language is inherently repressive. The segment allows Colbert to effectively satirize O'Reilly and his kin, while also suggesting that the struggle over the meaning of words has significant political consequences, which demand that words have meaning and that those committed to progressive politics need to struggle to communicate those meanings.

As Colbert explained during an out-of-character interview with Terry Gross, "The Wørd" segment is an essay based on a single word: "I'm speaking a completely self-sufficient, standalone essay, hopefully comedic. And on the left side of the screen it's giving bullet points that are excerpting parts of what I said, or commenting on what I just said. And the bullet points end up being their own character. Sometimes they're reinforcing my argument, sometimes they're sort of countermanding my argument. But it's sort of a textual addition of jokes or satire to the verbal essay I'm doing at the moment."[95] Baym has suggested that the bullet points function as a corrective to Colbert's spoken words: "the written text provides an unspoken voice, a second level of meaning that often contradicts, challenges, and undermines the spoken words."[96] But I would suggest that the bullet points don't offer a unified discursive position: Sometimes they further exaggerate what Colbert is saying, critically contradict him, just add a silly aside, or express a sense of frustration and defeat with his use of rhetoric. The brilliance of the bullet points, then, is their varied discursive registers. Because the bullet points are not simply one unified foil to Colbert, they don't merely create a single additional layer; instead, they add many discursive layers. This form of deconstructing language within a critical and politically motivated project that hopes to re-infuse language with socially relevant meaning (while also having fun) offers viewers an extremely rich linguistic experience. Colbert demonstrates to viewers that satire's political critique is always aesthetic; it always depends on art as well as an appeal to reason.

The segment provides an extremely complex source of wordplay, but to illustrate these practices, consider an especially salient example: "The Wørd" segment featuring *Clarity* from August 9, 2007, when the presidential primaries were in full swing. As the lead in, Colbert showed a series of clips of Rudy Giuliani complaining that the Democratic candidates were not using the phrase "Islamic terrorist" during their debates, which led Colbert to claim that "Rudy has used the words *Islamic terrorism* so many times that the phrase 'September 11th' is getting jealous."[97] In "The Wørd" segment on *Clarity* that followed, the primary argument was dedicated to the idea that it was simply not possible to use a single overarching term to describe the current connections between Islam, terrorism, and the United States. Colbert's satire was aimed at showing how political positions that attempted to define our "enemy" with one simple phrase would not only *not help* the current crisis, but would actually exacerbate it. To illustrate the complexity of this segment, below I reproduce it in its entirety, adding comments in brackets along the way.

Colbert: And that brings us to tonight's word: *Clarity*.

Bullet: Clarity [Here the bullet point simply mirrors Colbert.]

Colbert: You see, folks, Giuliani knows you cannot win, if it's not clear who you are fighting.

Bullet: Usually ex-Wives. [Here the bullet mocks Giuliani's marital history.]

Colbert: But the Democrats insist on muddying the waters. Here's who the Democrats say we are up against: [We then see a series of clips from Democratic debates where candidates refer to our "enemy." Obama to Al-Qaeda operatives, Hillary Clinton to the resurgent Taliban and Al-Qaeda fighters, Dodd to the Islamic Fundamentalist State, Edwards to Radical Islam] That's four *different* enemies. They make it sound like we are in the middle of a complex, nuanced struggle requiring deep understanding of the differences between politically and religiously diverse groups. How are you going to fit *that* on a bumper sticker?

Bullet: Gives a sample bumper sticker covered by the words Colbert has just spoken. [Here he shows how silly it is to choose political positions based on marketing.]

Colbert: You see, ladies and gentlemen, our enemies are a massive group of religious fanatics bent on destroying us at all costs. They're "Islamic Terrorists." I can't think of a better term to describe them.

Bullet: Or Unite Them. [Ironically, he suggests that by lumping these groups together in our discourse and actions, we have united these different groups more than before.]

Colbert: Not using that phrase is just an example of political correctness.

Bullet: We're "Differently Terrified." [This is a silly pun on the term "differently abled." The pun might be funny, but it certainly does not make the left look good; if anything, it makes the left arguments for politically correct language seem pretty silly. This is an example of the ways that Colbert also mocks what he considers to be absurd left positions.]

Colbert: No, no folks. It is worse than political correctness. It is actual correctness. [This is a moment when Colbert seems to be speaking out of character.] And we all know too often correctness gets bogged down in detail.

Bullet: Fails to see bigger caricature. [This is another mostly silly pun that also has a political resonance.]

Colbert: And we all know that if we really want to win this war, we have to paint with broad strokes. I mean, we'd have stamped out organized crime by now if we referred to the Mafia as Italian terrorists. [Here Colbert takes a common right-wing view and takes it to an exaggerated place that reveals logical flaws.]

Bullet: That's a Spicy-A Car Bomb. [This time, it's a totally silly pun with no political reference.]

Colbert: If we're not careful, we could get stuck in an ill-defined, unwinnable, indefinite commitment to understanding who we are up against.

Bullet: The War on Error. [In direct contrast to the silly pun above, this pun is a highly potent political wordplay that underlines the fact that those who orchestrated the War on Terror committed the error of never trying to fully understand the enemy.]

Colbert: We need to return to the clarity of the good, old days, before there was any difference between Sunnis and Shiites.

Bullet: 632 AD [This is the date when the Prophet Mohammed died and the distinction between Sunnis and Shiites began to develop. This bullet point uses satire to add some truth to the atmosphere of truthiness.]

Colbert: Back when there were "freedom fries" and our justification for war was three simple letters: W-M-D.

Bullet: L-I-E [A powerful example of the bullet offering truth to truthiness. The audience explodes in applause.]

Colbert: Nation, whenever America finds itself in a never-ending conflict between good and ultimate evil, like the War on Drugs, the government appoints a czar. Well I propose Rudy Giuliani be America's language czar.

Bullet: First Issue: "Czar" or "Tsar"? [Another purely silly pun.]

Colbert: He can decide what words help America, ...

Bullet: President Giuliani. [The bullet reveals the fact that Giuliani will say anything to get elected.]

Colbert: and which words weaken us.

Bullet: Habeas Corpus? [Here the bullet packs another punch by reminding viewers of a major way in which the Bush government had used the War on Terror to undercut our own democratic principles.]

Colbert: Now we can let America's Mayor pick America's language. After all, if we don't use his simple, all-encompassing label for all of our enemies, he knows there's no way to win.

Bullet: The Election. [Here the bullet emphasizes the manipulation of language for political gain.]

As Baym points out, this segment shows how "The Wørd" "is an exercise in rhetorical criticism, an interrogation of public discourse."[98] He further explains that this segment allows Colbert to critique "the pitfalls of reductive characterizations of complex situations and the use of language to mask dangerous government policies."[99] By using the word *Clarity* to define the segment, Colbert revealed that if we seek a clear understanding of a complex problem, then we need to use complex and nuanced language. Bumper-sticker tag lines, campaign mantras, and sound bites will not do. Ironically, though, his own satire demonstrates how short, witty puns are capable of deflating the political power of such misappropriated language. The moment when the bullet offers L-I-E as a foil for W-M-D is a classic example of the simple elegance of satirical irony. It is also important to remember though, that such powerful and potent use of satirical language is not meant to substitute for reasoned debate and informed decision making. It is merely meant to illustrate the folly of political discourse to the public and encourage them to produce a critical response. The fact that satire is not meant as a substitute, but remains a form of comedy, is illustrated by noting that, regardless of how politically powerful "The Wørd" segment is on a given night of *The Colbert Report*, it constantly includes the sort of silly non-politically referential puns of the sort found in the joke on "Italian Terrorists." My point is that the bullet comments are varied and multi-discursive. I would suggest that the bullet points' uneven registers of commentary, varying from silly to incisive, are even more politically powerful than if they were consistently critical. The viewer never knows what sort of information the bullet will offer and that destabilizing effect keeps the audience in a highly active mode of watching the exchange between Colbert and his textual counterpart.

Thus "The Wørd" segment is an artful deconstruction, reconstruction, and construction of language that has come to symbolize Colbert's powerful use of language on his show. There are more excellent examples of wørds that have appeared on the segment than I have the space to highlight. Beyond *truthiness* and *clarity,* which I have analyzed here, there have been countless others. What is also important to note is that the segment has offered neologisms like *wikiality* and *freem* as well as everyday words like *silence* and silly words like *jacksquat.* In each of these cases, the segment has offered viewers an extremely complex linguistic interplay between Colbert and the bullet points that, rather than spoon-feed ideas to the viewer, calls on them to produce their own active and engaged interpretation and analysis. This highly critical exchange between Colbert, the bullet points, and the viewer, then, prepares the stage for the show's next section—the interview.

In order to understand the interview segment, it is worth remembering Colbert's statement to Terry Gross that the title of the show is an unintentional pun on *rapport.* During the interview, he described a rapport as "a sense of understanding between the speaker and the listener. We're the same people you and me, we get it. The rest of the people out there, they don't understand the things that we understand. The show is like an invitation to the audience to be part of the club."[100] What is interesting, in light of that statement, is that the interview often is not a rapport, or at least it simulates a lack of it. When Colbert interviews someone on the right, he takes an über-right position, and feigns rapport with his guest. When he has a left-leaning guest, he feigns contrariness. Because he is in character, the rapport is simulated, just as the contentious confrontation is a joke as well. Consequently, it is the performance of these sorts of false dialogue that creates the real hope of a rapport between Colbert and his viewers.

Everything that Colbert says in character comes to us as parody, making each word he utters double-layered with meaning. As Baym puts it, "Colbert's ironic performance is continuously double voiced—his literal language always placed in juxtaposition with its implied meaning."[101] From the opening rundown, to the credit sequence, to "The Wørd," to the interview, each section of the show offers viewers a complex example of linguistic satire. But Colbert plays with language in even more ways. For instance, he often bases arguments on the ways that words are constructed, telling readers of his book, *I Am America*, "Think books aren't scary? Well, think about this: You can't spell 'Book' without 'Boo!'"[102] This is a nonsensical deconstruction of the word, but its silliness also draws readers' attention to the ways that words are constructed. Colbert uses reductive arguments and logical fallacies, plays with metaphors (most notoriously on the Meta-Free-Phor-All where he went head to head with Sean Penn after Penn underwent criticism for using a metaphor to attack President Bush), believes that things that rhyme must be true, and loves to link non sequiturs to prove a point.

Here is an example of this last technique: "Let's try a current mystery. Varying reports on the Hurricane Katrina debacle are pointing fingers in many directions. Who's really to blame for the slow response to the disaster? Let's think about it: Hurricane Katrina...Katrina and the Waves...Waves in the Oceans...Ocean's full of Fish...One Fish Two Fish Red Fish Blue Fish...Dr. Seuss...The Cat in the Hat...Mike Myers. Oh, my God, it's Mike Myers' fault! No wonder he kept quiet when Kanye West started blaming President Bush!"[103] This is yet another example of the way that the show combines silliness and seriousness. On the one hand, it is just a ridiculous string of connections. But, on the other hand, it is a biting parody of the sorts of so-called logical associations that are made by pundits on cable news all the time, a habit he has linked especially to Glenn Beck and his use of the chalkboard to make nonsensical connections.

Colbert also loves to play with analogies. In one example, he deconstructed Rick Santorum's analogy between J. R. R. Tolkien's *Lord of the Rings* and the Iraq War. He puts up a Santorum quote where he says: "As the hobbits are going up Mount Doom, the eye of Mordor is being drawn somewhere else. It's being drawn to Iraq. You know what? I want to keep it on Iraq. I don't want it to come back to the United States."[104] Colbert is delighted by the use of an analogy he can "understand," and he breaks it down step by step, showing that, according to Santorum, the United States is Mordor and Mount Doom is the midterm elections.

Colbert also relishes highlighting when pundits create false distinctions between words when they try to backtrack from inflammatory statements, such as when Beck accused Obama of having a deep-seated hatred of whites, but then said he didn't say, "Obama didn't like white people." This leads Colbert to conclude: "Deep-seated hatred and dislike are two different things. They're as different as putting your foot in your mouth or your head up your ass."[105] Here we have another excellent example of a simple, yet immensely effective way that Colbert can satirize the mass media through an artful use of language, simultaneously making us laugh and making us think critically. Again and again, from puns to malapropisms to neologisms to irony, parody, and farce, Colbert uses absurd language to expose absurd language. While he deconstructs the use of words, he always does this with an eye to building meaningful rapport with his audience. And that's tonight's wordplay.

AN IMAGE OF AN IMAGE: QUESTIONS OF IDENTITY

"The funny thing is, I knew when we were developing this show, we were doing a show that parodies the cult of personality. And yet, if the show was successful, it would generate a cult of personality. It had to. That means it's working."[106]

One of the distinctive features of Colbert's satire is his persona, which is modeled on the cult of personality that drives right-wing punditry. His character is so convincing that it has allowed him to create a significant scandal through his "Better Know a District" series, where he interviews politicians and encourages them to make compromising statements. This led Democrats Nancy Pelosi and Rahm Emanuel to warn politicians not to speak to him. Of course, his current fame and public visibility have hindered his ability to influence guests, but it is

Photo 4.8   Colbert stands in front of his original double-layered portrait.

still impressive that he can get guests to engage in fairly absurd debates and conversations. Unlike other comedians who assume a variety of roles (like Sacha Baron Cohen, for instance), Colbert adopts the position of one character for his show, revealing his "real" side publicly only in brief moments and occasional interviews. That this persona is a version of a right-wing pundit like Bill O'Reilly allows Colbert to parody O'Reilly-esque posturing on important social issues and to question the "character" of such figures. While this is the most obvious consequence of his satirical parody, Colbert's simulated identity has three further features that are essential to understand. First, his obsession with representations of himself (as seen, for instance, in his portrait of a portrait of himself) connect his persona to certain postmodern ideas, especially those of Jean Baudrillard, about identity as simulation and as performance. These connections reveal the conceptual limits of some postmodern positions while also commenting on the negative effects of a media-saturated society. Likewise, his constant claim that he "doesn't see race" coupled with his own impersonation of a racist allow him to critique right and left positions on identity issues relating to the Culture Wars. Evidence of his success at satirizing both extremes is found in his coverage of the Obama candidacy, where he was able to critique the racism of the right at the same time that he mocked those on the left who considered Obama not "black enough" because he was not a descendent of slaves. As a simulacrum of an identity category,

Colbert's persona is uniquely positioned to satirically question the role that identity categories based on race, gender, political affiliation, and more play in contemporary politics. However, this leads to the third point: such a practice runs a risk. It also creates a cult of personality, and since sometimes Colbert's vituperative examples of intolerance and bigotry are so entertainingly delivered, they could actually reinforce right-wing rhetoric rather than reverse it. All these issues coalesce together to create a complex picture of the way that identity issues connect with *The Colbert Report.*

Colbert is not what he seems. As he explained during an interview with Charlie Rose, when Rose asked him to comment on a cover of *Rolling Stone* that featured the two comedians: "That's Jon being Jon. That's me being *not me*. That's me being the Stephen Colbert guy."[107] When performing as the "Colbert guy," Colbert is always a representation of something else that is not himself. This is further exacerbated by the fact that some of the pundits he parodies seem to be performing themselves. Does O'Reilly *really* mean what he says? Or is he acting? As cited above, when Colbert and O'Reilly faced off on *The O'Reilly Factor,* O'Reilly stated: "It's hard to be me. Is it hard to be you?," to which Colbert replied: "It's hard to be me being you."[108] Clearly, Colbert is referencing his own performance, but beneath the statement is the idea that he is a performance of a performance. O'Reilly as much admitted that he was all an act, albeit oddly, when he later appeared on Colbert's show. In that interview Colbert asked O'Reilly if he could take Hannity in a fight. O'Reilly responded by saying Hannity would take him: "I'm effete. I'm not a tough guy. This is all an act." Which led Colbert to respond: "If you're an act, then what am I?"[109]

There are multiple references to Colbert as a simulation, as an act, as a copy, as a representation of a representation throughout his show. From the opening where a digitized Colbert runs and leaps holding a U.S. flag, to his portraits which each year include another layer of Colberts in front of Colberts, to the animated series *Tek Jensen,* to Colbert performing as Esteban Colberto, *The Colbert Report* makes a point of creating copies, other versions, and representations of Colbert. As if that weren't enough, he even markets his own "man seed" so that fans can reproduce him on their own.

All of these layers of representation point to a central question: Is Colbert just a representation of a representation with no reference to a reality? Or does the representation point to something, implying an original source? If so, what?

In order to answer these questions, it is necessary to recall an important postmodern theorist, Jean Baudrillard, whose widely influential

Photo 4.9   Colbert emphasizes that he is a representation.

book appeared in English in 1994 as *Simulacra and Simulation*. The book's main thesis was that current society has replaced reality with a procession of signs and symbols that only refer to each other and that have no connection to reality. He describes representation as having gone through phases that have increasingly taken the representational form farther and farther from the object it is meant to reflect. Hence, while at one time a representation reflected reality, he claims that is now no longer the case. In the current moment, he suggests that often the representation itself precedes and supersedes that which it represents. He especially notes that in a televisually mediated world, society consumes a flow of images disconnected from the reality they supposedly reflect. Let's consider the barrage of images that come at the viewer on a CNN news show. There are often so many competing images—anchor, photo connected to story, word scroll on the bottom of the screen, story graphics, and a visually complex set—that the idea that the anchor is telling a story connected to a "real" world often gets lost. According to Baudrillard, this process has gotten so intense that it is no longer possible to connect the image with a referent in the real world. One of his most famous examples was the way that the Gulf War was televised. The digitized images seemed totally disconnected from any sense of real war. It felt more like a video game than a representation of reality. In another example, some of his ideas formed the basis for the film *The Matrix,* which made several direct references to his work.

Now it may seem to make little sense to claim that there is no longer any reality and that representations only refer to themselves and no longer to any object, but *The Colbert Report* does demonstrate some validity to Baudrillard's claims. First of all, Colbert's simulation of a right-wing pundit often does have a more powerful impact on viewers than the objects he emulates. Colbert's performance of punditry occasionally can be (1) indistinguishable from the real thing, (2) more compelling than the real thing, (3) an exaggeration and quasi-celebration of punditry. These moments are especially visible when he goes head-to-head with other pundits on his show. His goal is to out-pundit his guest, but the result can sometimes feel like a disturbing celebration of punditry. As referenced in the opening quote to this section, the show's creators knew that they were likely to create a cult of personality. And without question the show has succeeded in doing that. But isn't it a bit troubling to create a cult of personality in order to satirize the disturbing ways that cults of personality occupy national consciousness?

The answer to this question lies in the difference between the persona of Colbert and that of those, like Beck and O'Reilly, he parodies. There is a huge difference between being an admiring fan of an effective satirist, who plays someone with a huge ego, and admiring a demagogue who fosters a culture of fear, intolerance, and self-interest. Moreover, satirical parody, while drawn from an original object (in this case, an amalgamation of mainstream right-wing pundits), represents the object through critique and humor. Thus, it is not exactly a simulation of the sort that Baudrillard describes. In Baudrillard's world, the simulations are copies—not ironic copies. And to add to the complexity, Colbert is actually a parody of a performance. So much of contemporary punditry is itself a self-styled performance. It can be difficult to discern any actual reference to reality when one tries to follow the fallacious reasoning of a pundit like Glenn Beck describing the evils of China or the logic of investing in gold. So, a parody of that may actually seem more real than the original performance.

Or it might just seem ridiculous and over the top, as in the segment where Esteban Colberto interviewed Lou Dobbs.[110] Colberto spoke Spanish and interviewed Dobbs about his views on immigration. The segment was not really that critical in a satirical way, although there were some fairly effective jabs, especially with regard to the barbed-wire fence that they had installed on the set. What must be noted from this segment is that no matter how satirically powerful his parody is, there is also a level of comedy that may make the object of satire turn to simple entertaining mockery. To add to the complexity, not all pundits are equal. Some appear to be performing more outrageously than others. Colbert, himself, made this distinction during an out-of-character interview when he explained why he would not have Ann Coulter on his show: "She's a self-generating bogeyman. She's like someone who wants attention for having been bad. My sense is that she's playing a character," he says. "I don't need another character. There's one character on my show, and that's me."[111] Colbert dismisses the punditry of Coulter for being too ridiculous. But certainly O'Reilly and Beck and Hannity have had their Coulter-like moments as well.

Regardless of the degree to which Colbert's object of parody is performing, the important issue is that his own identity is quite complex, since, on the one hand, it is a performance of a performance, but, on the other hand, Colbert's performance satirizes the way that news is performed. It calls on viewers to expect more from the news and from those who editorialize it. For these reasons, an issue that it most regularly turns to is the role of identity politics in debates connected to the Culture Wars.

Viewers might recall that when O'Reilly was on Colbert, Colbert brought out O'Reilly's book *Culture Warrior*—in it O'Reilly details what he sees as the demise of America, ruined by a "secular-progressive" cult that advocates gay marriage and threatens traditional

Photo 4.10   Colbert discusses O'Reilly's book during their interview.

values: "If these people win the culture war, the United States as we have come to know it for 230 years will cease to exist."[112] This sort of hysteria over the collapse of traditional U.S. values has been on the rise since the 1980s when the Culture Wars replaced the Cold War as the primary conflict between progressives and conservatives. The Culture Wars have been a central focus for right-wing punditry. The basic idea is that progressive arguments for the rights of minority groups threaten the core, traditional values of the country. Thus, anyone who fights for immigrant rights, women's rights, or gay rights advocates dangerous policies that must be vigorously opposed. If those advocating minority rights "win" the war, the nation will be destroyed.

As explained in chapter 2, the Culture Wars were a conservative backlash in response to the progressive advances of the 1960s when a number of disenfranchised groups were able to effectively lobby for better civil rights. Colbert, as the mega-pundit, makes this point in *I Am America* when he describes the 1960s as a turning point after which the nation has been in crisis: "See, at one time America was pure. Men were men, women were women, and gays were 'confirmed bachelors.' But somewhere around the late 60s, it became 'groovy' to 'let it all hang out' while you 'kept on truckin'' stopping only to 'give a hoot.' And today, Lady Liberty is under attack from the cable channels, the Internet blogs, and the Hollywood celebritocracy, out there spewing 'facts' like so many locusts descending on America's crop of ripe, tender values."[113] This passage effectively satirizes the right's manufactured hysteria over the demise of U.S. values. The key to the rhetoric of the right is the language of war and the idea that the nation is under threat. This use of language allows them to paint a picture of a battle that must be waged against people who want to hurt "the American way of life," but, of course, that language is performative, since the premise of the left progressives is that everyone should have a voice and should have a chance to actively participate in democracy. So the only threat advanced by liberal progressives is the threat to a non-participatory democracy governed by a power elite. The point is that it is the right that is waging the war—a war against allowing all groups in U.S. society to have a voice and to have equal access to rights and protections. The art of the right's strategy, though, is that they use rhetoric to turn their aggressive intolerance into a language of victimhood and national defense.

One of the successes of Colbert's parody of the right's culture-war rhetoric is his ability to satirize the idea of the right as a victim in a vicious battle. At the center of the battle is the fight over who gets to define U.S. values. After the 1960s when minority groups gained a stronger public voice, conservatives worried that diversity would dilute their values. Subsequently, it became the case that the right imagined itself as the model for traditional U.S. values, and the progressives were labeled as immoral, valueless hippies who wanted to destroy all that America stands for. Colbert satirizes the right's position in the Culture Wars throughout his show and in his book, *I Am America*. While the right claims that they are defending true, American values, their discourse often seems to do nothing more than stir up intolerance, bigotry, and Christian fundamentalism. For this reason, O'Reilly goes on and on about the "gay agenda" and gay marriage as one of the greatest threats to the nation. Colbert satirizes this view in his book when he states that gay marriage, which he calls the "Lavender Armageddon," is "the biggest threat facing America."[114] Of course, many pundits have said the same thing. He then pretends he is fending off a naysayer who might suggest that the Iraq War has been a bigger threat to the country than gay marriage, to which he responds; "Yes, Iraq is the central front in the War on Terror and We're Fighting Them Over There So We Don't Have to Fight Them Over Here. But consider this: who, other than terrorists, wants to destroy our way of life? The Gays. Allowing them to marry would be like strapping on a suicide vest with a matching cummerbund."[115]

Colbert takes up these issues all the time on his show. In a lead up to the Rally to Restore Fear on the National Mall, Colbert did a segment called the "Fear for All" where he identified five types of men that represented the nation's biggest threats: a Mexican, a gay man, a Muslim, a grizzly coddler, and a man who could be a robot. He had five guests: one for each group. He started by asking the group: "Why shouldn't I be afraid of you?"[116] The premise was that he *should* be afraid. As a classic satire of the way that news-show interviews are often slanted toward the opinions of the host, Colbert took his position as the assumed correct position and forced his guests to prove him wrong. The bit was highly effective satire since the inclusion of a "man who could be a robot" alongside a Muslim exposed the way that fear is manufactured. The inclusion of the "grizzly coddler"—whose lack of fear of bears frightens Colbert—also revealed the way that pundits adopt pet causes and project them onto the national space. Even better, the men who represented groups that suffer intolerance today all offered Colbert convincing arguments against prejudice, racism, and homophobia. As they worked on convincing him, they offered the show's viewers a rare opportunity to see these groups eloquently defend themselves.

In addition, he has hosted a number of progressive public figures that have worked for equal rights, such as Jane Fonda and Cornel

West, giving them a platform to argue for the rights of disenfranchised groups and for the fact that the right should not be the sole source of national values. But he also mocks those on the progressive left who have taken reductive positions on diversity, satirizing those who suggest that diversity requires that one has lived an experience in order to understand it. This position was lampooned on the show when Colbert suggested that one way to respond to the idea that Obama wasn't "black" enough because he was not a descendent of slaves would be to enslave him for a time to Jesse Jackson, so that he, too, could live the authentic African-American descendant-of-slaves experience.

One of the best examples of Colbert's commitment to advancing the struggles of marginalized groups was his appearance before Congress as an expert on farm workers and immigration. On September 24, 2010, Colbert testified in character before the House Judiciary Subcommittee on Immigration, Citizenship, and Border Security, having been invited by committee chairwoman Zoe Lofgren to describe his experience participating in the United Farm Workers' "Take Our Jobs" program, where he spent a day working alongside migrant workers in upstate New York. He submitted his speech beforehand, then proceeded to deliver something entirely different while there. He used the opportunity to satirize right-wing views on immigrant labor, exposing many of the logical flaws in their arguments. "This is America," he told the panel. "I don't want a tomato picked by a Mexican," he said. "We do not want immigrants doing this labor."[117] Of course, the joke is that "we" do. The position of the right seems to suggest that they are protecting U.S. jobs for U.S. workers, but that is a cover for the notion that what really is disturbing is that undocumented workers would have rights or protections. Colbert also used the opportunity to describe himself as an instant expert on anything, mocking the pundit tendency to opine on issues of which they know little. When ranking Republican Lamar Smith of Texas asked Colbert if one day on the farm made him an expert, Colbert replied, "I believe one day of me studying anything makes me an expert."[118] This comment satirizes the fact that most arguments against immigrant rights today come from sources with little if no knowledge of the issues and experiences involved. Colbert also used the opportunity to expose the incongruity between neoliberal free-market fundamentalism and hyper-patriotic conservative populism: "Now I'm a free-market guy. Normally I would leave this to the invisible hand of the market, but the invisible hand of the market has already moved over 84,000 acres of production and over 22,000 farm jobs to Mexico."[119]

Photo 4.11 Colbert at Congress.

The most telling moment came when Colbert broke character. His performance had included off-color and silly humor about his colon and its need for roughage, about solving the migrant labor problem by developing vegetables that pick themselves, and other goofy statements. It also rehashed most of the conservative claims about the reasons not to support citizenship or rights for undocumented labor. But it was hard for Colbert to hold the pundit performance even in his prepared in-character statement. For instance, he urged the committee to work to address the problem: "Now I'm not a fan of the government doing anything, but I've got to ask: why isn't the government doing anything?"[120] He also suggested that it was necessary to provide government protection for these workers: "Maybe we could offer visas to the immigrants who, let's face it, will probably be doing these jobs anyway. And this improved legal status might offer immigrants recourse if they're abused."[121] During the question-and-answer part of the session, Colbert answered questions from the committee out-of-character, giving Democratic Representative Judy Chu a chance to ask him why of all of the causes he could choose to work on he had chosen this one: "I like talking about people who don't have any power, and it seems like one of the least powerful people in the United States are migrant workers who come and do our work, but don't have any rights as a result. And yet we still invite them to come here and at the same time ask them to leave…Migrant workers suffer and have no rights."[122] What made this statement so effective as a comment on the United States' ongoing mistreatment of undocumented labor was the fact that it came after his in-character performance where he had satirized the commonly advanced conservative and neoliberal views about immigration and labor issues. This is an example of how his in-character satire of right-wing intolerance had the ability to make his out-of-character statements carry even more weight. When the simulation of punditry gave way to Colbert's own views about justice, rights, and compassion for fellow human beings, it made his true political position as an advocate for immigrant rights even more politically powerful.

There is a darker side to Colbert's simulation of right-wing views on U.S. identity issues, though, and that is its sometimes all-too-convincing quality. As Adam Sternbergh explains, most of Colbert's fans will catch themselves in the awkward position where they are laughing at his rendition of an extreme view that sometimes feels too eerily similar to laughing at a non-satirical version of the same statement: "Colbert's on-air personality, so distinct from Stewart's, leads to a peculiar comedic alchemy on the show. During one taping I attended, Colbert did a bit about eating disorders that ended with his addressing the camera and saying flatly, 'Girls, if we can't see your ribs, you're ugly.' The audience laughed. I laughed. The line was obviously, purposefully outrageous. But it was weird to think that this no-doubt self-identified progressive-liberal crowd was howling at a line that, if it had been delivered verbatim by Ann Coulter on *Today*, would have them sputtering with rage."[123] As Sternbergh points out, no one wants to associate Colbert with Coulter: Coulter is the real deal, and Colbert is merely a simulation of her shrill, offensive, demagogic behavior. Nevertheless, the fact remains that in some moments Colbert's cult of personality and simulation of intolerance come disturbingly close to getting us to laugh at jokes we would otherwise find offensive. Are we only laughing at Colbert's performance, or has he made mockery, derision, and bigotry fun and funny?

Sternbergh is not suggesting that Colbert is Coulter, but that their over-the-top sorts of statements have an uncanny resemblance. In his piece for *New York Magazine*, he offers readers a test where he lists ten offensive statements and asks readers to guess who uttered them: Coulter or Colbert? Here is one comparison:[124]

> "Even Islamic terrorists don't hate America like liberals do. They don't have the energy. If they had that much energy, they'd have indoor plumbing by now."

"There's nothing wrong with being gay. I have plenty of friends who
are going to hell."

Can you tell the difference? Probably not. The first is Colbert and
the second is Coulter. While Sternbergh makes a valuable point, and
one that should not be overlooked, he misses a crucial aspect of what
makes these utterances different: It is all in the messenger. It is not
just the delivery that makes such statements resonate with an audience in a different way, but the statement's actual source makes all
the difference in the world. As I have explained, understanding the
"source" of Colbert's statements can be tricky because his simulated
punditry is a parody of a performance. But helping his audience "get"
that process is a huge part of the way that Colbert's satire works.
When Colbert says things like, "Opinions are like assholes, in that I
have more than most people," it is hard to suggest that he is not constantly signaling to his audience not to take what he says seriously.[125]
Part of what makes Colbert's project so difficult, however, is that
the performance that Colbert parodies has become so extraordinarily
pervasive in U.S. culture that we regularly encounter these sorts of
biased and bigoted statements every day. It is hard to filter the difference between Colbert and someone like Coulter when voices like
Coulter's are much more dominant. In a world where the public is
commonly told that everything America stands for is under siege,
where the idea of providing an undocumented laborer shade and a
break for water is presented as a dangerous dissolution of national
resources, and where it is possible to claim on national television that
the first African-American president has a "deep-seated hatred" of
whites with absolutely no proof, the public needs to be aware of how
these ideas threaten democratic principles. What Colbert has done in
his performance of a performance of an intolerant pundit is manage
to draw attention to the disconnect between the absurdity of right-
wing Culture Wars rhetoric and to the very real ways that rhetoric
continues to foster a society of intolerance and inequality.

I AM AMERICA: COLBERT REDEFINES PATRIOTISM

Terry Gross: "You don't only love your country, you love yourself."
Colbert: "By loving myself, I am loving the country."[126]

Modeling himself on the massive patriotic egos of pundits as well as
those of many politicians, Colbert's self-obsession dovetails with his
claim that he, himself, stands for America. A common theme in his

show is that he is America, that he defines it, and that he speaks for it: He is "Lincolnish," "Megamerican," "Patriotic," "Star-Spangled." His set is full of Americana, and its design is an over-the-top tribute to Americanness. This satirical performance of hyper-patriotism allows Colbert to highlight the way that the right holds a monopoly on defining what it means to be patriotic. His performance also offers a critique of the way that self-absorption has become an American way of life precisely in a moment when the nation needs greater commitment to community, rights, and other collective social structures. Here I will analyze the extent to which Colbert's self-association with America offers his audience an opportunity to reflect on how hubris, megalomania, and self-satisfaction have become synonymous with U.S. identity. More importantly, I look at how Colbert has tried to satirize the right's claim to define U.S. patriotism. How does the Colbert Nation offer an alternative patriotism to the right-wing nation? I also analyze how Colbert has found a way to be critical of features of U.S. society while remaining committed to U.S. ideals of democracy, equality, and justice.

Geoffrey Nunberg notes that in other parts of the developed world, U.S. patriotism seems extreme. For instance, British journalists John Micklethwait and Adrian Wooldridge write: "American

Photo 4.12 A patriotic Colbert compares himself to a bald eagle.

Patriotism runs deep. No other developed country displays its flags more obsessively or sings its national anthem more frequently."[127] In polls done before and after 9/11, 83 to 90 percent of U.S. citizens described themselves as "extremely proud" or "very proud" to be an American.[128] While Republicans are slightly more likely than Democrats to say that they are "extremely proud," there is little question that U.S. patriotism runs high regardless of party affiliation. But if you listen to right-wing talk radio or watch Fox News, that isn't the view of patriotism you will get. Instead, you will hear that the only patriots are Republicans and that Democrats are not only unpatriotic, they hate their country and are trying to destroy it. Republicans have effectively cornered the market on patriotism, professing loudly and aggressively that they and only they know what it means to be an "American." The effect of this is that even the concept of a liberal patriot feels like an oxymoron. Nunberg notes that on the web the phrase "patriotic liberal" is outnumbered 40 to 1 by the phrase "patriotic conservative."[129]

One reason for the discrepancy between perceived liberal patriotism and conservative patriotism is linked to the fallout of the 1960s and the debates, conflicts, and controversies in connection with the Vietnam War. In this era, the right expressed their patriotism by asserting that criticism of the war was akin to treason. Their cars sported the bumper sticker: "America. Love it or leave it!" But, as public intellectuals like Martin Luther King, Jr., explained, there were other versions of what America could and should stand for. The American Civil Rights Movement had fought hard in the 1950s and 1960s to include other versions of America, versions that included people of color, women, and other marginalized groups. In 1963 King stood at the Lincoln Memorial and spoke to a crowd gathered on the National Mall. He told his audience that he had a dream of a time when the nation would live up to its ideals: "I have a dream that one day this nation will rise up and live out the true meaning of its creed: 'We hold these truths to be self-evident: that all men are created equal.'"[130] As King explained, this dream was not un-American. While it differed from the vision of America offered by those critical of the civil rights movement, for King, it was more accurate and more true to the ideals of the nation. It was "a dream deeply rooted in the American dream."[131]

As I've explained, these ideas seemed extremely threatening to the right, and they led later to the Culture Wars, where any effort to advocate for rights for minority groups was perceived as an attack on U.S. ideals. Colbert satirized the way that the right demonizes the civil rights struggles in his "The Wørd" segment on October 25, 2005, after the death of activist Rosa Parks: "Yesterday was full of loss for America, the greatest of which was beloved civil rights pioneer Rosa Parks. Which brings us to tonight's Wørd: 'Overrated'...Now, I know this isn't going to win me any popularity contests, but am I the only person who remembers that Rosa Parks got famous for breaking the rules?...You start disobeying laws simply because they are unjust, pretty soon you got yourself a country full of Gandhis. Look, there were other options. How about renting a car? If so many people were upset, why not start your own bus company? Let the free market do what it does best: bring justice to the disenfranchised."[132] Colbert really hammers his point when he suggests that what makes people like Parks threatening is that they try to change the country to make it better: "So tonight, let me be the first—the Rosa Parks, if you will—of saying to those malcontents out there that the best way to change the system is to wait till it changes."[133] Colbert attempts to use satire to reclaim the idea that patriotism can also be a commitment to fighting to change the nation.

Another angle to the critique of patriotism cannot be overlooked, however. And that is the critique of American exceptionalism. American exceptionalism is the longstanding belief that the United States differs qualitatively from other developed nations—a difference that makes it possible, for instance, for the United States to be critical of British or Soviet imperialism but not its own. That the United States is superior to developing or undeveloped nations is taken for granted. Thus, the bombing of civilians in Iraq or Afghanistan is justified, whereas the terrorist bombings of U.S. civilians are not. The Vietnam War was seen by many of its critics to be an outrageous example of American exceptionalism, as the United States entered a proxy war and practiced what appeared to many to be a new form of imperialism. Unlike the ideas of Martin Luther King Jr., where he wants to wrest a different and more equitable view of America, those critical of American exceptionalism tend to have little tolerance for hyper-patriotism. This does not mean that they advocate treason, but rather that they oppose U.S. imperialism and that they feel that the United States should be held accountable for its actions in the same way as any other nation. Consequently, to wage war in Iraq as a response to the attacks of 9/11, when there was no connection between Iraq and 9/11, reveals the hypocrisy of American patriotism. How can a nation that considers itself a beacon for freedom and a role model for democracy invade other nations with countless civilian casualties on false and misleading evidence?

The post-9/11 era took the tensions of the civil rights era over what it meant to support the nation and the criticism of U.S. imperialism from the Vienam War to an extreme. At the heart of the dilemma was: how could one condemn the attacks but also question the Bush administration's response to them? Anyone who criticized the government's response was described as supporting the terrorists. And anyone whose discomfort with American exceptionalism made them uncomfortable with overt symbols of nationalism was called a traitor. Days after the 9/11 attacks, before the full body count was known, Don Feder of *The Boston Herald* chastised liberals for not sufficiently displaying the flag: "Even after an unprovoked attack on their homeland, by creatures so evil that hell would spurn them, and 5,500 of their fellow American dead, public-broadcast donors just can't get over their red, white, and blue aversion."[134] But as Nunberg explains, by any reasonable measure of patriotism, most liberals are patriotic. "If they have reservations about past and present policies, it's most often because they believe that those policies fail to live up to the best American ideals, usually a sign of patriotism and optimism itself."[135] And those on the left who are not patriotic generally oppose nationalism tout court. They associate the idea of the "Homeland" with the militaristic nationalism of Hitler or the blind obedience to national authority demanded by Mao. They might not want to fly the flag, but they certainly don't root for another nation or for terrorists; instead, they advocate a version of global connectedness or cosmopolitanism that transcends national borders and sees all human beings as related.

The battle over who defines patriotism, though, is not really grounded in the actual beliefs of U.S. citizens; rather, it has been highly rhetorical, with the right virtually monopolizing the term. It is worth remembering the Democrats' efforts to regain the concept of patriotism during the 2004 Democratic National Convention when presidential candidate John Kerry emphasized his service to his country by saying: "I'm John Kerry and I'm reporting for duty."[136] Kerry was pushed to this place in response to the way that the Bush administration used rhetoric to insinuate that their projects were inherently patriotic. Recall the legislation named the USA PATRIOT Act or the opening of the Department of Homeland Security. After 9/11 Bush became the premiere icon for U.S. patriotism, so much so that it was even suggested that anyone who ran against him was unpatriotic. The chairman of the Republican National Committee made this point when he said: "Senator Kerry crossed a grave line when he dared to suggest the replacement of America's commander-in-chief at a time when America is at war."[137]

If the political campaign was a battlefield over who had the right to be patriotic, the war was even more intense in the realm of punditry. Rush Limbaugh blatantly called Kerry "anti-American," and Kerry was repeatedly accused of giving comfort to the enemy. Similarly, Obama's own citizenship has been frequently called into question. Politicians and pundits on the right have waged a nonstop campaign to define patriotism, and it is a campaign they have largely won. As Nunberg puts it: "So long as the right owns patriotism, the Democrats will be unable to change the conversation...Democrats have tried to reclaim the word in its dictionary meaning while ignoring the narrative it's embedded in."[138]

That's where Colbert comes in. He is able to artfully satirize the exaggerated patriotism of the right by calling attention to the ways that the right has co-opted the very idea of the nation. The right has constructed a version of nationalism that is exclusive, fear-based, and self-serving. It is a nationalism fundamentally opposed to debate, dialogue, and democratic ideals since it is a nationalism grounded on affect, authoritarianism, and intolerance. Colbert inserts himself in this narrative in a highly parodic and exaggerated fashion that is funny and critically incisive. He calls his book *I Am America (And So Can You!)* in direct parody of the types of books published by pundits like O'Reilly (*Culture Warrior*), Beck (*Glenn Beck's Common Sense*), Joe Scarborough (*The Last Best Hope: Restoring Conservatism and America's Promise*), and Ann Coulter (*Guilty: Liberal "Victims" and Their Assault on America*). While the books by these pundits are divisive and aggressively critical of the left, Colbert's is able to mock those positions and reveal the hubris involved with imagining that the right is the only viable source of patriotism. Readers who buy his book open the inside flap and read: "Congratulations—just by opening the cover of this book you became 25% more patriotic."

The introduction to the book highlights its satire of pundits who self-identify with the nation and who imagine that they and they alone know what it means to be patriotic: "This book is My Story and as such it is the American Story...Read this book. Be me. I Am America (And So Can You!)"[139] Here Colbert blends the genre of the right-wing autobiography/vision for America with a self-help book. And while the title, *I Am America (And So Can You!)*, is simply silly, the link Colbert makes is telling. Self-help books attempt to teach the public how to be better people, but they are often intensely patronizing to the reader and can be examples of the ego of the author who imagines himself or herself as a proper role model for the public at large. Similarly, the books by right-wing pundits generally suggest that the nation is on the brink of disaster and that good, traditional right-wing values (which are some sort of combination of conservative, fundamentalist Christian, hyper-patriotic, militarist, and neoliberal values) are under threat. In a sense, they are self-help books for the nation, not just individuals. Most importantly, both genres of books are not designed to encourage critical thinking or active dialogue; rather, they are meant to be a blueprint for future behavior. They offer the reader the freedom to agree with what is proposed or be wrong. Colbert's title takes the concept of these books to an extreme, exposing the problems with suggesting that one's patriotism is grounded in the U.S. ideals of freedom, democracy, and equality while, at the same time, constructing an authoritative and intolerant view of what it means to support the nation.

The entire book is effectively a satire of the concept that the right owns the idea of America, and it builds on Jon Stewart's book *America: A Citizen's Guide to Democracy Inaction*, a project Colbert participated in while still working for *The Daily Show*. Stewart's book, like his show, is organized around a satire of ridiculous and illogical arguments about the history and idea of America. Colbert's book, like his show, comes to the reader fully in character, adding another layer to the parody. Stewart's book simulated a civics textbook on the history and democratic structure of the United States. In contrast, Colbert's is structured like an autobiography with sections on "My American Childhood," "My American Adolescence," and "My American Maturity." Within each section Colbert has several chapters that allow him to opine on major issues and themes from the perspective of a conservative, pro-free-market, fundamentalist Christian pundit. Thus, the structure of the book literally maps America to Colbert's personal life, intertwining his own life with larger social issues. This technique allows the book to expose the fallacy of assuming that one life can serve as the model for a diverse democracy, while also satirizing the right's urge to imagine itself as the source of American identity.

In an example of this same line of satirical critique from *The Colbert Report*, Colbert riffed on Newt Gingrich's claim that he had cheated on his wife because he felt passionately about his country. Colbert (in-character) suggests that this makes perfect sense, since "patriotism takes many forms: some people join the army, some people wear a flag pin, and some people cheat on their wife while she is in the hospital with cancer."[140] He goes on: "Who can blame these guys for getting a little randy. Just looking at America's purple mountain's majesty can make my rocket red glare. So with this patriotic defense of his inappropriate behavior, Newt is just saying that all he ever wanted to do was screw America. And if we elect him, he will keep that promise." In one short bit, Colbert was able to connect the right's idea that they are the quintessential patriots and the sources of its best values to the reality that their hypocritical policies and practices "screw America."

In another example, Colbert satirized Glenn Beck's rally on August 28, 2010, which happened to be on the anniversary of Martin Luther King's "I Have a Dream" speech. After showing clips where Beck explains that he is not trying to be King, and that, for instance, he will speak "several steps lower down" than where King stood, Colbert then shows clips of Beck projecting the impact of his speech: "It's going to provide a shock wave to this nation. Something miraculous is going to happen...This event at the Lincoln Memorial—it's a defibrillator to the heart of America."[141] Colbert responds by showing great enthusiasm for following Beck's every word, saying that he is ready: "And what is the truth that you are asking all of America to gather at your feet to hear?" Next we see a clip of Beck shouting at the camera "Two plus two equals four." Colbert responds by just staring at the screen, looking disappointed, and then telling viewers that, in that case, he plans on going to the Emmys. Colbert effectively satirized the absurdity with which pundits like Beck hijack icons of American identity like Martin Luther King, attempting to refashion them in their own image. He gets at the way that right-wing patriotism is often indistinguishable from religious fervor, and he powerfully points out that such rhetoric is all hype, no substance.

If one of Colbert's goals is to satirically and exaggeratedly equate himself with America so that he can comment on the problematic way that concept serves as the central tenet for all right-wing pundits and politicians, another major goal is to critique the United States, calling attention to practices that contrast its ideals. This critique generally takes two tacks: the first, analyzed in the section above, relates to the problem of democratic participation and the marginalization of major social voices within the U.S. landscape; the second relates to American exceptionalism. Colbert points to U.S. arrogance in his chapter on "Religion," where he summarizes the "win-loss record of the Judeo-Christian God." His summary on the "Revolutionary War" reads: "Sorry, Great Britain, but if you go up against 'One nation, under God,' you're going to get your ass handed to you *twice* as hard. (Historico-linguistical note: At this point, 'God' became synonymous with 'America')."[142] He then explains that God didn't lose the war in Vietnam; it was the Democratic

Congress's fault since they refused to fund God's war. "He may be omnipotent, but he's not made of money."[143]

Critique of U.S. imperialism is also a common theme on *The Colbert Report*, appearing frequently, for instance, in debates about the Iraq War in "Formidable Opponent" segments and during interviews. He has also done a lot of work to draw attention to the ongoing war in Iraq. These efforts are best exemplified by the series of shows he shot from Baghdad and his guest-edited issue of *Newsweek* dedicated to the war. His entire show on September 8, 2010, focused on returning vets and was ironically called "Been There, Won That." He shot his introduction that night from a tank, popping out of different hatches and ending by shooting a letter "C" into the side of the building. His first line was "Tonight, the Iraq War is over; media, now you have an excuse for not covering it."[144] As this show demonstrates, Colbert's coverage of the war has balanced a concern for the soldiers with a constant critique of the way that the war has been handled.

In the midst of all of this hyper-American parody—from the set, to the opening words, to his book, to his short-lived run for president, to his Ben & Jerry's ice-cream flavor "Stephen's Americone Dream"— we find the Colbert Nation. As Colbert recounts, the concept of the Colbert Nation was originally a fictitious ploy to parody the sort of fan loyalty encouraged by other pundits. But shortly after the first show, fans created a Colbert Nation webpage, which eventually migrated to a hosted site under the Comedy Central domain. Colbert explained the process in an interview with Neil Strauss for *Rolling Stone*:

> *It's interesting how by joking about the Colbert Nation, you made it exist.*
> Yeah, they want in on the fun. That was something we didn't expect, because we joked about the Colbert Nation and then we said, "Oh shit, it's real." That's an interesting thing, and that's another improvisational aspect—that discovery is better than invention. We invented the Colbert Nation, but then we discovered it was real. We didn't make it happen, they self-organized it. I love that relationship.[145]

The Colbert Nation is both a metaphor for pundit fans and an actually existing active fan base that takes seriously Colbert's call to wrest patriotism back from the domain of the right. As a concept, it is multilayered—simultaneously parody and reality. When it functions as a metaphor for pundit fans, it mocks the idea that one man can stand for the nation and determine what it means to be a patriot. When it functions as a counter to that metaphor, it offers viewers an opportunity to envision an-other America, one which defines patriotism as a

Photo 4.13   Colbert directs fans to the Colbert Nation website.

commitment to democratic ideals rather than a quasi-religious fanaticism. *The Colbert Report* teaches viewers that we are in a battle over who gets to define the nation and who gets to represent it. It shows the extent to which the right has monopolized the narrative of the nation and asks the Colbert Nation to work to offer another alternative.

The Public Sphere Can Be Fun

"The greatest enemy of authority is contempt, and the surest way to undermine it is laughter."

—Hannah Arendt[146]

When compared to most cable satirist shows, *The Colbert Report* is noteworthy for its efforts to attract a younger audience. It attempts to appeal to youth culture via green-screen challenges posted on YouTube, the use of Wikipedia and other Internet venues, cartoon segments, and other gimmicks like Colbert's dance-off with Korean pop-icon Rain. These fun segments are often simply silly, but they must be considered part of a larger project that aims to suggest to younger viewers that political engagement can be "fun." This section analyzes how *The Colbert Report* engages young viewers by linking entertainment with political empowerment. As I've explained throughout this book, a key aspect of Colbert's satire is his interest in emphasizing democracy's dependence on a public sphere: i.e., a collective space through which social equality can be nourished via active and engaged civic participation and debate of important issues. At a time when U.S. youth is exceptionally disenfranchised, Colbert has used his program to suggest that collectives do have power, even if that power is evidenced by voting to name a bridge in Hungary after Colbert.

Colbert has used his satire of the United States' decrepit public sphere, especially with regard to elected representatives who are mocked on segments like "Better Know a District," to suggest that citizens have more power than they recognize and to underscore the degree to which the public has lost interest in the political process. The power of the public begins when it demands more from its representatives, but it also depends on civic commitment, on an active and engaged population that is willing to participate in public debate in order to strengthen democracy. By aiming much of his program at youth culture, and by repeatedly using ploys to force his audience to recognize their collective power, Colbert has stressed that the public sphere can be fun as well as politically powerful. This is exemplified by his efforts to mobilize fans to get him on the ballot for president in South Carolina and then later when he asked fans to lobby for him as a debate moderator. And yet, by cloaking these activities in satire, Colbert's political critique runs the risk of simply seeming frivolous, more entertainment than activism. What *The Colbert Report* teaches us, though, is that the opposition between entertainment and political debate no longer holds in a media-saturated society where viewers learn more of their news from blogs and cable comedy than from newspapers. Thus, I close this chapter by arguing that youth-oriented political satire offers one of the most powerful ways of reinvigorating the public sphere.

The evidence of the connection between Colbert and a youthful audience abounds. Segment after segment is aimed at a young audience. In 2008, a Pew Research Center for the People & the Press study found that both *The Colbert Report* and *The Daily Show* attracted a youthful audience.[147] The study found that "the audiences for radio and cable talk shows tend to be dominated by older Americans, with two notable exceptions—the Colbert Report and the Daily Show. Fully 43% of Colbert's regular viewers are younger than 30, as are 42% of Stewart's regular viewers. That is roughly double the proportion of people younger than 30 in the general public (21%)."[148] While only 57 percent of the population is below 50, 77 percent of *The Colbert Report* viewers are under 50. Two years later, the Pew Research Center conducted another poll and found that the trend of attracting a youthful audience had continued.[149] They summarized the results of their survey as follows: "Most of those who regularly watch O'Reilly (63%) and Hannity (65%) are 50 or older; 44% of the public is 50 or older. By contrast, *The Daily Show* and *Colbert Report* have the youngest audiences of any outlet included in the survey. Large majorities of those who say they regularly watch *The Colbert Report* (80%) and *The Daily Show* (74%) are younger than 50; 55% of public is 18 to 49."[150]

These results indicate that the target audience for Colbert's show is under 50, and while that is the most lucrative demographic for cable shows, I would argue that *The Colbert Report* and *The Daily Show* also target this age range because of the ability of this segment of the population to make an impact in the public sphere. And one of the key ways that *The Colbert Report* attracts young viewers is by being fun and by including segments that are hip, up-to-date, and in touch with the lives of a young audience. To do this, Colbert includes lots of references to pop culture. Recall that his first green-screen challenge was modeled on the "Star Wars Kid" video meme. He appeals to a youthful audience by engaging bands like The Decemberists and Coldplay, by having a cartoon sci-fi series with an animated version of himself as Tek Jensen, by doing silly segments like Colbert's "Ballz for Kidz," and more.

The appeal to youth culture goes well beyond the segments on the show, however. Colbert has made his show more interactive with

Photo 4.14 In a rare shot that shows Colbert with his audience, we get a glimpse of the young demographic that attends the live taping of his show.

viewers in two ways. First, he includes pieces that ask his viewers to do something. There are two types of these interactions: he asks viewers to compete to create content, which may or may not air on the show (green-screen challenges, portrait alterations, etc.), and he asks viewers to do something, usually to vote for him in some naming competition. An example of this second instance that doesn't simply ask viewers to promote his ego, though, was his call to viewers to donate to the Red Cross to help victims of the Japanese tsunami. He also encouraged viewers to contribute to Donors Choose, ramping up this effort with a fun exchange with Jimmy Fallon that led him to appear on Fallon's show and sing a pop song if Fallon's viewers would contribute to the cause as well.

Then, in addition to segments that offer viewers fun ways to interact with the show, the show is not limited to a nightly block on cable television. It has a complex Colbert Nation blog website, where fans post comments in threads, upload images, and engage in a variety of interactive communications. In addition, the show sponsors a Facebook page, Colbert is a regular tweeter on Twitter, and *The Colbert Report* is connected to a series of iPhone applications. Fans can get automated emails and text messages, post on the Colbert Nation blog, start conversation threads on the Facebook site, and follow Colbert on Twitter. And that doesn't even include all the fan-driven media (websites, blogs, tweets, social media) connected to the show. It's worth remembering that one of the principal sites that circulated the video of Colbert's performance at the White House Correspondents' Association Dinner was the website: ThankYouStephenColbert.org. This site, created by a fan, had a huge impact on the circulation of the video of that event. As I explained in chapter 1, fans played a huge role in drawing public and media attention to Colbert's performance.

Attracting young viewers and finding evidence of their energetic fandom does not necessarily lead, however, to the conclusion that *The Colbert Report* helps young viewers envision themselves as part of a democratic public sphere. Even though Bonnie R., the winner of the first green-screen challenge, stated that winning made her "feel empowered," it is not entirely clear what sort of empowerment results from making a silly video of Colbert that gets national attention.[151] Thus, understanding the show's relationship to a youth-driven public sphere first requires attention to the state of youth culture today. To explore this issue, we need to return to the idea of the public sphere explained in detail in chapter 2 and to understand the connection between youth and the public sphere in the contemporary moment.

As Henry Giroux explains in *Youth in a Suspect Society,* the current era of neoliberalism has converted the nation's young from promise and potential to suspect and commodity. In today's context of militarized schools and zero tolerance, youth become subject to a whole host of punitive measures "governing them through a logic of punishment, surveillance, and control."[152] The introductory chapter to Giroux's book, "Expendable Futures: Youth and Democracy at Risk," charts the direct link between the decline of democratic values required by neoliberal demands for market sovereignty and the rise in the criminalization and commodification of youth. He shows how rising malnutrition, declining healthcare, burgeoning juvenile prison populations, and militarized schools link to a media culture that tends to present youth as either stupid or dangerous. Giroux offers example after example of representations of young people in the media that depict them as "dangerous, unstable, or simply without merit."[153] He explains that these depictions have led to the removal of youth from "the register of public concern, civic commitment, and ethical responsibility;" they are now considered a "bad social investment," lingering only in the public imagination as "dim-witted, if not dangerous, ingrates unworthy of compassion and so justifiably relegated to the civic rubbish pile."[154]

Young people are perceived as having attention spans that last only slightly longer than a nanosecond. They are perceived as selfish and unfocused. If they write, it is a post on Facebook. If they read, it is a short inane blog. The media doesn't only portray youth as stupid and lazy and threatening, but the growth in reality TV and the rise in programs that highlight the basest human qualities only serve to further depict a society incapable of civic commitment and democratic action. In addition, social media constructs an egocentric, frivolous space of human interaction that contrasts any sense of a politically engaged public sphere.

But there is another side to the story of contemporary youth culture, and it is evident on *The Colbert Report.* Colbert may play with the Colbert Nation and he may harness his star power in the cult of his personality, but there is little doubt that *The Colbert Report* offers a different view of youth culture and its prospects for democratic action. Through its association with many of the media forms that most connect to young people—blogs, tweets, YouTube, chats, Facebook, phone apps—*The Colbert Report* gives viewers an opportunity to interact with these media forms in a way that supports the development of a public sphere. And as I've described throughout this book, it does so through the art and fun of satire.

Without doubt, the blogosphere has a complex connection to the distribution of meaningful information to the public, but there is little question that the blogosphere has also served as a corrective to mainstream news media that presents spectacle under the guise of news. Similarly, it would be hard to make the case that Facebook is the future of the public sphere, since so much of its content exhibits narcissism and mindless superficiality. These forms of media, though, signal a new era in media, entertainment, and democratic engagement—one which is always ambiguous, offering both possibility and risk for the public sphere. As Liesbet van Zoonen explains in *Entertaining the Citizen,* it is no longer possible to separate entertainment from politics. She points out that there are a few common views on the ties between entertainment society and politics, most of which fail to grasp the current reality of entertainment-saturated political communication. One common view is nostalgia for a time when these realms were separate; another is denunciation of the ways that politics has become spectacle. These positions, however tempting, are out of date. Vilification of the connections between entertainment and politics misses the reality that these ties have only intensified since the 1960s and the growth of television culture. Celebration is not in order either, she claims, since not all forms of entertaining politics are created equal.[155] What she suggests is that (1) the intersection between entertainment and politics is irreversible, and that (2) determining whether the connection is damaging to citizenship or potentially productive requires case-by-case consideration.

An additional consideration, as mentioned above, is that youth today are especially disenfranchised from a sense of civic engagement. Thus, when Bonnie R. says that winning the green-screen challenge makes her feel empowered, perhaps such a sense of public impact does, in fact, have a larger effect on her sense of civic agency. How can we tell the difference between frivolous youth culture and one with potentially productive effects for a vibrant public sphere? Such differences are not easy to measure, but I would suggest that Colbert actually offers viewers a lesson in determining the differences on his show. Clearly, his show is meant to be a lot of fun, and it is not only interested in creating political impact. It also is an extremely effective example of politically progressive media. Colbert navigates these poles by offering viewers critical examples of the difference between fun for fun's sake, politically purposeful fun, and deceptive misinformation.

An excellent example of this distinction came the night when Colbert introduced his neologism *wikiality* on July 31, 2006. The piece began with Colbert telling fans that he had gone to Wikipedia, since it was such a good source of information about his show,

Photo 4.15   Colbert changes a Wikipedia site while he explains his theory of "wikiality."

to check it to find out whether his preferred term for Oregon was "California's Canada or Washington's Mexico." He went on to explain that he loves Wikipedia since any "site that's got a longer entry on 'truthiness' than it has on 'Lutherans' has its priorities straight."[156] After checking the site, he finds that he has used both terms. Not satisfied, he decides to log in and change the history of what he has called Oregon, since anyone can change anything on Wikipedia. He then explains to his viewers a bit about how Wikipedia works.

Wikipedia is a web-based, free-content encyclopedia project based on an openly editable model that allows users to change and update content. Many of its encyclopedia entries can be immediately changed, and in all cases, users can suggest changes that will be posted after passing a review. As Wikipedia explains on its own page:

> People of all ages, cultures and backgrounds can add or edit article prose, references, images and other media here. What is contributed is more important than the expertise or qualifications of the contributor. What will remain depends upon whether it fits within Wikipedia's policies, including being verifiable against a published reliable source, so excluding editors' opinions and beliefs and unreviewed research, and is free of copyright restrictions and contentious material about living people. Contributions cannot damage Wikipedia because the software allows easy reversal of mistakes and many experienced

editors are watching to help and ensure that edits are cumulative improvements. Begin by simply clicking the *edit* link at the top of any editable page![157]

Despite the fact that Wikipedia claims that content is subject to review and to being verifiable, Colbert keys into the idea that all that is needed is for enough users to agree an idea to become a fact. The problem with this, Colbert satirically suggests, is that truth can become subject to mob mentalities, much in the same way that the culture of punditry has repeatedly influenced public perceptions of the truth.

Colbert makes this point by satirically taking an extreme position. He tells his viewers that he is no fan of reality (while the bullet point reads "It has a Liberal bias"). He then invokes much of his critique of current perceptions of the truth that he referenced in his word segment on *truthiness*. "We should apply these principles to all information. All we need to do is to convince a majority of people that some factoid is true. For instance, that Africa has more elephants today than it did ten years ago." Colbert points out that that "truth" might create trouble for environmentalists. His real goal, though, is to critique the way that the Bush government created false truths that led us to war in Iraq: He calls them masters at "information

Photo 4.16 Colbert tells viewers he is "no fan of reality."

management": "While they've admitted that Saddam did not have weapons of mass destruction, they also insinuated he *did* have weapons of mass destruction. Insinuations that have been repeated over and over again on cable news for the past three and a half years. And now the result is 18 months ago only 36% of Americans believed it, but 50% of Americans believe it now." Colbert describes this ironically as "bringing democracy to knowledge," and he references Fox News and what he dubs the "24,000-hour news cycle" as accomplices in this production of truthiness.

This is the aspect of Colbert's definition of wikiality that has most often been analyzed. This version of wikiality exemplifies Colbert's critique of relativist truth that has no basis in evidence, and, without question, it is a central feature of the term's meaning. But I would further suggest that what makes the term so creatively powerful is that it has another equally potent layer of meaning. The second layer of meaning suggests the power of the public to challenge existing mainstream views. So, if wikiality, on the one hand, means an abusive and authoritative imposition of relativist truth, then, on the other, it suggests the power of a collective to challenge that claim to truth. As the piece ends, Colbert shifts gears and explains the second layer of meaning: "If you go against what the majority of people perceive to be reality, you're the one who's crazy. Nation, it's time we use the power of our numbers for a real Internet revolution. We're going to stampede across the web like that giant horde of elephants in Africa. In fact, that's where we can start. Find the page on elephants on Wikipedia and create an entry that says the number of elephants has tripled in the last six months... Together we can create a reality that we can all agree on—the reality we just agreed on." Here Colbert suggests that his viewers have the power to change the truth regime within which they live.

The brilliance of the definition of *wikiality* is that it has two possible reference points to the idea of agreeing together on reality: In one instance, the public has been dictated a false reality, but they have passively consumed it and agreed to it. In the second version—the one he advocates as he calls on viewers to stampede the Internet—is the idea that if we work together, we can create a different, more accurate, more verifiable reality. What Colbert artfully shows is that wikiality always remains the tension point in democracy—the masses can be deceived or they can be actively engaged. What makes the difference? A vibrant public sphere and a tradition of dialogue, debate, and civic commitment. The "entries," just like the public sphere itself, can be created by an active and informed citizenry or by a manipulative power structure that caters to corporate influence and political blocs.

After the segment, Wikipedia had to shut down the site for elephants since so many fans had logged on to make the change that Colbert suggested. The ploy—as seemingly silly as it was—worked. Viewers followed Colbert's charge, logged on to their computers and changed an encyclopedia entry. It was fun, but it also directly had the ability to teach viewers a lesson in civic activity. Not only can we question the information that we are fed by the government and media, but in the Internet age we can also do small things that can make a difference and that can challenge the status quo. Wikipedia offers a metaphor for democracy: it is a resource that can be manipulated by lobbyists and corporations, but it is also a public sphere open to user participation. The first step in challenging the hegemony of the power elite in a sphere like Wikipedia is to be active. Colbert's irony, though, teaches viewers that for such a plan to work, they must do more than simply follow his instructions; they have to become active citizens themselves. As Colbert explained when asked about the power of the Colbert Nation for an interview with *Rolling Stone,* he doesn't always know what his fan base will do with his suggestions. And he doesn't want to: "Our actions plant seeds, and then we'll go, 'Oh look, someone responded to that in a way we hadn't intended, let's acknowledge that.' Because the game is in the acknowledgement of their acceptance—that's what's improvisational about it. You make initiations beyond even your knowledge of them, because if you have the knowledge of all of your initiations, you're not initiating, you're writing."[158] Thus, Colbert is attempting to instigate, initiate, and spark an active citizenry that combines activism and critical reflection with a healthy dose of fun.

This call to action has special meaning when aimed at a younger audience, and it marks a shift away from the skeptical and suspicious attitude about young citizens so common in much mainstream media. Colbert's focus on appealing and interacting with young people was reflected in Barak Obama's own treatment of young people in his 2008 campaign. Perhaps coincidentally, perhaps not, it turns out that the Obama campaign was the first major campaign to use social media effectively to connect with the nation's youth, both voting age and younger, to inspire them to be engaged with the election process. And while analysis of the connections between Colbert's and Obama's ability to reach out to the younger sectors of the nation is beyond the scope of the space I have here, it is worth noting that they both suggest that being actively involved in shaping the public sphere should be both fun and socially significant.

Without question, Colbert's satire has served as model for how to reach out to younger audiences. *The Colbert Report* has been creative in thinking of ways to get the audience actively involved creating content linked to the show. These activities succeed in showing viewers the sort of public power they wield—power that can be used frivolously to alter entries about elephants or to create videos of Colbert fighting aliens as well as power that can have deep social relevance and can demand more from public institutions. The art of his comedy combines with the punch of his satire to further show a young audience that we can all be like Colbert. It is not necessary to choose between entertainment and politics. The Colbert Nation can have fun and can make a difference at the same time. And so can you!

5

AMUSING OURSELVES TO ACTIVISM?

"The 'Save Our Starbucks' campaign is the kind of grass-roots activism Stephen likes—the kind that helps sprawling corporate behemoths."[1]

On July 23, 2008, Colbert presented his audience with a crisis that needed their attention. Over 600 Starbucks stores nationwide were about to close. Colbert asked fans to imagine the drastic consequences to such closings when they might have to walk more than two blocks to get a latte. He then urged viewers to sign the "SOS: Save Our Starbucks" petition and explained that this grass-roots campaign had helped him avoid signing a much less important petition to stop the genocide in Darfur. How could Darfur compare with the closing of Starbucks? Colbert exclaimed: "They don't make lattes in Darfur!"[2] By mocking the so-called Starbucks activists, Colbert made a number of crucial points. First, activism is possible and relatively easy, and second, it is worth reflecting on the sort of causes that deserve activism. What does it mean when U.S. citizens are willing to petition to save a Starbucks but not to save Darfur?

This last, concluding chapter asks what happens when counter-culture goes mainstream. What are the risks of claiming satire TV as a primary source of critical public pedagogy? How can a critique of the media take place via mainstream media? The arguments here build on Neil Postman's analysis of television from *Amusing Ourselves to Death*, where he suggests that the fundamentally passive form of television makes it incompatible with critical reflection. Agreeing with Postman's assessment of the real limits implied by television's commercialized, episodic, and passive cultural form, I would like to argue that contemporary satire television, especially that of Colbert, works to undermine some of those very same flaws. After surveying Postman's claims and situating them in the current era of post-network television, I return to the tricky question of whether we can amuse ourselves to activism. I survey a few studies of *The Colbert*

Report that have tried to determine the actual impact it has on viewers, which allows me to ask how one might measure the success of satire TV. This last chapter weighs the strengths and weaknesses of this form of public culture especially with regard to its potential to encourage passive viewers to become active citizens.

Postman's *Amusing Ourselves to Death* focuses on how television influences the public's ability to practice rational decision-making. Rephrasing Marshall McLuhan's famous dictum that the "medium is the message" to the "medium is a metaphor," Postman claimed that the medium creates the frames through which we can see the world: "Whether we are experiencing the world through the lens of speech or the printed word or the television camera, our media-metaphors classify the world for us, sequence it, frame it, enlarge it, reduce it, color it, argue a case for what the world is like."[3] The main argument of Postman's book is that "form excludes content," by which he means that each medium can only sustain particular types of ideas. He suggests that print media is the ideal form to coax the content of rational argument whereas the medium of television makes rational thinking impossible. Television is a visual form that projects images rapidly and for the sake of commercially lucrative entertainment. Thus, when televised, the "news of the day" becomes nothing more than a packaged commodity. Postman explains, "on television, discourse is conducted largely through visual imagery, which is to say that television gives us a conversation in images, not words. The emergence of the image-manager in the political arena and the concomitant decline of the speech writer attest to the fact that television demands a different kind of content from other media. You cannot do political philosophy on television. Its form works against the content."[4] One of Postman's key arguments is that reading is inherently interactive and dialectical, since the reader must engage the use of reason to make sense of the words on the page. Television, in contrast, only asks viewers to passively consume content. From Postman's view, television is not a medium suited for the communication of news, much less of critical satire. Nothing about it enables critical thinking or encourages civic engagement. If we think of Colbert's comments about the way that cable news presents the public with information, it would be fair to assume that he would agree with much of Postman's assertions. Colbert ironically referenced the unlikely link between television and activism on his first show, when he told viewers: "You're doing something right now. You're watching TV."[5] Satirical statements like this leave little doubt that Colbert hopes to remind his audience that watching TV is not akin to being an activist.

The main point of distinction between Postman's views and Colbert's, however, would have to be that television as a medium today is substantially different than it was in the 1980s. Programs like *The Colbert Report* differ from the television analyzed by Postman in a number of ways. First of all, television today is more complex and mediated than it was at the time of Postman's assessments. Now it is always linked to other more active forms of media, like the Internet (via official sites, blogs, fan sites, Facebook pages, etc.), that allow viewers to engage with the programs they watch in ways not previously possible. In addition, the post-network era of television further signals a shift in the medium, since viewers have far more choice than before. Perhaps more importantly, television and other forms of screen culture are increasingly the means through which citizens acquire information about political issues. The centrality of the medium demands, then, a reconsideration of its potential for encouraging critical reflection. These observations become even more complicated when we speak of satire TV, because it is a television form that calls into question mass-mediated sources of public information. And since 9/11, satire TV has been a particularly potent form of public critique.

Postman's book was published in 1985, when the U.S. president, Ronald Reagan, had been a movie star and when the top television shows were *Dynasty* and *Dallas*. The Internet had yet to become a major public medium, and we were just beginning to enter the cable age. As explained in chapter 2, *The Colbert Report* is an example of post-network television. To watch *The Colbert Report,* it is not even necessary to own a television. Shows are not simply screened in their entirety on the Internet. They are posted in short segments that range from 30 seconds to several minutes, which allows users to view content in the order they desire. The Colbert Nation website, hosted by Comedy Central, tags all *The Colbert Show* clips and cross-references them so that viewers can watch, for instance, a segment on Sarah Palin, then see others on the same topic. In contrast to television, the flow of information is at the user's discretion. On the same site, a fan forum allows conversation across a range of Colbert-related topics. An off-topic section, called "Politics in General," allows users to post on a wide range of political topics, often with the goal of encouraging engagement (votes, petition signing, word spreading, debate) from other users.

While the million or more viewers who watch *The Colbert Report* on television still outnumber the viewers who access his clips online, Geoffrey Baym argues that new media forms like the Internet are not driven by mass appeal but rather by "deep engagement among a narrow and highly committed subset of people."[6] The Internet, due to its presentation of information through images, text, and hypertext, further allows linkages "to wider networks of information and conversation."[7] The point is that *The Colbert Report* is not simply a television show; it is part of a networked media environment. As such, if we are to follow Postman's arguments above, it exists in a new medium that produces new opportunities for viewer interaction. Neither wholly dominated by the sort of rational deliberation Postman associates with reading, nor by the frivolous, passive, and entertainment-oriented medium of commercial television, programs like *The Colbert Report* exist in a new hybrid space that offers both opportunities and risks for the development of an active and informed citizenry.

Of course the Internet is not uniformly a space of activism or user interaction, and much of what is available on the Internet is as mindless and inane as what is found on cable television. As Nicolas Carr argued in his article for *The Atlantic* "Is Google Making Us Stupid?": "Thanks to the ubiquity of text on the Internet, not to mention the popularity of text-messaging on cell phones, we may well be reading more today than we did in the 1970s or 1980s, when television was our medium of choice. But it's a different kind of reading, and behind it lies a different kind of thinking—perhaps even a new sense of the self."[8] Carr's main argument is that the way that users consume information on the Internet (his article does not only focus on Google) might have detrimental effects on cognition. Because most of the material consumed on the Internet comes in snippets and flashes, it discourages more reflective and sustained patterns of reading, thereby diminishing our capacity for concentration and contemplation. In addition, much of the material consumed is far removed from the sort of information useful to educating a citizenry. Carr claims that he sees "within us all . . . the replacement of complex inner density with a new kind of self—evolving under the pressure of information overload and the technology of the 'instantly available.'"[9] There are two problems, then, with Internet reading: its short, easily digestible form, and its content, which too often is simply superficial and base.

Colbert has made a similar point via his own in-character views on blogging: "The vast majority of bloggers out there are responsible correspondents doing fine work in niche reporting fields like *Gilmore Girls* fan fiction, or cute things their cats do, or photoshopped images of the *Gilmore Girls* as cats. That's great. Where I draw the line is with these attack-bloggers. Just someone with a computer who gathers, collates, and publishes accurate information that is then read by the general public. They have no credibility. All they have is facts. Spare me."[10] In contrast to Carr, who sees the Internet as nothing more than a threat to critical thinking, Colbert suggests a key nuance: there is a huge difference between frivolous, silly blogs and ones that offer meaningful alternatives to the information offered on mainstream news outlets. A key feature of the Internet is that it is a medium that allows users the opportunity to create content that can have a public impact. Of course, corporate-sponsored sites pop up higher in Google searches. But it is now possible for citizens to create sites that challenge those sources of information. Internet sites like Media Matters for America or Crooks and Liars regularly offer alternatives to mainstream news sources. Before the Internet, the reach of such alternative information was severely limited.

Colbert's satire is deeply committed to the idea that it is possible to challenge the misinformation and spectacle of mainstream news through alternative media. His work takes as a given the fact that most of the nation gets its information from cable news and from the Internet. The problem is that the bulk of this information does not help citizens make sense of the major issues facing the nation. Instead of turning away from entertainment and spectacle, he uses it to satirize the role of entertainment and spectacle in politics and news reporting. By exaggerating the connection between entertainment and politics, *The Colbert Report* uses comedy to expose the extent to which entertainment has infected news reporting. This mixing of comedy and news, though, sometimes leads to confusion when shows like *The Colbert Report* and *The Daily Show* are taken as straight news. What Colbert and Jon Stewart have had to explain repeatedly is that these are actually comedy shows, not news shows. Thus, in their line of work, entertainment is not only appropriate, it remains fundamental.

But, perhaps more importantly, entertaining television and other forms of screen culture are increasingly the means through which citizens acquire information about political issues. The centrality of screen culture and its bias toward commercially successful entertainment demands a reconsideration of its potential for encouraging political action. It no longer makes sense to yearn for an entertainment–free public sphere, for a time when citizens were more likely to recall the words of a president's speech than to recognize that a major political figure has changed his hairstyle. Those days long ended with the first televised presidential-candidate debates. Liesbet van Zoonen makes this point in *Entertaining the Citizen*. Her argument is that, rather than wallow in nostalgia for a bygone era when print news could compete with television, we must recognize the extent that new media forms have radically altered the means by which citizens become informed about current events and political issues.

She argues that entertainment may be pervasive, but it is not all created equal: blanket arguments about the evils of TV news or the benefits of blogs are inadequate since case-by-case studies are needed. According to van Zoonen: "Entertainment in politics comes in various formats and qualities that need to be analyzed in their particular contexts, with their particular features and their particular effects on the democratic project, before they can be denounced, cheered, or blissfully ignored. Only by such situated analyses will we know whether, when, and how entertainment functions to *entertain the citizen* in the triple sense of the word: does entertainment provide a context to contemplate the concept of citizenship, does it provide an environment in which citizenship can flourish, and does it make citizenship pleasurable?"[11] One of the biggest problems, she argues, is the notion that politics must be serious and must not be tainted by entertainment, since such a position strips politics from everyday life. Separating it from entertainment culture, then, means that it becomes even less accessible and less meaningful to a public that spends more and more time consuming entertainment media. If we are going to reach citizens today, she claims, then we must use entertainment.

Within this hybrid space, which combines citizenship with entertainment and flows across television through the Internet and into peer-to-peer media, *The Colbert Report* stands as an exemplary case of the effective crossing and mixing of these arenas. As I've argued throughout this book, what makes *The Colbert Report* and the Colbert persona different is their unique form of satire. Not only is Colbert's comedy a highly complex media form that offers users many ways to engage with content, but it does this through satire of the media. It constantly calls attention to the dangerous ways that the public is fed false, damaging, and misleading information that runs the risk of negatively influencing public opinion. Quite simply, the Colbert persona has created a media spectacle that exposes the problems with media spectacles. The layering of irony, parody, farce, and satire on the show means that the audience always receives multiple registers of information. Navigating those multiple layers creates a highly productive critical space for the viewer, since the viewer must always work to make sense of the show's messages and metaphors.

The Colbert Report is noteworthy for its hybrid media form and its ability to encourage fans to act. Shortly after the show first aired, Rachel Sklar, writing for *The Huffington Post,* highlighted the way that the show was "fast becoming the leader in web-TV integration."

She writes: "The people behind 'The Colbert Report' may be the smartest minds in television: While everyone else frets about YouTube, web TV, and platform integration Stephen Colbert & Co are already galvanizing the online to action and integrating fan content into the show, to hilarious effect. It is, in a word, freaking brilliant."[12] She then lists some of the various ways that he has encouraged viewers to take action, creating videos, entering his name in polls, and more. At the time of her writing, most viewer interaction with the show had still been more on the silly rather than the serious side—naming a Hungarian bridge after Colbert does not necessarily directly link to civic engagement. Since then, Colbert has also had viewers contribute to DonorsChoose.org, sign petitions for his presidential candidacy, help victims of the Japanese tsunami, attend a rally on the National Mall, and asked viewers to "Make McCain exciting" by editing one of his dry-speech appearances.

A recent example of *The Colbert Report*'s use of a hybrid media space that uses satire and fun to provoke activism took place as I was finalizing this manuscript. It was too perfect an example of this process to leave out. The story begins with Senator Jon Kyl, a Republican from Arizona, stating during the budget debates held on April 11, 2011, that 90 percent of Planned Parenthood activities are abortions. *Politifact* reported that the actual figure is 3 percent.[13] When Colbert covered the story that night, he described Kyl's statement as "rounding up to the nearest ninety."[14] He then showed a CNN clip that offered astonishing proof of the culture of "truthiness" that governs U.S. politics: When asked about the 87 percent difference between Kyl's figure and the reality of Planned Parenthood's activities, Kyl's office responded that the senator's "remark was not intended to be a factual statement but rather to illustrate that Planned Parenthood, an organization that receives millions in taxpayer dollars, does subsidize abortions."[15] Colbert told viewers: "You can't call him out for being wrong, when he never intended to be right."[16] The next night Colbert highlighted Kyl's truthiness when he explained that even though the truth is that the number is only 3 percent, "ninety percent feels true, especially since thanks to Jon Kyl that number is now in the Congressional record."[17] Kyl's actions showed how politicians blatantly disregard the facts, offer misinformation as true, and then refuse to take responsibility for the damage done by their misrepresentations. Colbert used Kyl's explanation to reiterate the dangers of truthiness in U.S. politics.

But he didn't stop there. Colbert continued to have fun by explaining that he had "celebrated Jon Kyl's groundbreaking 'excuse-planation' by tweeting round-the-clock non-facts about him."[18] He then read out to viewers a couple of the tweets he had sent out, such as "Jon Kyl calls all Asians 'Neil' no matter what their name is," all of which ended with the hash tag: "#NotIntendedToBeAFactualStatement." The use of the hash tag here is crucial. For those unfamiliar to Twitter, the hash tag allows users to tag a tweet so that it is connected to others with the same tag. So, say, for instance, that your tweet is about Justin Bieber. If you use the hash tag #JustinBieber your tweet will then be visible to anyone looking for tweets with that key word. It allows those tweeting to link their tweets to others who are posting on the same topic. When Colbert created the hash tag "#NotIntendedToBeAFactualStatement" he opened a space for tweeters to follow his lead and tweet any number of statements about Kyl, all of which would then be connected through the common tag. Little did Colbert know, he had started something that would be picked up by the Colbert Nation. As he explained that night, "Well, nation, you picked this up and ran with it. Using my hash tag to tweet your own nonfacts at an unprece-tweeted rate of 46.2 posts per minute, which incidentally is the rate at which Jon Kyl catapults puppies into the sea." As he said this last part, the screen below him read: "NotIntendedToBeAFactualStatement." He then went on to read some of the tweets that his own tweeting had inspired. He put up a tweet by "bloominoctober" that said "Jon Kyl throws babies at the elderly." He ended the piece reminding viewers that if they tweet something about Jon Kyl or anyone else that they know not to be true that they should "make sure to include the hash tag #NotIntendedToBeAFactualStatement, because Jon Kyl taught us that makes it OK."

This story is an excellent example of a few of the ways that Colbert's show amuses viewers to activism. It starts with Colbert deciding that, if Kyl could say whatever he wanted in front of Congress, as long as he stipulated that it was "not intended to be a factual statement," then Colbert could say whatever he wanted about anything or anyone . . . even Jon Kyl. This is similar to what he did when he called Sarah Palin a "F—king Retard." He takes the unbelievably absurd excuses made by public figures for their misstatements and then aims them right back at them. The satire is extremely effective humor and critique at the same time. But in this example, Colbert took it a step further and launched it into another media realm where he has a huge presence. Colbert has over 2.2 million followers on Twitter, and he has posted over 1,500 tweets. He won the Golden Tweet in 2010 for the most retweeted tweet. But his use of this form of social media to attack the truthiness of Kyl created an unprecedented response. Lauren Duggan reported on Mediabistro that "According to trendistic, #NotIntendedToBeAFactualStatement was 0.13% of all tweets on Wednesday at 12AM Eastern, which means about 18,571,428 tweets and retweets containing that hash tag were sent out that hour alone."[19] Reading some of these tweets makes it clear that some are simply goofy, but the vast majority are actually satirical interventions that specifically reference right-wing rhetoric. Either way, it is hard not to credit Colbert with having had an impact on activating the public sphere when there were more than eighteen million tweets that stemmed from his tweet intervention within the space of an hour. While Twitter is a media space that has been criticized for being especially silly, this is yet another example of a way that Colbert has managed to use it for political satire while keeping it fun. Here no line exists between amusement and activism; the two activities are productively and hilariously intertwined.

As evidenced by the example above, Colbert has repeatedly offered viewers a way to combine amusement and activism. He provokes his audience, and they offer a vast array of responses, some of which Colbert and his team did not even anticipate. Baym calls this a "new and hybrid form of public voice": "professional and amateur, consumer and activist, corporate and citizen."[20] In this way, Colbert's satire refuses binaries and oppositions common to most arguments about the connections between the public sphere, the media environment, and political activism. Nevertheless, a couple of research studies have concluded that *The Colbert Report* does not lead viewers to be more critical and that, if anything, it serves to simply reinforce right-wing pundit-like thinking.

A study published in 2008 by Jody C. Baumgartner and Jonathan S. Morris concluded that "when young adults are exposed to *The Colbert Report*'s humor, they are not led to be more critical of the far right. Instead, the opposite happens."[21] They suggest that his parody of the hyper-partisan rhetoric of right-wing pundits confuses viewers who, they suggest, cannot always differentiate between the direct message (what the character of Colbert satirically says to the audience) and the indirect message (what the satire implies). Because the "true" message is implied, they argue, audiences often fail to get the joke. "In other words, the 'true message' that the satiric humorist is attempting to convey may not be the one that audiences are processing."[22] According to them, one problem is the degree to which Colbert's exaggerated rhetoric is only slightly different from that of the pundits he parodies. In contrast, their research suggests that *The*

Daily Show clarified politics for viewers and helped them feel more confident about their own political sophistication.[23] "But the mixed messages contained in Colbert's presentation create the possibility that young viewers may actually become more confused about politics."[24]

Such a study might seem to suggest that all that I have argued thus far regarding the critical impact of Colbert's work is not true; that Colbert's satire not only is not politically powerful, but that it is actually deleterious to the creation of the public sphere. The authors of the study, however, explain that there are a few pitfalls to their research design. First, the data they used came from a lab setting. Those polled in it were not regular viewers of the show and only had a short-term exposure to the program. Then, the questions they answered happened shortly after viewing, denying the participants time to reflect on what they had seen. That said, the study did point out the reality that simply viewing an episode or two of *The Colbert Report* will not necessarily enhance one's ability to critically assess the rhetoric of cable pundits.

The second study produced slightly different findings. Research conducted by Heather Lamarre, Kristen Landreville, and Michael Beam found that both liberal and conservative viewers are amused by Colbert's presentation of the news. The catch is that conservative viewers thought that Colbert was presenting a comedic view of liberal political ideologies, while liberal viewers believed that Colbert shared their political ideology. Similar to the study above, they concluded that *The Daily Show* had a better chance of encouraging critical reflection about social issues, since "Jon Stewart provides context for viewers as he interjects commentary during segments, moves in and out of character and even laughs at himself."[25] Colbert, however, does not offer the same sort of disambiguation of the ambiguous: he stays in character. They conclude that "Colbert's deadpan satire and commitment to character do not provide viewers with the external cues of source recognition that Stewart offers. Thus, Colbert creates conditions under which biased processing is likely to occur."[26] To conduct their study, the researchers showed a group of undergraduates a clip of *The Colbert Report* via the Internet, after which they were asked a series of questions. What they found was that students who had self-identified as conservative thought Colbert was conservative, too; whereas self-identified liberal students thought he was just kidding. Both groups found him equally funny. What this study suggests is that one short clip of Colbert shown out of context may be misunderstood by conservatives. It certainly proves that showing one clip of Colbert will not alter a viewer's political affiliation.

Both studies teach us that a clip of Colbert will not save the world nor will it change the political biases of the viewer. Beyond that, they teach us relatively little about the impact of the show or its role in using satire to intervene in the public sphere. They also miss the already existing evidence that Colbert has had a major influence on young viewers. A study by the Pew Research Center published on January 28, 2010, found that one thing that young people could correctly identify was that Colbert was a comedian. "About four-in-ten (41%) correctly say that Stephen Colbert is a comedian and television talk show host. This is the only question on the quiz that more people younger than 30 than older people answer correctly (49% vs. 39%)."[27] Just because they know he is a comedian does not mean, however, that they appreciate his satire. Nor does it mean that his show has led them to be active citizens.

It is worth noting that Colbert has said that his main goal is to create effective comedy, not change the world. As he explained in an interview with Charlie Rose, "If you're going for the joke and if you're going to be successful at all in comedy, you have to go for what's funny. You can't be disappointed if you actually don't change things because it can't have been your intention."[28] Both Colbert and Stewart reiterated this point during an interview with Maureen Dowd for *Rolling Stone*:

> *Dowd*: I don't understand why you always say, "I'm just a comedian," because from Shakespeare to Jonathan Swift, humor is the best way to get through to people.
>
> *Colbert*: Peter Cook was once asked if he thought that satire had a political effect. He said, "Absolutely. The greatest satire of the twentieth century was the Weimar cabaret, and they stopped Hitler in his tracks." It doesn't mean that what we do is worthless. It's hard to do, and people like it, and it's great. But it doesn't mean that it has an effect politically.
>
> *Stewart*: Or that it has an agenda of social change. We are not warriors in anyone's army. And that is not trying to be self-deprecating. I'm proud of what we do. I really like these two shows. I like making 'em. I like watching them. I'm really proud of them. But I understand their place. I don't view us as people who lead social movements.[29]

Stewart and Colbert make a key point: satire is not the same as a social movement. Politics is for politicians, and activism is for activists, just as satire is for satirists. One thing the satirist cannot do is dictate to the audience what to think or what to do. The satirist exposes farce and folly, points to public arenas that demand greater scrutiny, and mocks patterns of behavior that damage society. And successful satire is always amusing. It may not lead to belly laughs, but it is always funny in a way that allows the audience to feel like they are "in on the joke." Most importantly, it structures its performances in layers between direct and indirect meaning, asking the audience to use their critical reasoning to differentiate what the satirist says from what is actually meant. And because it asks for such patterns of thinking, it won't influence everyone the same way.

If it did influence everyone the same way, it would be brainwashing, dogma, or propaganda, not satire. If the goal is to create a space through which society can reflect on the "important issues of the day," to quote the show's description on its Facebook site, then it has to encourage questioning, analysis, and critique: it cannot offer readymade conclusions of the sort circulated on cable news programs. Its ability to comment on the media is especially complicated by the fact that it is a part of the very same media circuits. It can't solve problems and it can't tell the audience how to either. It can, in contrast, give

Photo 5.1   Colbert shown in a rare moment of reflection.

the viewer a welcome opportunity to reflect critically on the media landscape and political posturing.

So, does *The Colbert Report* amuse us into activism? There is no easy answer to this question. The majority of the show's content is a direct commentary on issues central to democracy, the public sphere, and the future of the nation. But this content comes to us through humor and satire. Clearly, much evidence suggests that it has had a major impact on young viewers and has encouraged them to engage in the public sphere. But proving a direct sphere of influence would be nearly impossible. What we do know is that Colbert's satire breaks down the opposition between fun and serious, between comedy and critique, between amusing television and politically powerful culture. We also know that Colbert's satire is founded on dispelling the power of "truthiness." Citizens need to make their own decisions about what to believe and what to advocate and what to condemn. Democracy is founded on the notion that citizens should determine how the government can best serve the nation. For citizens to exercise their civic duty, they need to be able to arrive at good decisions. *The Colbert Report* reminds viewers of the various impediments to civic deliberation that exist today. The show does not give answers, but it does use satire to help viewers critique the information we receive and the process by which we receive it. When the show first aired, the public sphere was in decline, the news media was a circus, and the government was withholding information from the public. Colbert showed us how to have fun and ask questions at the same time. *The Colbert Report* has changed the social force of satire to make it play a major role in mobilizing a young audience to rethink their role in the democratic process. In an era where entertainment is a way of life, it has shown the public that engaged citizenship can be fun. Pleasure does not have to be separate from politics. Not sure whether we can amuse ourselves to activism? Watch Colbert. Night after night, he does a show where he has a bunch of fun and raises viewer awareness of a range of major social issues. Even more, he lets his viewers in on the fun. What they do after they turn off their televisions is up to them.

NOTES

INTRODUCTION

1. George Monbiot, "How These Gibbering Numbskulls Came to Dominate Washington," *The Guardian*, October 28, 2008, http://www.guardian.co.uk/commentisfree/2008/oct/28/us-education -election-obama-bush-mccain?INTCMP=ILCNETTXT3487.
2. This context will be discussed in greater detail in chapter 2, but it is worth remembering that this was the period that marked the passage of the USA PATRIOT Act, which limited citizens' rights. It was also the era of the creation of the No Fly List, which occasionally targeted people who happened to have similar names to suspected terrorists, and of "extraordinary rendition," the CIA practice of abducting suspects and transferring them to other countries for interrogation and detention.
3. For an overview of Giroux on public pedagogy, see: *America on the Edge: Henry Giroux on Politics, Culture, and Education* (New York: Palgrave Macmillan, 2006).
4. See the Wikipedia entry on Stephen Colbert for an up-to-date list of his awards and honors.
5. Anthony Crupy, "Comedy Colbert Report Gets 1.13 Mil. Viewers," *Mediaweek*, October 18, 2005. http://www.mediaweek.com/mw /news/cabletv/article_display.jsp?vnu_content_id=1001307981.
6. Stephen Colbert, *The Colbert Report*, "The Wørd–Wikiality," broadcast on Comedy Central on July 31, 2006, http://www.colbertnation.com /the-colbert-report-videos/72347/july-31-2006/the-word--wikiality.
7. After the Obama election, Rahm Emmanuel, former White House Chief of Staff in the Obama administration, counseled Democrats not to speak to Colbert for fear that their words could also be similarly twisted.
8. Pew Research Center for the People & the Press, "Public Knowledge of Current Affairs Little Changed by News and Information Revolutions What Americans Know: 1989–2007," People-press.org, April 15, 2007, http://people-press.org/report/319/public-knowledge-of-current -affairs-little-changed-by-news-and-information-revolutions.
9. For a breakdown of the responses to his announcement see: Nick Hezel, "Colbert for President. Is He Kidding?" ABCNews.com, October 19, 2007, http://abcnews.go.com/Entertainment/story?id=3747746&page=1.

10. I'll discuss some of the precursors to these comedians in chapter 3, which focuses on satire in the United States.
11. *PostPartisan Blog*, "Colbert Turns Truthiness into Truth," blog entry by E. J. Dionne, in the *The Washington Post*, October 1, 2010, http://voices.washingtonpost.com/postpartisan/2010/10/colbert_turns_truthiness_into.html.
12. Nellie Andreeva, "Jon Stewart/Stephen Colbert Rally Draws Total Audience of Almost 3 Million," *Deadline.com*, November 1, 2010, http://www.deadline.com/2010/11/jon-stewartstephen-colbert-rally-draws-total-audience-of-almost-3-million/.
13. See Jonathan Grey, Jeffrey P. Jones and Ethan Thompson, eds. *Satire TV: Politics and Comedy in the Post-Network Era* (New York UP: New York, 2009).
14. There are a number of edited volumes that have studied Colbert's work, most of which appear as citations throughout this book. But, as of yet, there is no book by a single author dedicated entirely to the various features of his show.

1   I Stand by This Man: Colbert Speaks Truthiness to Power

1. Colbert at the White House Correspondents' Association Dinner 4/29/2006. The full text is also printed in Stephen, Colbert, *I Am America (And So Can You!)* (New York: Hachette Book Group, 2007), 218–227.
2. John Stewart referred to Colbert's performance as "balls-alicious" on a segment on is show. For text see: *BoingBoing: A Directory of Wonderful Things*, "John Stewart Praises Colbert's White House Gig," a blog entry by Corey Doctorow, May 2, 2006, http://www.boingboing.net/2006/05/02/jon-stewart-praises-.html.
3. "History of the WHCA," *White House Correspondents' Association*, http://www.whca.net/history.htm.
4. Ibid.
5. Frank Rich, "All the President's Press," *The New York Times*, April 29, 2007, http://query.nytimes.com/gst/fullpage.html?res=9F06E1D712 3EF93AA15757C0A9619C8B63&scp=4&sq=frank%20rich%20all%20 the%20president%27s%20press&st=cse.
6. White House Correspondents' Association, http://www.whca.net/history.htm.
7. Justine Schuchard Holcomb, "In the Culture of Truthiness: Comic Criticism and the Performative Politics of Stephen Colbert" (2009), *Communication Theses*, Paper 51, http://digitalarchive.gsu.edu/communication_theses/51, 80.
8. Rem Rieder, "The Party Is Over," American Journalism Association, May 3, 2006, http://www.ajr.org/article.asp?id=4110.

9. Ibid.
10. Scott McClellan, *What Happened. Inside the Bush White House and Washington's Culture of Deception* (New York: Public Affairs, 2008), 135.
11. Ibid., XIII.
12. Peter Daou, "Time to Revisit a Media Low Point (and to Heed the implicit Warning)," *Huffingtonpost.com*, April 27, 2006, http://www.huffingtonpost.com/peter-daou/time-to-revisit-a-media-1_b_19961.html.
13. Holcomb, "In the Culture of Truthiness," 83.
14. William Vitka, "Bush Lampoons Self at Press Dinner," *CBSNEWS.com*, April 29, 2006, http://www.cbsnews.com/stories/2006/04/29/national/main1561619.shtml.
15. Jacques Steinberg, "After Press Dinner, the Blogosphere Is Alive with the Sound of Colbert Chatter," *NYTimes.com*, May 3, 2006, http://www.nytimes.com/2006/05/03/arts/03colb.html?ex=1304308800&en=6586b30be2b4067c&ei=5090&partner=rssuserland&emc=rss.
16. Stephen, Colbert, *I Am America (And So Can You!)* (New York: Hachette Book Group, 2007), 218-227. 221.
17. Ibid.
18. Ibid.
19. Paul Bedard, "Skewering Comedy Skit Angers Bush and Aide," *USNews.com*, January 5, 2006, http://www.usnews.com/usnews/news/articles/060501/1whwatch.htm.
20. Associated Press, "Bush in 'Chipper' Mood at Reporters' Dinner," *msnbc.com*, April 30, 2006, http://www.msnbc.msn.com/id/12555176/ .
21. Colbert, *I Am America*, 222.
22. Ibid.
23. Ibid.
24. Ibid.
25. Ibid.
26. Ibid.
27. It is interesting that Bush cited his approval rating as 36 percent. The actual number as cited by CNN was 32 percent. See for details: Opinion Research Corporation, "Bush's Approval ratings Down to New Low," *CNN.com*, April 25, 2006, http://articles.cnn.com/2006-04-24/politics/bush.poll_1_approval-rating-opinion-research-corporation-gallup-poll?_s=PM:POLITICS.
28. Holcomb, "In the Culture of Truthiness," 94.
29. Colbert, *I Am America*, 223.
30. "George Bush and Steve Bridges at the WHCA Dinner," YouTube video, http://www.youtube.com/watch?v=BDPAUi3VPSo.
31. Geoffrey Nunberg, *Talking Right. How Conservatives Turned Liberalism into a Tax-Raising, Latte-Drinking, Sushi-Eating, Volvo-Driving, New York Times-Reading, Body-Piercing, Hollywood-Loving, Left-Wing Freak Show* (Cambridge, MA: PublicAffairs™, 2006), 34.

32. Ibid., 171.
33. Colbert, *I Am America*, 224.
34. Chris Cocoran, "A Conversation with Stephen Colbert," Institute of Politics, Harvard University, April 1, 2006, http://www.iop.harvard .edu/Multimedia-Center/All-Videos/A-Conversation-With-Steven -Colbert2.
35. Dan Eggen, "Justice Dept. Investigating Leak of NSA Wiretapping," *Washingtonpost.com*, December 31, 2005, http://www.washingtonpost .com/wp-dyn/content/article/2005/12/30/AR2005123000538 .html.
36. Colbert, *I Am America*, 224.
37. Ibid.
38. Ibid.
39. Sachs's name is misspelled as Sacks in Colbert's book.
40. Colbert ended the list mentioning Frank Rich (whom he would "bump" if the President came on his show). Rich has appeared on the show three times since Colbert's WHCA speech: 5/19/2006, 9/19/2006, and 1/19/2006.
41. Stephen Colbert, "Bob Schieffer," *The Colbert Report*, broadcast on Comedy Central on March 6, 2006, http://www.colbertnation.com /the-colbert-report-videos/59958/march-06-2006/bob-schieffer.
42. Transcript of the video available in Stephen, Colbert, "Stephen Colbert at the White House Correspondents' Dinner," Transcript, *About.com*, accessed February 15, 2010, http://politicalhumor.about.com/od /stephencolbert/a/colbertbush_4.htm.
43. Colbert, *I Am America*, 226.
44. Ibid., 227.
45. James Poniewozik, "Stephen Colbert and the Death of 'the Room,'" in *Tuned In* (blog), *Time.com*, accessed November 23, 2009, http://tunedin .blogs.time.com/2006/05/03/stephen_colbert_and_the_death/.
46. Holcomb, "In the Culture of Truthiness," 81.
47. J. K. & S. S. M, "Media Touted Bush's Routine at Correspondents' Dinner, Ignored Colbert's Skewering," *Media Matters for America*, May 1, 2006, http://mediamatters.org/research/200605010005.
48. Ibid.
49. Elisabeth Bumiller, "A New Set of Bush Twins Appears at Annual Correspondents' Dinner," *New York Times*, May 1, 2006, http:// www.nytimes.com/2006/05/01/washington/01letter.html?ex=1304 136000&en=11242248c2a671a1&ei=5090&partner=rssuserland&e mc=rss.
50. See, for instance, the response in William Vitka, "Bush Lampoons Self at Press Dinner," *CBSNEWS.com*, April 29, 2006, http://www .cbsnews.com/stories/2006/04/29/national/main1561619.shtml; and in "George Bush and Steve Bridges at the WHCA Dinner," YouTube video, http://www.youtube.com/watch?v=BDPAUi3VPSo.

51. It is worth noting that others didn't think the jokes were funny given the dire state of the nation and the disasters of his presidency.
52. Amy Argetsinger, Roxanne Roberts. "The New Bush Twins: the Double Dubya," *Washington Post,* May 2, 2006, http://www.washingtonpost.com/wp-dyn/content/article/2006/05/01/AR2006050101917.html. Of course, that certainly wasn't the case when Don Imus roasted President Clinton at the Radio/TV Correspondents Association Annual Dinner, on Thursday, March 21, 1996, leading again to controversy.
53. Stephen Spruiell, "Reporters Are Shielding Colbert Not Bush from Bad Publicity," in *Media* (blog), *National Review Online,* May 1, 2006, http://www.nationalreview.com/media-blog/37459/reporters-are-shielding-colbert-not-bush-bad-publicity/stephen-spruiell.
54. Holcomb, "In the Culture of Truthiness," 91–92.
55. Bedard, "Skewering Comedy Skit Angers Bush and Aide."
56. Ibid.
57. Ibid.
58. Jacques Steinberg, "After Press Dinner, the Blogosphere Is Alive with the Sound of Colbert Chatter."
59. Noam Cohen, "The After-Dinner Speech Remains a Favorite Dish," *NYTimes.com,* May 22, 2006, http://www.nytimes.com/2006/05/22/business/media/22colbert.html?_r=1.
60. "Stephen Colbert at the 2006 White House Correspondents' Association Dinner," *Wikipedia,* last modified March 17, 2011, http://en.wikipedia.org/wiki/Stephen_Colbert_at_the_2006_White_House_Correspondents%27_Association_Dinner.
61. Ibid.
62. Martin Kaplan, "I love Ray McGovern," *HuffingtonPost.com,* May 5, 2006, http://www.huffingtonpost.com/marty-kaplan/i-love-ray-mcgovern_b_20398.html.
63. "New York Times Runs Article on Colbert Blogstorm," *BloggersBlog,* May 3, 2006, http://www.bloggersblog.com/stephencolbert/.
64. Holcomb, "In the Culture of Truthiness," 92.
65. "New York Times Runs Article on Colbert Blogstorm," *Bloggers Blog.*
66. Ibid.
67. "Gawker Poll: Stephen Colbert Hero or Doofus?" *Gawker* (blog), May 2, 2006, http://gawker.com/#!170977/gawker-poll-stephen-colbert-hero-or-doofus.
68. Jesse, "Colbert Is A Great Patriot, Now Scientifically Proven!" *Gawker* (blog), May 3, 2006, http://gawker.com/#!171309/colbert-is-a-great-patriot-now-scientifically-proven.
69. "Blogstorm Follows Stephen Colbert's Performance," *Bloggersblog,* Last update May 5, 2006, http://www.bloggersblog.com/stephencolbert/.
70. Holcomb, "In the Culture of Truthiness," 92.
71. In an interview with Charlie Rose, Colbert suggests that he was only focused on the "room," and he also describes being quite shocked by

the responses to his speech. This contradicts the idea that he had meant for the speech to reach an audience not in the room. That said, however, Colbert knew by the time of his appearance that he had already mobilized an active fan base that would likely access the speech online. See the interview here: http://www.charlierose.com/view/interview/93.
72. Poniewozik, "Stephen Colbert and the Death of 'the Room.'"
73. Ibid.
74. Ibid.
75. Sophia Stone, "Why Is Stephen Colbert So Funny?" in *Stephen Colbert and Philosophy*, ed. Aaron Allen Schiller, (Open Court, Chicago, IL: 2009). Kindle edition.
76. "Spike Guys' Choice Awards," *Wikipedia*, last modified November 28, 2010, http://en.wikipedia.org/wiki/Spike_TV_Guys%27_Choice_Awards.
77. Colbert, *I Am America*, 228.

2   THE PUBLIC AT RISK: DISSENT AND DEMOCRACY AFTER 9/11

1. Colbert actually referenced Habermas in a monologue on his December 8, 2010, show.
2. Habermas's theories have been debated by a number of U.S. scholars. To gain entry into this debate, see: Craig Calhoun ed., *Rethinking the Public Sphere: A Contribution to the Critique of Actually Existing Democracy* (Boston, MA: MIT Press, 1993).
3. Douglas Kellner, *Media Culture: Cultural Studies, Identity and Politics Between the Modern and the Postmodern*, (London: Routledge, 1995), 59.
4. *Ibid.*
5. Gerard A. Hauser, "Civil Society and the Principle of the Public Sphere." *Philosophy & Rhetoric*. 31, no. 1 (1998): 19–40. p. 20–21.
6. Some of my comments on neoliberalism presented here have been included in previous work. See in particular: "Neoliberalism and the Crisis of Intellectual Engagement," in *Academic Freedom in the Post-9/11 Era*, edited by Edward J. Carvalho and David B. Downing (New York: Palgrave-Macmillan, 2010), 203–213. And "The Humanities, Human Rights, and the Comparative Imagination," in *Representing Humanity in an Age of Terror*, eds., Sophia A. McClennen and Henry James Morello (West Lafayette, IN: Purdue UP, 2010), 36-57.
7. Henry A. Giroux. *The Terror of Neoliberalism: The New Authoritarianism and the Eclipse of Democracy* (Boulder, CO: Paradigm Press, 2004), xxii.
8. Ibid., 105.
9. Henry A. Giroux, *Beyond the Spectacle of Terrorism: Global Uncertainty and the Challenge of the New Media*. (Boulder, Co.: Paradigm, 2006), 1.
10. Geoffrey Nunberg, *Talking Right. How Conservatives Turned Liberalism into a Tax-Raising, Latte-Drinking, Sushi-Eating, Volvo-Driving, New*

York Times-Reading, Body-Piercing, Hollywood-Loving, Left-Wing Freak Show. (Cambridge, MA: PublicAffairs, 2006), 126.

11. Markos Moulitsas, *American Taliban: How War, Sex, Sin, and Power Bind Jihadists and the Radical Right,* (Sausalito, CA: Polipoint Press, 2010), 6.
12. Ibid.
13. Ibid.
14. Stephen Colbert, "This Week in God," *The Daily Show,* broadcast on Comedy Central on July 28, 2005, http://www.thedailyshow.com/watch/thu-july-28-2005/this-week-in-god---scientology.
15. Stephen Colbert, "The Wørd," *The Colbert Report,* broadcast on Comedy Central on September 29, 2008,http://www.colbertnation.com/the-colbert-report-videos/186456/september-29-2008/the-word---ye-of-little-faith.
16. George W. Bush, Press Conference of the President, September 15, 2006. Transcript available at http://georgewbush-whitehouse.archives.gov/news/releases/2006/09/20060915-2.html.
17. Masao Miyoshi, "Ivory Tower in Escrow," in *Learning Places: The Afterlives of Area Studies,* eds., Masao Miyoshi, H. D. Harootunian (Durham, NC: Duke University Press, 2002), 42.
18. Susan Searls Giroux, "Playing in the Dark: Racial Repression and the New Campus Crusade for Diversity," *College Literature* 33, no. 4 (2006): 93–112. p. 94.
19. Henry A. Giroux, *Hearts of Darkness: Torturing Children in the War of Terror* (Paradigm Publishers: Boulder, CO, 2010), 4.
20. Stephen Colbert, "The Wørd: Stressed Position," *The Colbert Report,* broadcast on Comedy Central on April 21, 2009, http://www.colbertnation.com/the-colbert-report-videos/225298/april-21-2009/the-word---stressed-position.
21. Ibid.
22. Lauren Berlant, "The Epistemologies of State Emotions," in *Dissent In Dangerous Times,* ed., Austin Sarat (Ann Arbor: University of Michigan Press, 2005), 46.
23. Ibid.
24. Ibid.
25. Steve Gimbel, "Formidable Opponent and the Necessity of Moral Doubt," in *Stephen Colbert and Philosophy. I Am Philosophy (and So Can You),* ed., Aaron A. Schiller (New York: Open Court, 2009). Kindle edition.
26. Ibid., 1061–1075.
27. Berlant, "The Epistemologies of State Emotions," 47.
28. Austin Sarat, *Dissent in Dangerous Times,* 6.
29. Stephen Colbert, "ThreatDown-Threat," *The Colbert Report,* broadcast on Comedy Central on December 7, 2005, http://www.colbertnation.com/the-colbert-report-videos/181308/december-07-2005/threatdown---threats.

30. Stephen Colbert, *The Colbert Report*, "March to Keep Fear Alive Announcement," broadcast on Comedy Central on September 16, 2010, http://www.colbertnation.com/the-colbert-report-videos/359382 /september-16-2010/march-to-keep-fear-alive-announcement.
31. Bill Nichols, "The Terrorist Event," in "Representing Humanity in an Age of Terror," eds., Sophia A. McClennen and Henry James Morello, 2–12, http://docs.lib.purdue.edu/clcweb/vol9/iss1/15. P. 2.
32. Ibid., 3.
33. Douglas Kellner, "9/11, Spectacles of Terror, and Media Manipulation: A Critique of Jihadist and Bush Media Politics," accessed August 22, 2009, http://gseis.ucla.edu/faculty/kellner/essays/911terrorspectaclemedia .pdf. p. 3-4.
34. Ibid., 4–5.
35. Ibid., 7.
36. Geoffrey Baym, *From Cronkite to Colbert: The Evolution of Broadcast News* (Boulder, CO: Paradigm Publishers, 2009), 34.
37. Ibid.
38. Ibid., 35.
39. Ibid., 37.
40. Ibid., 38.
41. For Colbert's thoughts on the news, see his interview at Harvard: Chris Cocoran, "A Conversation with Stephen Colbert," May 2, 2006, http://www.iop.harvard.edu/Multimedia-Center/All-Videos/A -Conversation-With-Steven-Colbert2.
42. Stephen Colbert, "Mika Brzezinski Experiences Palin Fatigue," *The Colbert Report*, broadcast on Comedy Central on January 18, 2011, http://www.colbertnation.com/the-colbert-report-videos/371413 /january-18-2011/mika-brzezinski-experiences-palin-fatigue.
43. Stephen Colbert, "Morning Shows," *The Colbert Report*, broadcast on Comedy Central on July 25, 2006, http://www.colbertnation.com /the-colbert-report-videos/182106/july-25-2006/morning-shows.
44. Dan D. Nimmo and James E. Combs, *The Political Pundits* (New York: Praeger, 1992), 12.
45. François Debrix, *Tabloid Terror: War, Culture, and Geopolitics* (New York: Routledge, 2008), 145.
46. Ibid., 145–146.
47. Stewart has said in interviews that the Stewart/Colbert rally was not a response to Beck's. However, its timing suggests otherwise.
48. Stephen Colbert, "Glenn to the Mountaintop," *The Colbert Report*, broadcast on Comedy Central on May 13, 2010, http://www.colbertnation .com/the-colbert-report-videos/309295/may-13-2010/glenn-to-the -mountaintop.
49. Stephen Colbert, "Bend It Like Beck," *The Colbert Report*, broadcast on Comedy Central on October 28, 2009, http://www.colbertnation .com/the-colbert-report-videos/252013/october-08-2009/bend-it-like -beck.

50. Ibid.
51. Baym, *From Cronkite to Colbert*, 7.
52. Ibid., 5.
53. Anthony R. DiMaggio, *Mass Media, Mass Propaganda. Examining American News in the "War on Terror,"* (Lanham, MD: Lexington Books, 2008), 148.
54. Ibid., 197.
55. Achter, "Comedy in Unfunny Times," 274.
56. Chris Raphael, "Politically Incorrect: A Eulogy," *The Big Story*. June 3, 2002. http://thebigstory.org/ov/ov-politicallyincorrect.html.
57. Ibid.
58. Ibid.
59. He later moved to HBO with a new show, *Real Time with Bill Maher*, that had a different, more politically engaged format.
60. Theodore Hamm, "Reading The Onion Seriously," *In These Times*, June 26, 2008, http://www.inthesetimes.com/article/3778/ .
61. Achter, "Comedy in Unfunny Times," 299.
62. Baym, *From Cronkite to Colbert*, 110.

3   PROUD TO BE AN AMERICAN SATIRIST

1. It is important to note that using the word *American* to refer to only the United States elides the fact that the Americas run from Canada to Argentina. I'll cover the idea of America—as an imperial force—in chapter 4 in more detail, but want to point out that my use of the word *America* simply follows Colbert's satirical use of it.
2. Colin Wells, "Satire," *The Encyclopedia of the New American Nation*, ed. Paul Finkelman (New York: Charles Scribners' Sons, 2006), 158.
3. Paul J. Achter, "Comedy in Unfunny Times: News Parody and Carnival After 9/11," *Critical Studies in Media Communication* 25, no. 3 (2008): 274–303. p. 275.
4. Quoted in Paul Lewis, *Cracking Up: American Humor in A Time of Conflict*, (Chicago: Chicago UP, 2006), 10.
5. Ibid., 3.
6. Ibid., 17.
7. David Marc, Foreword to *Satire TV: Comedy and Politics in the Post-Network Era*, eds. Jonathan Gray, Jeffrey P. Jones, Ethan Thompson (New York: New York UP, 2009), ix.
8. Henry A. Giroux, "Private Satisfactions and Public Disorders: *Fight Club*, Patriarchy, and the Politics of Masculine Violence," accessed October 26, 2010, http://www.henryagiroux.com/online_articles /fight_club.htm.
9. "Cultural Studies in Dark Times, Public Pedagogy and the Challenges of Neoliberalism," accessed October 22, 2010, http://www.henryagiroux.com /online_articles/DarkTimes.htm. Previously published in *Fast Capitalism* 1, no. 2 (2005), http://www.fastcapitalism.com.

10. Ibid.
11. Ibid.
12. Ibid.
13. Ibid.
14. Russell L. Petersen, *Strange Bedfellows: How Late-Night Comedy Turns Democracy into a Joke* (Piscataway, NJ: Rutgers UP, 2008), 22.
15. Pew Research Center for the People & the Press, "Cable and Internet Loom Large in Fragmented Political News Universe," *People-press. org.* January 11, 2004, http://people-press.org/report/200/cable-and -internet-loom-large-in-fragmented-political-news-universe.
16. Pew Research Center for the People & the Press, "Today's Journalists Less Prominent," *People-press.org*, March 8, 2007, http://people-press .org/report/309/todays-journalists-less-prominent.
17. Petersen, *Strange Bedfellows*, 23.
18. Jonathan Gray, Jeffrey P. Jones, Ethan Thompson, "The State of Satire, the Satire of State," in *Satire TV*, 7.
19. Ibid., 11.
20. Ibid., 13.
21. Ibid., 14.
22. George A. Test, *Satire: Spirit and Art* (Gainesville, FL: University Press of Florida, 1991), 30.
23. Ibid., 32.
24. Gray, Jones, Thompson, "The State of Satire," 15.
25. Ibid., 18. Emphasis in the original.
26. Stephen Colbert, "The Swift Payment," *The Colbert Nation*, broadcast on Comedy Central on December 13, 2010, http://www.colbertnation.com/the -colbert-report-videos/368379/december-13-2010/the-word---swift-payment.
27. George Wittkowsky, "Swift's Modest Proposal: The Biography of an Early Georgian Pamphlet," *Journal of the History of Ideas*, 4, no. 1 (Jan., 1943), 75–104, 88.
28. Stephen Colbert, "The Wørd—Disintegration," *The Colbert Report*, broadcast on Comedy Central on January 18, 2011, http://www.colbertnation .com/the-colbert-report-videos/371414/january-18-2011/the-word ---disintegration.
29. Stephen Colbert, "Andre Bauer Is Not Against Animals," *The Colbert Report*, broadcast on Comedy Central on January 26, 2010, http:// www.colbertnation.com/the-colbert-report-videos/262595/january -26-2010/andre-bauer-is-not-against-animals.
30. Morris A. Linda, "American Satire: Beginnings through Mark Twain," in *A Companion to Satire*, ed. Ruben Quintero (Malden, MA: Blackwell Publishing, 2007), 377.
31. Stephen Colbert, "Better Know a Founder," *The Colbert Report*, broadcast on Comedy Central on March 1, 2006, http://www.colbertnation .com/the-colbert-report-videos/59707/march-01-2006/better-know -a-founder---benjamin-franklin.

32. For more on this, see the introduction and the section on language and "The Wørd" in chapter 4.
33. Ingham B. Granger, *Political Satire in the American Revolution, 1763–1783* (Ithaca, NY: Cornell UP, 1960), 28. Emphasis in the original.
34. Morris, "American Satire," 377.
35. Colin Wells, "Satire," in *The Encyclopedia of the New American Nation,* ed. Paul Finkelman (New York: Charles Scribners' Sons, 2006), 158.
36. Ibid.
37. Stephen Colbert, "Huckleberry Finn Censorship," *The Colbert Nation,* broadcast on Comedy Central on January 5, 2011, http://www.colbertnation.com/the-colbert-report-videos/369991/january-05-2011/huckleberry-finn-censorship.
38. Quoted in Jeffrey A. Trachtenberg, "Mark Twain's New Book," *WSJ.com,* April 18, 2009, http://online.wsj.com/article/SB124000246279630121.html.
39. Colbert and Twain share another common bond: they both delivered controversial roasts. Twain's was a speech at the *Atlantic Monthly's* seventieth birthday dinner for John Greenleaf Whittier on December 17, 1877. For more on that event see: Jerome Loving, "Birthday Party Brouhaha. Mark Twain's Infamous Toast," *Humanities* 29, no. 6 (2008), http://www.neh.gov/news/humanities/2008-11/Twain_Toast.html.
40. Don Bliss, "Stephen Colbert Hill Visit: A Twist on Twain," *WashingtonPost.com,* September 28, 2010, http://www.washingtonpost.com/wp-dyn/content/article/2010/09/27/AR2010092706125.html.
41. Ibid.
42. Ibid.
43. Devonia Smith, "Stephen Colbert's Congress Routine Fell Flat (full transcript & video of testimony)," *Examiner.com,* September 24, 2010, http://www.examiner.com/political-buzz-in-dallas/stephen-colbert-s-congress-routine-fell-flat-full-transcript-video-of-testimony#ixzz1GCPJ70IB.
44. Ibid.
45. Ibid.
46. Gray, Jones, Thompson, "The State of Satire," 11.
47. Marc, Foreword to *Satire TV,* 10.
48. Ibid., 11.
49. Ibid., 12.
50. "The Smothers Brothers Comedy Hour," *Wikipedia,* Last modified February 11, 2011, http://en.wikipedia.org/wiki/The_Smothers_Brothers_Comedy_Hour.
51. Heather Osborne Thompson, "Tracing the "Fake" Candidate in American Television Comedy," in *Satire TV,* 66.
52. Gray, Jones, Thompson, "The State of Satire," 24.
53. Ibid., 26.

54. Don Waisanen, "A Citizen's Guides to Democracy Inaction: Jon Stewart and Stephen Colbert's Comic Rhetorical Criticism," *Southern Communication Journal* 74, no. 2 (2009), 119–140. p. 123.
55. Ibid., 125.
56. Geoffrey Baym, *From Cronkite to Colbert: The Evolution of Broadcast News* (Boulder, CO: Paradigm Publishers, 2010), 5.
57. Ibid., 1.
58. Pew Research Center for the People & the Press, "Journalism, Satire or Just Laugh?" *People-press.org*, May 8, 2008, http://pewresearch.org /pubs/829/the-daily-show-journalism-satire-or-just-laughs.
59. Ibid.
60. "Stewart Slams Tucker Carlson and Paul Begala," *About.com*, accessed December 13, 2010, http://politicalhumor.about.com/library/bljon stewartcrossfire.htm.
61. Ibid.
62. Stephen Colbert, "Stone Phillips' Gravitas Off," *The Colbert Nation*, broadcast on Comedy Central on October 17, 2005, http://www.colbertnation .com/the-colbert-report-videos/24040/october-17-2005/stone-phillips ---gravitas-off
63. Ibid.
64. Baym, *Cronkite*, 6.
65. Geoffrey Baym, "Representation and the Politics of Play: Stephen Colbert's *Better Know a District*," *Political Communication* 24, no. 4 (2007): 359-376.
66. Stephen Colbert, "Better Know A District," *The Colbert Nation*, broadcast on Comedy Central on November 7, 2006, http://www.colbertnation .com/the-colbert-report-videos/77981/november-07-2006/better -know-a-district---midterm-midtacular.
67. Baym, "Representation and the Politics of Play," 360.
68. "National Voter Turn Out in Federal Elections 1960–2008," *Infoplease. com*, accessed July 7, 2010, http://www.infoplease.com/ipa/A0781453 .html.
69. Baym, "Representation and the Politics of Play," 368.
70. Colbert, "Better Know A District."
71. Ibid.
72. Baym, "Representation and the Politics of Play," 363.
73. Stephen Colbert, "Why I Took This Crummy Job," *Newsweek.com*, June 6, 2009, http://www.newsweek.com/2009/06/05/why-i-took -this-crummy-job.html.
74. Jon Meacham, "A Reader's Guide to the Colbert Issue," *Newsweek.com*, June 06, 2009, http://www.newsweek.com/2009/06/05/a-reader-s -guide-to-the-colbert-issue.html.
75. Colbert, "Why I took This Crummy Job."
76. Baym, "Representation and the Politics of Play," 373.

4   AMERICA ACCORDING TO *THE COLBERT REPORT*: OR HOW A TV SHOW CAN CHANGE THE WAY A NATION THINKS

1. The Colbert Report's Facebook page, accessed September 19, 2009, http://www.facebook.com/thecolbertreport?sk=info.

2. In an interview with Terry Gross for National Public Radio, Colbert talked about how *The Daily Show* had made him more political, mentioning that Stewart asked him to have a political opinion. He explained that until that moment he had mostly done silly comedy, jokes about Ted Kennedy drinking too much for *Second City*, or comedy free of references to people, places, or politics with Amy Sedaris. According to Colbert, it wasn't until his work with Stewart that he began making politically passionate comedic choices. See: Terry Gross, "A Fake Newsman's Fake Newsman: Stephen Colbert," *Fresh Air from WHYY*, NPR, January 24, 2005, http://www.npr.org/templates/story/story.php?storyId=4464017.

3. Deborah Solomon, "Questions for Stephen Colbert: Funny About the News," *The New York Times Magazine*, September 25, 2005, http://www.nytimes.com/2005/09/25/magazine/25questions.html.

4. Stephen Colbert, "The Colbert Report—Introduction," *The Colbert Report*, broadcast on Comedy Central on October 17, 2005, http://www.colbertnation.com/the-colbert-report-videos/180900/october-17-2005/intro---10-17-05.

5. Ken P., "An Interview with Stephen Colbert," *IGN*, August 11, 2003, http://movies.ign.com/articles/433/433111p7.html.

6. Charlie Rose, "A conversation with comedian Stephen Colbert," *Charlie Rose*, December 8, 2006, http://www.charlierose.com/view/interview/93.

7. Ibid.

8. *Colbert Nation* homepage, accessed March 15, 2011, http://www.colbertnation.com/home.

9. Stephen Colbert, "Better Know a District—California's 6th—Lynn Woolsey," *The Colbert Report*, broadcast on Comedy Central on August 10, 2006, http://www.colbertnation.com/the-colbert-report-videos/72804/august-10-2006/better-know-a-district---california-s-6th---lynn-woolsey.

10. Stephen Colbert, "Green Screen Challenge—The Finalists," *The Colbert Report*, broadcast on Comedy Central on October 11, 2006, http://www.colbertnation.com/the-colbert-report-videos/76546/october-11-2006/green-screen-challenge---the-finalists.

11. "Recurring segments on *The Colbert Report*," *Wikipedia*, last modified March 31, 2011, http://en.wikipedia.org/wiki/Recurring_segments_on_The_Colbert_Report.

12. Stephen Colbert, "Sarah Palin Uses a Hand-O-Prompter," *The Colbert Report*, broadcast on Comedy Central on February 8, 2010, http://

www.colbertnation.com/the-colbert-report-videos/264042/february
-08-2010/sarah-palin-uses-a-hand-o-prompter.

13. "Reception" on "*The Colbert Report*," *Wikipedia,* last modified April 6,
2011, http://en.wikipedia.org/wiki/The_Colbert_Report#Reception.

14. Entries from "colabus" to "cold betty," *Urban Dictionary,* accessed March
3, 2011, http://www.urbandictionary.com/browse.php?word=colbert.

15. Maureen Dowd, "Oprah! How Could Ya?" *The New York Times,* January
14, 2006, http://select.nytimes.com/2006/01/14/opinion/14dowd
.html.

16. Ken P., "An Interview with Stephen Colbert," 4.

17. Ken P., "An Interview with Stephen Colbert," 4.

18. "Stephen Colbert (character)," *Wikipedia,* last modified March 18, 2011,
http://en.wikipedia.org/wiki/Stephen_Colbert_%28character%29.

19. Ibid.

20. Ken P., "An Interview with Stephen Colbert," 6.

21. Ibid., 6.

22. Ibid., 7.

23. "Stephen Colbert," *Wikipedia,* last modified April 5, 2011, http://
en.wikipedia.org/wiki/Stephen_Colbert.

24. Terry Gross, "Rob and Nate Corddry Find Their Place on TV," *Fresh
Air from WHYY,* NPR, March 8, 2007, http://www.npr.org/templates
/story/story.php?storyId=7773229.

25. Eric Deggans, "For Aasif Mandvi, cultural irreverence on 'The Daily
Show,'" *Tampabay.com.* June 1, 2008, http://www.tampabay.com
/features/media/article545843.ece.

26. Jon Stewart, "Carell—Colbert—10 F#@king Years—Even Stevphen,"
The Daily Show with Jon Stewart, broadcast on Comedy Central
on September 19, 2006, http://www.thedailyshow.com/watch/tue
-september-19-2006/10-f--king-years---even-stevphen.

27. The God Machine is a device that parodies the concept of the *deus
ex machina* (literally "god out of the machine"), a theatrical term
used to describe an abrupt and contrived resolution to a complex plot
problem performed by the addition of a new element, such as a new
character.

28. "This Week in God" on "List of *The Daily Show* recurring segments,"
Wikipedia, last modified March 25, 2011, http://en.wikipedia.org
/wiki/List_of_The_Daily_Show_recurring_segments#This_Week_in
_God.

29. Jon Stewart, "Colbert—This Week in God—Hurricane Katrina Coverage,"
The Daily Show with Jon Stewart, broadcast on Comedy Central on
September 26, 2005, http://www.thedailyshow.com/watch/mon
-september-26-2005/this-week-in-god---hurricane-katrina-coverage.

30. Adam Sternbergh, "Stephen Colbert Has America by the Ballots,"
New York Magazine, October 8, 2006: 2, http://nymag.com/news
/politics/22322/.

31. Gary Levin, "First 'Stewart,' now 'Colbert,'" *USA Today,* October 13, 2005, http://www.usatoday.com/life/television/news/2005-10-13 -colbert_x.htm.
32. Ibid.
33. Ibid.
34. *"The Colbert Report,"* *Wikipedia,* last modified April 6, 2011, http:// en.wikipedia.org/wiki/The_Colbert_Report.
35. "Stephen Colbert on *The O'Reilly Factor,"* YouTube video, accessed January 20, 2010. http://www.youtube.com/watch?v=QquTUR9 nbC4.
36. "Stephen Colbert," *Wikipedia.*
37. Stephen Colbert, "Obama Poster Debate—David Ross and Ed Colbert," *The Colbert Report,* broadcast on Comedy Central on February 12, 2009, http://www.colbertnation.com/the-colbert-report-videos/218732 /february-12-2009/obama-poster-debate---david-ross-and-ed-colbert.
38. "Jon Stewart on *The O'Reilly Factor,"* YouTube video, accessed February 20, 2010, http://www.youtube.com/watch?v=H5pK7sK0i4A.
39. Terry Gross, "Bluster and Satire: Stephen Colbert's 'Report,'" *Fresh Air from WHYY,* NPR, December 7, 2005, http://www.npr.org/templates /story/story.php?storyId=5040948&ps=rs.
40. Jon Stewart emphatically claimed it was not a response to Beck but was simply another vehicle for the work he and Colbert are doing. See: Daniel Kreps, "Jon Stewart: Rallies Not a Response to Glenn Beck," *Rolling Stone,* September 30, 2010, http://www.rollingstone.com/music /news/jon-stewart-rallies-not-a-response-to-glenn-beck-20100930.
41. Gross, "Bluster and Satire: Stephen Colbert's 'Report.'"
42. "The Colbert Report," *Wikiquote,* last modified March 5, 2011, http:// en.wikiquote.org/wiki/The_Colbert_Report.
43. Ibid.
44. Ibid.
45. Ibid.
46. Geoffrey Baym, "Stephen Colbert's Parody of the Postmodern," in *Satire TV: Politics and Comedy in the Post-Network Era,* eds. Jonathan Gray, Jeffrey P. Jones, and Ethan Thompson (New York: New York University Press, 2009), 132.
47. Stephen Colbert. "Harvey Mansfield," *The Colbert Report,* broadcast on Comedy Central on April 5, 2006, http://www.colbertnation.com/the -colbert-report-videos/61315/april-05-2006/harvey-mansfield.
48. Gail Chiasson, "Colbert Set Builders Praise Christie Micro Tiles," in *Daily DOOH* (blog), accessed January 10, 2009, http://www.dailydooh. com/archives/25526.
49. *"The Colbert Report,"* *Wikipedia.*
50. *"The Colbert Report,"* *Wikipedia.*
51. Stephen Colbert, "Sign Off—Fifth Anniversary Portrait," *The Colbert Report,* broadcast on Comedy Central on October 25, 2010, http://

www.colbertnation.com/the-colbert-report-videos/363112/october
-25-2010/sign-off---fifth-anniversary-portrait.

52. Stephen Colbert, "The Wørd—Truthiness," *The Colbert Report*, broadcast on Comedy Central on October 17, 2005, http://www.colbertnation
.com/the-colbert-report-videos/24039/october-17-2005/the-word
---truthiness.

53. Colbert called *truthiness* the "thesis statement" for the show during an interview with Charlie Rose. During the interview, he stated: "I was thinking of the idea of passion and emotion and certainty over information. And what you feel in your gut (as I said in the first Wørd we did, which was sort of a thesis statement of the whole show—however long it lasts—is that sentence, that one word), that's more important to, I think, the public at large, and not just the people who provide it in prime-time cable, than information." See: Charlie Rose, "A conversation with comedian Stephen Colbert."

54. Colbert, "The Wørd—Truthiness."

55. Mark Peyser, "The Truthiness Teller," *Newsweek*, February 13, 2006, http://web.archive.org/web/20060425101629/http://www.msnbc
.msn.com/id/11182033/site/newsweek/.

56. For coverage of its post-premiere appearance see: "Truthiness," *Wikipedia*, last modified February 26, 2011, http://en.wikipedia.org
/wiki/Truthiness.

57. "Where Words Come From," *Midmorning with Kerri Miller*, Minnesota Public Radio, January 5, 2006, http://news.minnesota.publicradio.org
/programs/midmorning/listings/mm20060102.shtml.

58. Allan Metcalf, "*Truthiness* Voted 2005 Word of the Year by American Dialect Society," January 6, 2006, http://www.americandialect.org
/Words_of_the_Year_2005.pdf.

59. "Word of the Year 2006," *Merriam-Webster Dictionary*, accessed January 24, 2010, http://www.merriam-webster.com/info/06words.htm.

60. Ibid.

61. Adam Gorlick, "Colbert's 'truthiness' pronounced Word of the Year," *Chron*, December 8, 2006, http://www.chron.com/disp/story.mpl
/chronicle/4389349.html.

62. "Truthiness," *Wikipedia*.

63. Sternbergh, "Stephen Colbert Has America by the Ballots," 2.

64. Baym, "Stephen Colbert's Parody of the Postmodern," 126.

65. Stephen Colbert, Interview by Nathan Rabin, *The A.V. Club*, January 25, 2006, http://www.avclub.com/articles/stephen-colbert,13970/.

66. Colbert, "The Wørd—Truthiness," *The Colbert Report*.

67. Stephen Colbert, "Introduction," in *I Am America (And So Can You!)* (New York: Hachette Book Group, 2007), viii.

68. Ibid.

69. Ibid.

70. There isn't sufficient space to explore the idea here, but Colbert demonstrates the way that postmodern relativism plays into the hands of right-wing bullying. During the 1980s, it had been common for left

progressives to suggest that there was no one truth and that truth depended on perspective. The problem with that position was that, rather than open up the space for minority views, it seemed to justify the imposition of the power elite's ideas about the truth.

71. Colbert Interview by Nathan Rabin.
72. Ibid.
73. David Corn, "Cheney, 9/11 and the Truth about Iraq," *HuffingtonPost. com*, September 11, 2006, http://www.huffingtonpost.com/david -corn/cheney-911-and-the-truth-_b_29154.html.
74. David Detmer, "Philosophy in the Age of Truthiness," in *Stephen Colbert and Philosophy. I Am Philosophy (And So Can You!)*, ed. Aaron A. Schiller (New York: Open Court, 2009), Kindle edition.
75. Ibid.
76. Colbert, "The Wørd—Truthiness."
77. Rose, "A conversation with comedian Stephen Colbert."
78. Colbert, "The Wørd—Truthiness."
79. Stephen Colbert, "Ron Suskind," *The Colbert Report*, broadcast on Comedy Central on July 13, 2006, http://www.colbertnation.com /the-colbert-report-videos/71739/july-13-2006/ron-suskind.
80. David Leonhardt, "Truth, Fiction and Lou Dobbs," *The New York Times*, May 30, 2007, http://www.nytimes.com/2007/05/30 /business/30leonhardt.html.
81. Stephen Colbert, "Tim Robbins," *The Colbert Report*, broadcast on Comedy Central on November 17, 2005, http://www.colbertnation .com/the-colbert-report-videos/25367/november-17-2005/tim-robbins.
82. Colbert, "The Wørd—Truthiness."
83. Stephen Colbert, "Formidable Opponent—Iraq Withdrawal," *The Colbert Report*, broadcast on Comedy Central on September 13, 2006, http://www.colbertnation.com/the-colbert-report-videos/182249 /september-13-2006/formidable-opponent---iraq-withdrawal.
84. Neil Strauss, "Stephen Colbert on Deconstructing the News, Religion, and the Colbert Nation: More from Neil Strauss' conversation with TV's most dangerous man," *Rolling Stone*, September 2, 2009, http://www .rollingstone.com/culture/news/stephen-colbert-on-deconstructing -the-news-religion-and-the-colbert-nation-20090902.
85. Rose, "A Conversation with Comedian Stephen Colbert."
86. See: David Corn, *The Lies of George W. Bush: Mastering the Politics of Deception* (New York: Crown, 2003). Also see: Lauren Berlant, "The Epistemology of State Emotion," in *Dissent in Dangerous Times*, ed. Austin Sarat (Ann Arbor: University of Michigan Press, 2005), 46–80.
87. Susan Sontag, "Regarding the Torture of Others: Notes on What Has Been Done—and Why—to Prisoners, by Americans," *New York Times Magazine*, May 23, 2004: 24–29, 42. P. 25.
88. Oliver Poole and Alec Russell, "I Am a Survivor, Rumsfeld Tells His Troops," *Telegraph*, May 14, 2004, http://www.telegraph.co.uk

/news/main.jhtml?xml=/news/2004/05/14/wirql14.xml&sSheet=
/news/2004/05/14/ixnewstop.html.

89. Some ideas expressed here also appeared in my essay: "E Pluribus Unum/ Ex Uno Plura: Legislating and Deregulating American Studies post-9/11," in *Dangerous Professors*, eds. Malini Johar Schueller (Ann Arbor: University of Michigan Press, 2009), 145–72.

90. Sternbergh, "Stephen Colbert Has America by the Ballots,"1.

91. Ibid.

92. Stephen Colbert, "Opening rundown," *The Colbert Report*, broadcast on Comedy Central on April 3, 2008.

93. Stephen Colbert, "Opening rundown," *The Colbert Report*, broadcast on Comedy Central on October 20, 2005.

94. Sources of these words came from: "Colbert Intro: A list by nkocharh," *wordnik* (blog), accessed March 20, 2011, http://www.wordnik .com/lists/colbert-intro, and Eric D., "The Colbert Report's Opening sequence: Stephen Colbert's attributes?" *Sinopenn* (blog), November 10, 2010, http://www.sinopenn.com/2010/11/10/the-colbert-reports -opening-sequence-stephen-colberts-attributes.

95. Gross, "Bluster and Satire: Stephen Colbert's 'Report.'"

96. Baym, "Stephen Colbert's Parody of the Postmodern," 130.

97. Stephen Colbert, "The Wørd—Clarity," *The Colbert Report*, broadcast on Comedy Central on August 9, 2007, http://www.colbertnation .com/the-colbert-report-videos/183221/august-09-2007/the-word ---clarity.

98. Geoffrey Baym, *From Cronkite to Colbert: The Evolution of Broadcast News* (Boulder, CO: Paradigm Publishers, 2009), 132.

99. Ibid.

100. Gross. "Bluster and Satire: Stephen Colbert's 'Report.'"

101. Baym. *From Cronkite to Colbert: The Evolution of Broadcast News*, 130.

102. Colbert, *I Am America*, 122.

103. Stephen Colbert, *The Colbert Report*, broadcast on Comedy Central on March 2, 2006.

104. Stephen Colbert, "Santorum's Iraqi Lord of the Rings," *The Colbert Report*, broadcast on Comedy Central on October 18, 2006, http:// www.colbertnation.com/the-colbert-report-videos/76932/october-18-2006/santorum-s-iraqi-lord-of-the-rings.

105. Stephen Colbert, "Glenn-Harried Glenn-Lost," *The Colbert Report*, broadcast on Comedy Central on August 13, 2009, http://www .colbertnation.com/the-colbert-report-videos/246560/august-13 -2009/glenn-harried-glenn-lost.

106. Sternbergh, "Stephen Colbert Has America by the Ballots," 5.

107. Rose, "A conversation with comedian Stephen Colbert."

108. "Stephen Colbert on *The O'Reilly Factor*."

109. Stephen Colbert, "Bill O'Reilly," *The Colbert Report*, broadcast on Comedy Central on January 18, 2007, http://www.colbertnation

.com/the-colbert-report-videos/81003/january-18-2007/bill-o
-reilly.
110. Stephen Colbert, "Lou Dobbs," *The Colbert Report,* broadcast on
Comedy Central on January 24, 2007, http://www.colbertnation
.com/the-colbert-report-videos/81286/january-24-2007/lou-dobbs.
111. Sternbergh, "Stephen Colbert Has America by the Ballots," 4.
112. Bill O'Reilly, *Culture Warrior* (New York: Doubleday, 2006), 17–8.
113. Colbert, *I Am America,* viii.
114. Colbert, *I Am America,* 113.
115. Ibid.
116. Stephen Colbert, "Fear for All Pt. 1," *The Colbert Report,* broadcast
on Comedy Central on October 28, 2010, http://www.colbertnation
.com/the-colbert-report-videos/363665/october-28-2010/fear-for
-all-pt--1.
117. Matthew Jaffe and Z. Byron Wolf, "Stephen Colbert Takes On Congress,
Sarcastically Argues for Farm Workers: Comedian Testifies on Plight of
Farm Workers and Immigration Reform," *ABC News,* September 24,
2010, http://abcnews.go.com/Politics/stephen-colbert-asked-testify
-immigration/story?id=11717624.
118. Ibid.
119. "Immigrant Farm Workers," *C-SPAN Video Library,* September 24,
2010, http://www.c-spanvideo.org/program/295639-1.
120. Ibid.
121. Ibid.
122. Ibid.
123. Sternbergh. "Stephen Colbert Has America by the Ballots," 4.
124. Ibid.
125. Stephen Colbert, "Tip/Wag—Joe Reed & Levi's Ex-Girlfriend Jeans,"
The Colbert Report, broadcast on Comedy Central on February 28, 2011,
http://www.colbertnation.com/the-colbert-report-videos/375740
/february-28-2011/tip-wag---joe-reed---levi-s-ex-girlfriend-jeans.
126. Terry Gross, "Colbert Builds 'Report' with Viewers, Readers," *Fresh Air
from WHYY,* NPR, October 9, 2007, http://www.npr.org/templates
/story/story.php?storyId=15116383.
127. Geoff Nunberg, *Talking Right: How Conservatives Turned Liberalism
into a Tax-Raising, Latte-Drinking, Sushi-Eating, Volvo-Driving, New
York Times–Reading, Body-Piercing, Hollywood-Loving, Left-Wing
Freak Show* (New York: Public Affairs, 2006), 190.
128. Ibid.
129. Ibid, 189.
130. Martin Luther King, Jr., "I Have a Dream" speech, August 28, 1963,
Transcript available at *U.S. Constitution Online,* last modified March
3, 2010, http://www.usconstitution.net/dream.html.
131. Ibid.
132. Stephen Colbert, "The Wørd—Overrated," *The Colbert Report,*
broadcast on Comedy Central on October 25, 2005, http://www

.colbertnation.com/the-colbert-report-videos/24370/october-25-2005/the-word---overrated.

133. Ibid.
134. Nunberg, *Talking Right*, 189.
135. Ibid., 190.
136. John Kerry, "2004 Democratic National Convention Acceptance Address," Fleet Center, Boston, July 29, 2004, YouTube video, *American Rhetoric Online Speech Bank*, http://www.americanrhetoric.com/speeches/convention2004/johnkerry2004dnc.htm.
137. Cited in Nunberg, *Talking Right*, 193.
138. Nunberg, *Talking Right*, 195.
139. Colbert, *I Am America*, ix.
140. Stephen Colbert, "Newt Gingrich Wants to Screw America," *The Colbert Report*, broadcast on Comedy Central on March 1, 2011, http://www.colbertnation.com/the-colbert-report-videos/377118/march-10-2011/newt-gingrich-wants-to-screw-america.
141. Stephen Colbert, "Glenn—Livid," *The Colbert Report*, broadcast on Comedy Central on August 26, 2010, http://www.colbertnation.com/the-colbert-report-videos/351602/august-26-2010/glenn-livid.
142. Colbert, *I Am America*, 51.
143. Ibid., 52.
144. Stephen Colbert, "Intro 9/8/10," *The Colbert Report*, broadcast on Comedy Central on September 8, 2010, http://www.colbertnation.com/the-colbert-report-videos/352253/september-08-2010/intro---9-8-10.
145. Neil Strauss, "Stephen Colbert on Deconstructing the News, Religion and the Colbert Nation: More from Neil Strauss' conversation with TV's most dangerous man," *Rolling Stone*, September 2, 2009, http://www.rollingstone.com/culture/news/stephen-colbert-on-deconstructing-the-news-religion-and-the-colbert-nation-20090902.
146. Hannah Arendt, *On Violence* (Orlando: Harcourt Brace, 1969/1970), 45.
147. Pew Research Center for the People & the Press, "Key News Audiences Now Blend Online and Traditional Sources," *People-Press.org*, August 17, 2008: 3, http://people-press.org/2008/08/17/watching-reading-and-listening-to-the-news/.
148. Ibid.
149. Pew Research Center for the People & the Press, "Americans Spending More Time Following the News," *People-Press.org*, September 12, 2010, http://people-press.org/report/652/.
150. Ibid.
151. Colbert, "Green Screen Challenge—The Finalists."
152. Henry A. Giroux, *Youth in a Suspect Society: Democracy or Disposability?* (New York: Palgrave-Macmillan, 2009), xii.

153. Ibid., 15.
154. Ibid., 16.
155. Liesbet Van Zoonen, *Entertaining the Citizen: When Politics and Popular Culture Converge* (Lanham, MD: Rowman & Littlefield, 2005), 4.
156. Stephen Colbert, "The Wørd—Wikiality," *The Colbert Report*, broadcast on Comedy Central on July 31, 2006, http://www.colbertnation.com/the-colbert-report-videos/72347/july-31-2006/the-word---wikiality.
157. "Wikipedia: About," *Wikipedia*, last modified April 7, 2011, http://en.wikipedia.org/wiki/Wikipedia:About.
158. Strauss, "Stephen Colbert on Deconstructing the News, Religion and the Colbert Nation: More from Neil Strauss' conversation with TV's most dangerous man," *Rolling Stone*, September 2, 2009, http://www.rollingstone.com/culture/news/stephen-colbert-on-deconstructing-the-news-religion-and-the-colbert-nation-20090902.

5 Amusing Ourselves to Activism?

1. Stephen Colbert, "Starbucks Closing," *The Colbert Report*, broadcast on Comedy Central on July 23, 2008, http://www.colbertnation.com/the-colbert-report-videos/177511/july-23-2008/starbucks-closings.
2. Ibid.
3. Neil Postman, *Amusing Ourselves to Death: Public Discourse in the Age of Show Business* (New York: Penguin, 1985), 10.
4. Ibid., 7.
5. Stephen Colbert, "First Show," *The Colbert Report*, broadcast on Comedy Central on October 17, 2005, http://www.colbertnation.com/the-colbert-report-videos/180903/october-17-2005/first-show.
6. Geoffrey Baym, *From Cronkite to Colbert: The Evolution of Broadcast News* (Boulder, CO: Paradigm, 2009), 149.
7. Ibid.
8. Nicolas Carr, "Is Google Making Us Stupid?" *TheAtlantic.com*, July/August 2008, http://www.theatlantic.com/magazine/archive/2008/07/is-google-making-us-stupid/6868/.
9. Ibid.
10. Jon Stewart, "Colbert—Bloggers," *The Daily Show*, broadcast on Comedy Central on February 16, 2005, http://www.thedailyshow.com/watch/wed-february-16-2005/bloggers.
11. Liesbet van Zoonen, *Entertaining the Citizen: When Politics and Popular Culture Converge* (Lanham, MD: Rowman & Littlefield Publishers, Inc., 2005), 4.
12. Rachel Sklar, "Stephen Colbert's Web Dominance: How *The Colbert Report* Is Fast Becoming the Leader in Web-TV Integration," *TheHuffingtonPost.com*, August 22, 2006, http://www.huffingtonpost.com/eat-the-press/2006/08/22/stephen-colberts-web-dom_e_27670.html.

204   NOTES

13. "Jon Kyl says abortion services are "well over 90 percent of what Planned
    Parenthood does," *PolitiFact.com*, April 8, 2011, http://www.politifact
    .com/truth-o-meter/statements/2011/apr/08/jon-kyl/jon-kyl-says
    -abortion-services-are-well-over-90-pe/.
14. Steven Colbert, "Pap Smears at Walgreens," *The Colbert Report*, broad-
    cast on Comedy Central on April 11, 2011, http://www.colbertnation
    .com/the-colbert-report-videos/381282/april-11-2011/pap-smears-at
    -walgreens.
15. "Government Shutdown Nearing; Unrest in Syria; Republicans Want to
    Cut Funding to Planned Parenthood; Federal Government on the Brink
    of a Shutdown," *CNN Transcripts*, April 8, 2011, http://transcripts.cnn
    .com/TRANSCRIPTS/1104/08/cnr.07.html.
16. Colbert, "Pap Smears at Walgreens."
17. Stephen Colbert, "Jon Kyl Tweets Not Intended to Be Factual Statements,"
    The Colbert Report, broadcast on Comedy Central on April 12, 2011,
    http://www.colbertnation.com/the-colbert-report-videos/381484
    /april-12-2011/jon-kyl-tweets-not-intended-to-be-factual-statements.
18. Ibid.
19. Lauren Dugan, "Colbert Tweets: Jon Kyl's knees bend both ways. He's
    part racehorse #NotIntendedToBeAFactualStatement," *All Twitter:
    The Unofficial Twitter Source*, April 14, 2011, http://www.mediabistro
    .com/alltwitter/colbert-tweets-jon-kyls-knees-bend-both-ways-hes-
    part-racehorse-notintendedtobeafactualstatement_b7135.
20. Geoffrey Baym, *From Cronkite to Colbert: The Evolution of Broadcast
    News* (Boulder, CO: Paradigm, 2009), 163.
21. Jody C. Baumgartner, Jonathan S. Morris, "One Nation Under Stephen?
    The Effects of *The Colbert Report* on American Youth," *Journal of
    Broadcasting & Electronic Media* 52, no.4 (2008), 622–643. p. 623.
22. Ibid., 626
23. Ibid., 627.
24. Ibid., 627–628.
25. Heather L. La Marre, L., Kristen D. Landreville, Michael A. Beam,
    "The Irony of Satire: Political Ideology and the Motivation to See What
    You Want to See in *The Colbert Report*," *The International Journal of
    Press/Politics* 14, no. 2 (2009), 212–231. p. 216.
26. Ibid.
27. Pew Research Center for the People & the Press, "Senate Legislative
    Process A Mystery to Many," *Press-People.org*, January 28, 2010, http://
    people-press.org/report/586/.
28. Charlie Rose, "An Interview with Comedian Stephen Colbert,"
    CharlieRose.com, December 8, 2006, http://www.charlierose.com
    /view/interview/93.
29. Maureen Dowd, Dowd, "America's Anchors," *RollingStone.com*,
    November 16, 2006, http://www.rollingstone.com/news/coverstory
    /jon_stewart_stephen_colbert_americas_anchors/page/3.   Retrieved
    2008-09-02.

INDEX

Note: Page numbers in *italics* indicate photos.

CPSIA information can be obtained at www.ICGtesting.com
Printed in the USA
BVOW082308201212

308830BV00005B/15/P